Library of Congress Cataloging in Publication Data
Peabody Museum of Salem.
  The tribal style.
    Bibliography: p.
    1. Art, Black—Africa, Sub-Saharan—Exhibitions.
    2. Art, Primitive—Africa, Sub-Saharan—Exhibitions.
    3. Peabody Museum of Salem—Exhibitions. I. Grimes, John
        Richard,1959-   . II. Title
N7391.65.P42 1984   730′.0967′07401445   84-4961
ISBN 0-875-77-150-5

Designed by Frederick MacDougall Johnson
Typeset by Typesetters Unlimited
Printed by Deschamps Printing Company, Inc.
Manufactured in the United States of America

The Tribal Style

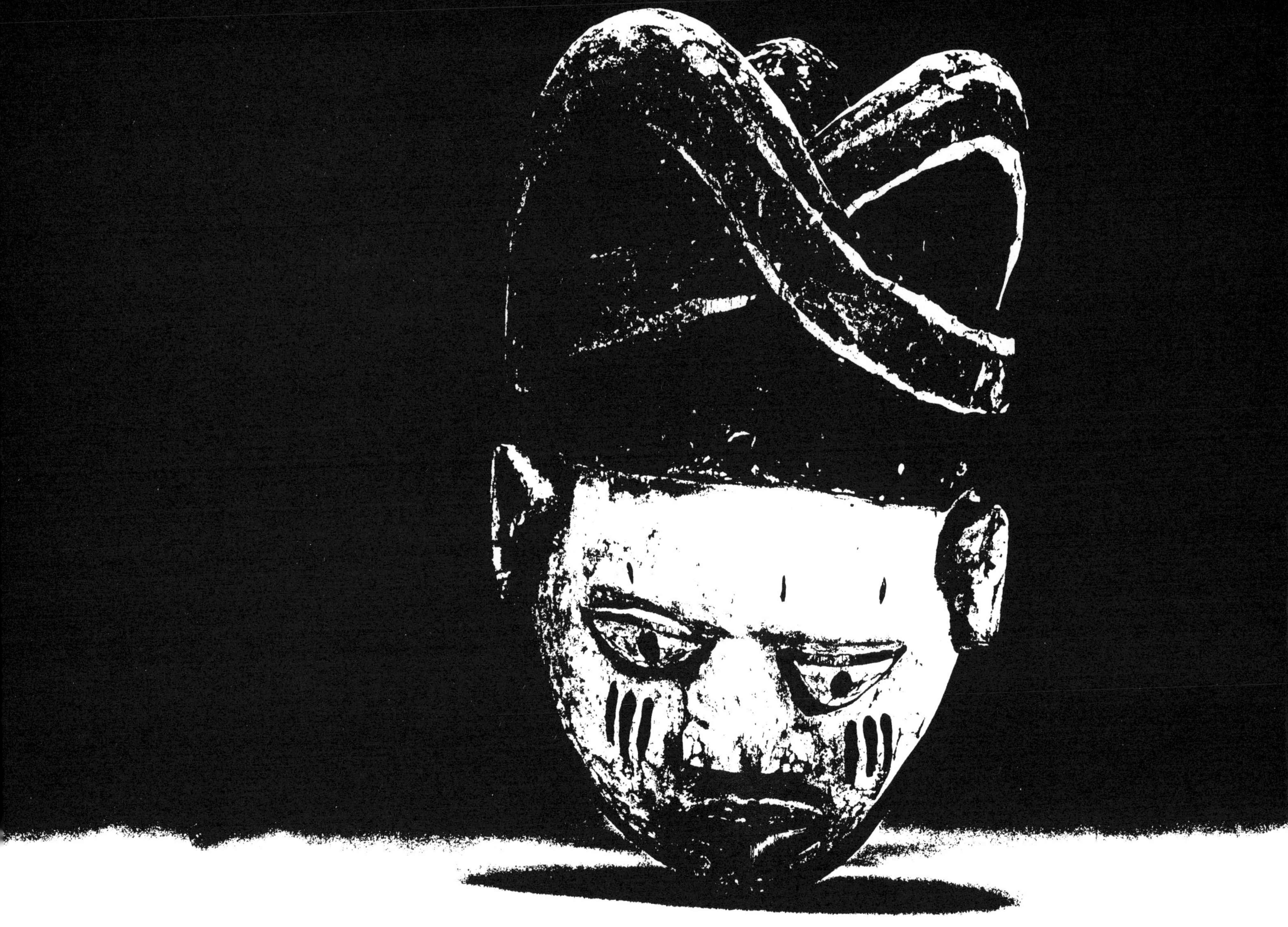

The Tribal Style

Selections from the African Collection at the Peabody Museum of Salem

by
John R. Grimes

Catalog Design by Frederick MacDougall Johnson
Photography by Markham Sexton

Peabody Museum of Salem, Salem, Massachusetts 1984

Preface

The African continent, second only to Asia in total landmass, is the home of diverse indigenous cultures, each with unique systems of coping with its environment, maintaining social balance, and interpreting and expressing its place in the universe. What is surprising, perhaps, is that it is only within the last several decades that the creative accomplishments of these people, including plastic arts, music, dance, folklore and crafts, have begun to be appreciated outside Africa. Objects which less than a century ago would have been regarded as little more than curiosities today form the basis of countless museum exhibitions and publications annually, while the influence of African art on that of the West is widely manifest in music, choreography, sculpture and painting.

Although it is entirely proper that African art assumes its place among Asian, Western and so-called "primitive" arts, its legitimacy as art does not necessarily derive from its acceptance or popularity outside the culture in which it was produced. Conceived and executed in response to specific personal, social, and religious needs, African art is, above all, for and about Africans. To an extent, therefore, it will always be foreign to us; the aesthetic and iconographic precepts which guided its creators are too far removed from our own perspective for us to view their art precisely as they did.

Clearly, it would be inaccurate to suggest that African art is completely beyond our comprehension. In fact, the work of anthropologists, art historians and other scholars provides us with powerful insights into its cultural context and meaning. Archaeological discoveries permit us to trace the development of a number of African artistic traditions, as well as the effects of cultural borrowing, both within Africa and without. In areas where the traditional idiom is preserved, the artists themselves have helped further our understanding of their work. Beyond this, African art embodies mastery of form, composition and medium; embraces basic human themes, and imparts a vitality characteristic of all great art.

This catalog, and the exhibit which it accompanies, was organized to fulfull two basic objectives. First, it is intended to bring to light the Peabody Museum of Salem's sub-Saharan African art collection, which is virtually unknown even though it was one of the first to be commenced in this hemisphere. Secondly, the catalog is meant to balance the tendency of most publications on African art to focus strictly on sculpture and masks, ignoring the wide variety of functional and personal artifacts which are a major part of African life. Included in the present work are personal accessories, domestic utensils, sculpture, masks, musical instruments and weapons, all of which display a high degree of artistic achievement.

The author readily acknowledges the contribution of many individuals, through their published works, to the development of this catalog and exhibit. Many of these sources are included in the bibliography, and the reader is encouraged to pursue them for fuller treatment of the cultures and artifacts described herein. Several individuals have been of great personal assistance through their expertise, comments, and direction, particularly William Teel, Peter Fetchko, Gregor Trinkaus-Randall, Margie Krebs and Susan Bean. Frederick MacDougall Johnson designed both catalog and exhibit, which were funded in part by a grant from the National Endowment for the Arts. Photography for the catalog was by Markham Sexton, and additional technical assistance was provided by John Koza, Kathleen Smith and Marjorie Detkin; Margaret Warner helped prepare the catalog manuscript.

Introduction

Salem and the African Trade

The origins of the Peabody Museum's African collection, like its Pacific, Asian and American collections, are deeply rooted in Salem's long history of maritime trade. Direct contact between Salem and Africa was established within decades of the town's founding in 1626. In 1645, Governor John Winthrop wrote:

"One of our ships, which went to the Canaries in the beginning of November last, returned now, and brought wine, and sugar, and salt, and some tobacco, which she had at Barbadoes, in exchange for Africoes [i.e. slaves], which she carried from Maio [in the Cape Verde islands, West Africa]."

(John Winthrop. *Journal, History of New England, 1630-1649.* As quoted in Donnan, E. *Documents Illustrative of the History of the Slave Trade to America.* Washington: Carnegie Institution. 1932.)

The pattern of trade which Winthrop describes characterized New England's occasional commerce with West Africa until the American Revolution. Although actual cargoes and destinations varied, generally tobacco and other goods carried to West Africa were exchanged for slaves destined for the plantation colonies of the West Indies, Virginia and the Carolinas. In the West Indies slaves were traded for rum, molasses, and sugar to be returned to New England, where the cycle began anew. This triangular trade became more profitable during the 18th century, when the establishment of distilleries in New England permitted the production of inexpensive rum suited to the African trade. Slaves were seldom imported directly to New England, since northern colonies lacked the large cash crops that required an extensive labor force.

Commerce with West Africa was interrupted by the Revolution, and trade with the West Indies was almost completely curtailed in 1783 when the British-controlled islands were closed to American vessels. Faced with the resulting loss of revenues, a chronic imbalance of payments and lack of credit abroad, American merchants hastened to establish new markets for their cargoes. Trade was opened in 1784 with China and India, both previously closed to Americans, while the African trade underwent a period of reorganization as New England traders gradually shifted from slaves to commodities such as gold dust and ivory. Legitimate commerce with Africa received additional impetus in 1788 when both Massachusetts and Rhode Island passed legislation prohibiting the slave trade. Even after 1808, however, when the governments of both the United States and Britain outlawed slave trading completely, New England's participation in the slave trade did not altogether cease. Demand for slaves in the southern states escalated with the growth of cotton plantations, and the large illicit traffic continued until the Civil War.

The outbreak of war in Europe in the 1790's stimulated the expansion of legitimate trade opportunities with West Africa. Scattered along the African coast, European forts and trading settlements, called factories, were deprived of regular provisioning from their homeland. Neutral American vessels quickly capitalized on this situation by supplying beef, flour, tobacco, rum and lumber in exchange for African products, specie, or credit with European trading firms. This relative prosperity was short-lived, however, for with the cessation of hostilities in Europe, and the end of the War of 1812, American trading at French and British factories was banned. Although trade with Dutch and Danish factories was unaffected, and exchanges with coastal natives continued as before, New England merchants looked toward East Africa for additional commercial opportunities.

The lucrative east coast trade network established a millennium earlier by Arabs had passed to the Portuguese about 1500, then to Omani Muslims. In the early 19th century, Zanzibar, lying at the crossroads of inland caravan routes and Indian Ocean shipping, was transformed into a thriving center for cloves, ivory and slaves by Sayyid Said, the Imam of Muscat (1804-56). New England vessels first arrived about 1817, and after some promising commerical returns, Edmund Roberts of Portsmouth, New Hampshire, began negotiations with the Imam to formalize American-Zanzibar trade relations. The resulting commercial treaty, ratified in 1835, provided for establishment of an American consulate at Zanzibar, and Richard Waters of Salem was named first consul. Salem ships consequently dominated the Zanzibar trade until 1841, when Britain installed its own consul and began to compete actively with the New Englanders.

West coast trade was resumed with British and French factories by the 1830's, but cargoes on both coasts were gradually changing. While ivory remained a valued export, hides, gum copal, and peanuts were favored commodities. African hides were an economical alternative to animal skins from South America and the western United States for the burgeoning New England tanning industry. Palm oil figured in the production of candles, and gum copal was an important component of varnish; Salem possessed processing plants for both. Peanuts, a native American crop that flourished in Africa, became a popular novelty food at fairs and circuses.

Through the 1840's and 1850's, New England's trade with Africa remained moderately active. Salem's growth as a leading center for this commerce coincided with a decrease in its importance as a center for trade with China. While Salem Harbor, which had silted in, was not deep enough for the larger, faster ships of the China trade, it was still adequate for the older, shallow-draft vessels that plied the Atlantic to Africa. By the 1860's, however, even the trade with Africa began to decline in Salem, as more commerce shifted to Boston and New York, and as European shipping firms increasingly turned to steamships.

Origins of the African Collection

The earliest artifacts in the Peabody Museum's African collection were assembled by the East India Marine Society, of which the museum is a direct outgrowth. Founded in 1799, the Society was composed of Salem captains and supercargoes who had sailed beyond the Cape of Good Hope or Cape Horn. Among the chartered goals of the Society, in addition to providing for families of members lost at sea, was the establishment of a "cabinet of natural and artificial curiosities" from the places they visited.

The Society's cabinet grew rapidly. The first catalog was published in 1821, followed by a second edition in 1831 and a supplement in 1837. By then, some 5,000 entries recorded assorted natural history specimens and ethnological objects from Asia, the Pacific Islands, the Americas, and Africa.

Donations of African artifacts were relatively rare during this early period, since most Society members were engaged in trade with other areas of the world. One

Society member, Henry Leavitt (1803-1830), sailed several times to the East Coast of Africa and returned with a collection of artifacts from Zanzibar and Madagascar for the Society. In following years, the African collection continued to grow through other gifts of utilitarian objects and weapons. As the reputation of the Society's cabinet spread, it attracted donations from non-members as well.

By the 1860's, faltering membership and lack of funds had brought the East India Marine Society close to bankruptcy. The noted philanthropist George Peabody rescued the Society's museum in 1867 by purchasing the building in which the collections were housed and establishing an endowment for their care. Ar-rangments were also made to acquire as permanent deposits both the Society's collection and the ethnological and natural history collections of the neighboring Essex Institute. These combined collections became the basis for a new museum, called the Peabody Academy of Science, re-named the Peabody Museum of Salem in 1915.

A number of artifacts acquired from the Essex Institute were of African origin. Particularly important were those collected by Edward D. Ropes and William G. Webb, both successors to Richard Waters as consuls to Zanzibar. Others came from Dr. George A. Perkins, who served with the Episcopal Mission at Cape Palmas, West Africa, in the 1830's and 1840's.

Collections by missionaries account for a sizable portion of the Museum's African holdings from the middle of the 19th century. In 1812, Salem became the head-quarters of the American Board of Commissioners for Foreign Missions, which subsequently established stations throughout the world, including West Africa (1834) and South Africa (1836). Missionaries serving the A.B.C.F.M. in Africa assembled large numbers of artifacts, particularly from the Zulu in South Africa, which have since come to the Museum. Reverend Thomas Adams, who worked in the Congo River basin in the 1890's, contributed important objects from that area.

Missionary activities in Africa during the second half of the nineteenth century coincided with increasing exploration of the African interior by such pioneers as Richard Burton, John Speke, David Livingstone and Henry Stanley. Remarkably, the Museum owns a number of mementos relating to Livingstone and Stanley, as well as several dozen artifacts gathered by E.J. Glave, who served as a field associate of Stanley in the 1880's.

Since 1900, the African collection has benefited from many gifts by collectors, to supplement limited museum purchases. Dr. C.G. Weld, known primarily for his gifts to the Museum's Japanese collections, donated a quantity of objects during the early years of the century. Recent gifts of sub-Saharan figural sculpture underscore the new recognition accorded African tribal carvings as, far from primitive, one of the meaningful artistic traditions of the world.

Through the generosity of individual donors and supporters of the Museum, these additions insure the long-standing historical continuity of a collection which reflects the changing character of a continent, and its peoples, that figured prominently in Salem's past.

Format

The existing literature on African art and ethnology testifies to the inherent problems in an undertaking such as this catalog. Foremost is the bewildering variety of names and spellings applied to given groups of people. The Chokwe, for example, are designated by at least 25 different terms, as diverse as Ahioko, Badjok, Chiboque, Makioko and Waschokwe, making it difficult to correlate information from varied sources, particularly older studies.

This selection of the most significant African artifacts in the Museum's collection is organized into three broad geographic regions: West Africa, the Congo River Basin, and the Lakes Region and Southern Africa. Within these areas, tribal designations follow George P. Murdock's ethnolinguistic compendium, *Africa: Its Peoples and Their Culture History* (McGraw-Hill). Murdock's classification dispenses with the German convention of adding a "Ba" prefix to the names of Bantu-speaking peoples, although in some cases his terms are not those most widely used in African art references. To insure consistency, Murdock's scheme is followed throughout, with important alternative names included in the explanatory captions and index.

Another obstacle is the paucity of literature on many aspects of African material culture. The functional objects of areas rich in plastic arts, such as West Africa and the Congo River basin, are frequently overlooked. East Africa, where sculpture and masks are less conspicuous, is often ignored altogether as are most southern African groups apart from the Zulu. A notable exception, Roy Sieber's exhibition catalog, *African Furniture and Household Objects* (Indiana University Press), was invaluable for the identification of functional objects.

Any collection with origins as distant and diverse as the Museum's has inherited numerous errors of attribution. Museum acquisition records may note only Africa, West Africa, Kenya, etc. for individual artifacts. In attributing these pieces, the author has benefited greatly from the comments of visiting scholars and expert associates of the Museum. Some identifications remain elusive, however, and it is hoped this catalog will elicit more information from knowledgeable readers.

Individual catalog entries are presented in the following format:

Object type (Museum catalog number)

Tribal/linguistic group, Country

Material(s)

Dimension, i.e. H.-height, L.-length, D.-diameter

Explanatory notes.
Donor, date received. Collector, date collected.

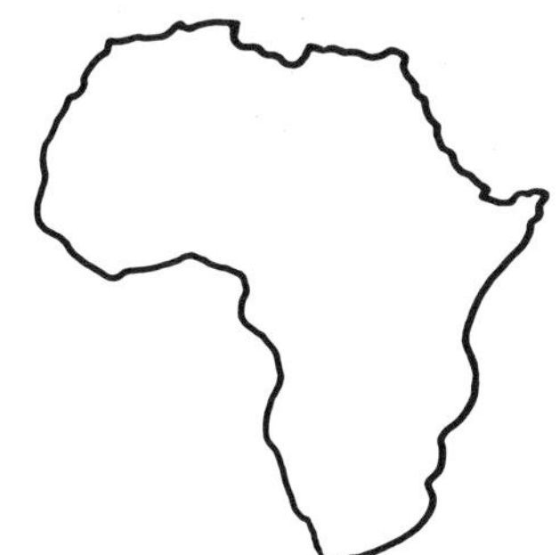

Maps indicate the approximate location of tribal/ linguistic groups.

9

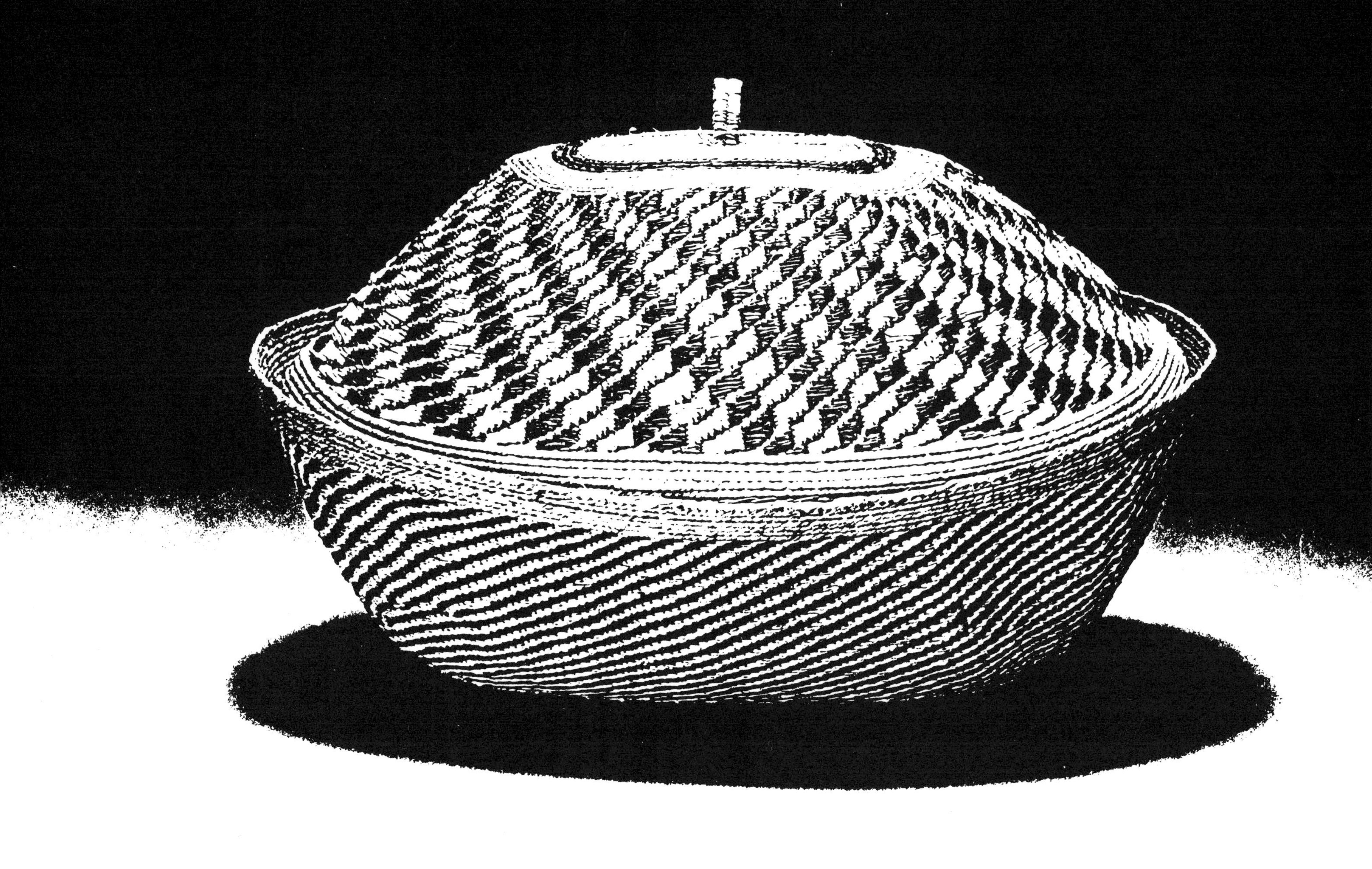

West Africa

West Africa, as defined here, comprises the broad band between the Gulf of Guinea and the Sahara Desert, together with the area south of Lake Chad to the edge of the Congo River basin. Rain forest stretches over much of the coastal plain from Guinea to Cameroon, where it merges with the large equatorial rain forest of the interior. North of the coastal forest, savanna blankets a succession of low plateaus. The dominant topographic feature in the region is the Niger River, which originates in the highlands of Guinea and flows northeastward through Mali, then southeastward to the Nigerian coast.

The peoples of West Africa speak languages of Negritic stock, except those living east of the Gulf of Guinea, where Bantu languages prevail. All subsist by shifting agriculture, leaving fields fallow after several plantings. Millet, rice, sorghum, bananas, maize, and yams are among the principal crops. Fishing is significant along the coast and inland waterways, and most groups hunt to some degree. Cattle are kept throughout the region, primarily for use as bride payments rather than for their milk or meat.

The area is divided culturally into two regions: the Western Sudan (from the Arabic, *Bilad as-Sudan*, "Land of the Blacks"), and the Guinea Coast, which parallels the equator to its south. The savanna-dwelling Sudanese, bounded by the northern desert and southern forest, maintained continual cultural and material exchanges with Islamic North Africa from at least the 11th century. It was in this region that the native medieval empires of Ghana, Mali and Songhai flourished. Inhabitants of the Guinea Coast rain forest belt, between the Atlantic and the northern savanna, included countless tribal groups, some of whom established powerful trading kingdoms along the Ivory and Gold Coasts, as well as in ancient and modern Nigeria. While many West African tribes and cities were Islamized, others stubbornly resisted both Islamic and Western influences upon their traditional ways of life, their ancient tribal beliefs, and the objects fashioned to serve them.

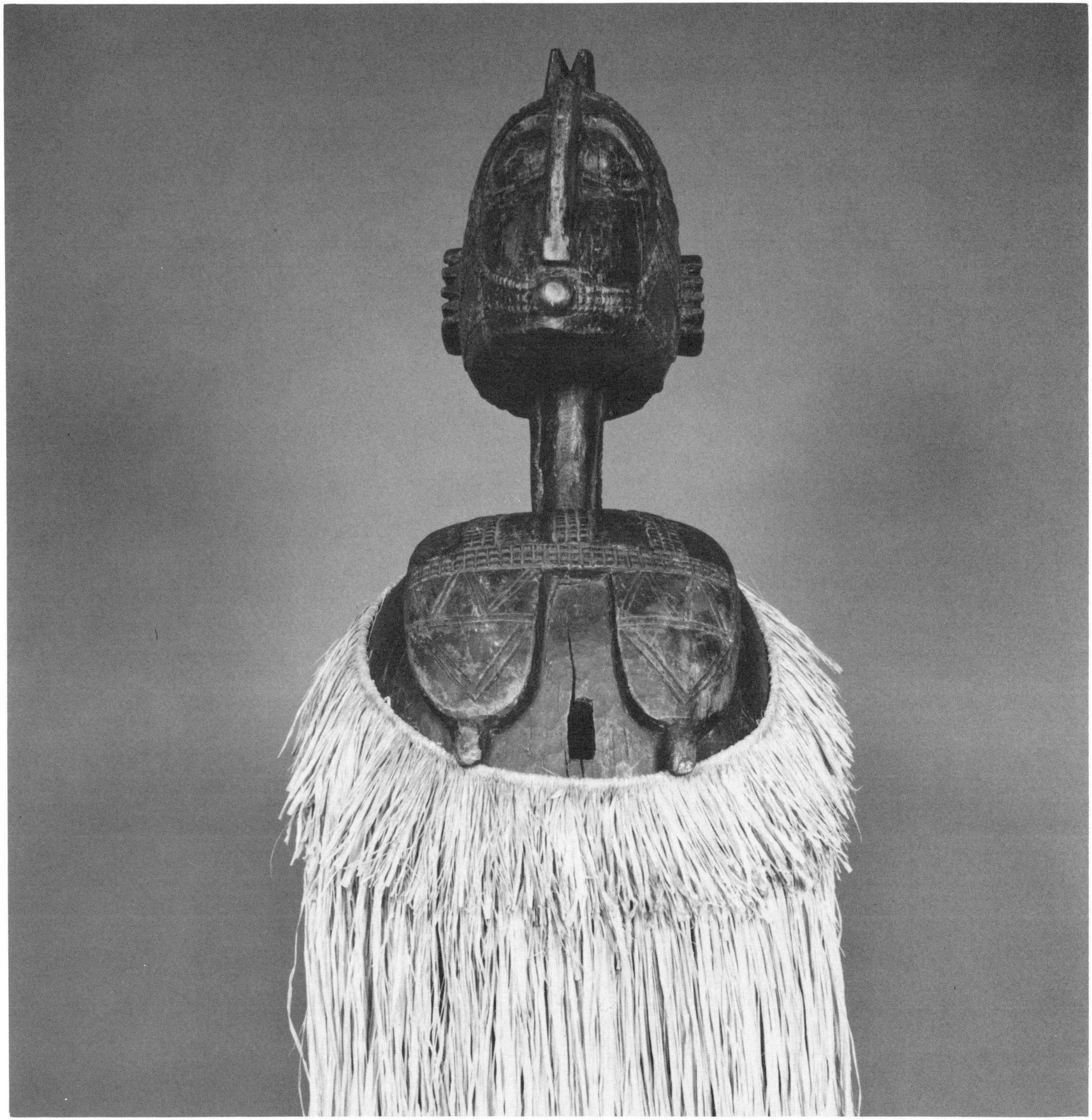

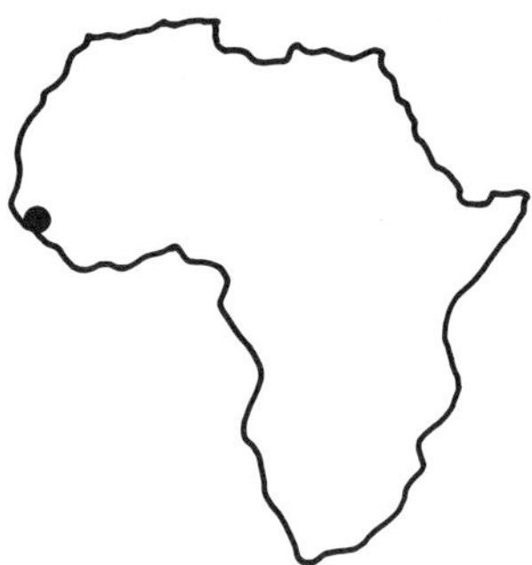

Mask (E72,850)

Baga, Guinea

Wood, pigment, replicated raffia skirt

H. (mask only) 112 cm.

The river-dwelling Baga of Guinea produce one of the most imposing of all African masks. Representing *Nimba*, a fertility goddess, they are used in *Simba* society rituals for the promotion of human fertility and crop success. *Nimba* masks may weigh over one hundred pounds, and require that dancers take turns during performances. This mask was collected in the village of Kema. *Anonymous gift, 1981.*

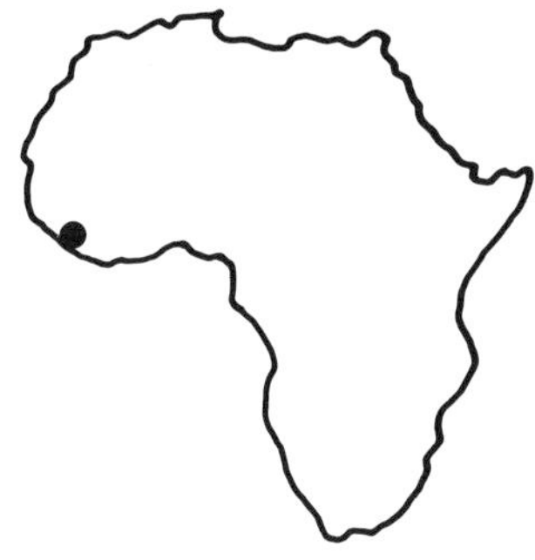

Covered Basket (E4,011 &
E4,012)

Group uncertain, Sierra
Leone

Vegetable fiber

H. 18 cm.

African baskets are seldom
displayed or illustrated, despite
the fact that many are as
aesthetically pleasing and finely
crafted as any in the world. This
example, from Sierra Leone, is
produced by a technique known
as twining. It is possible that the
cover is not original to the basket.
*Ex Essex Institute Collection,
1867. Collected by Capt. William
T. Julio, ca. 1843.*

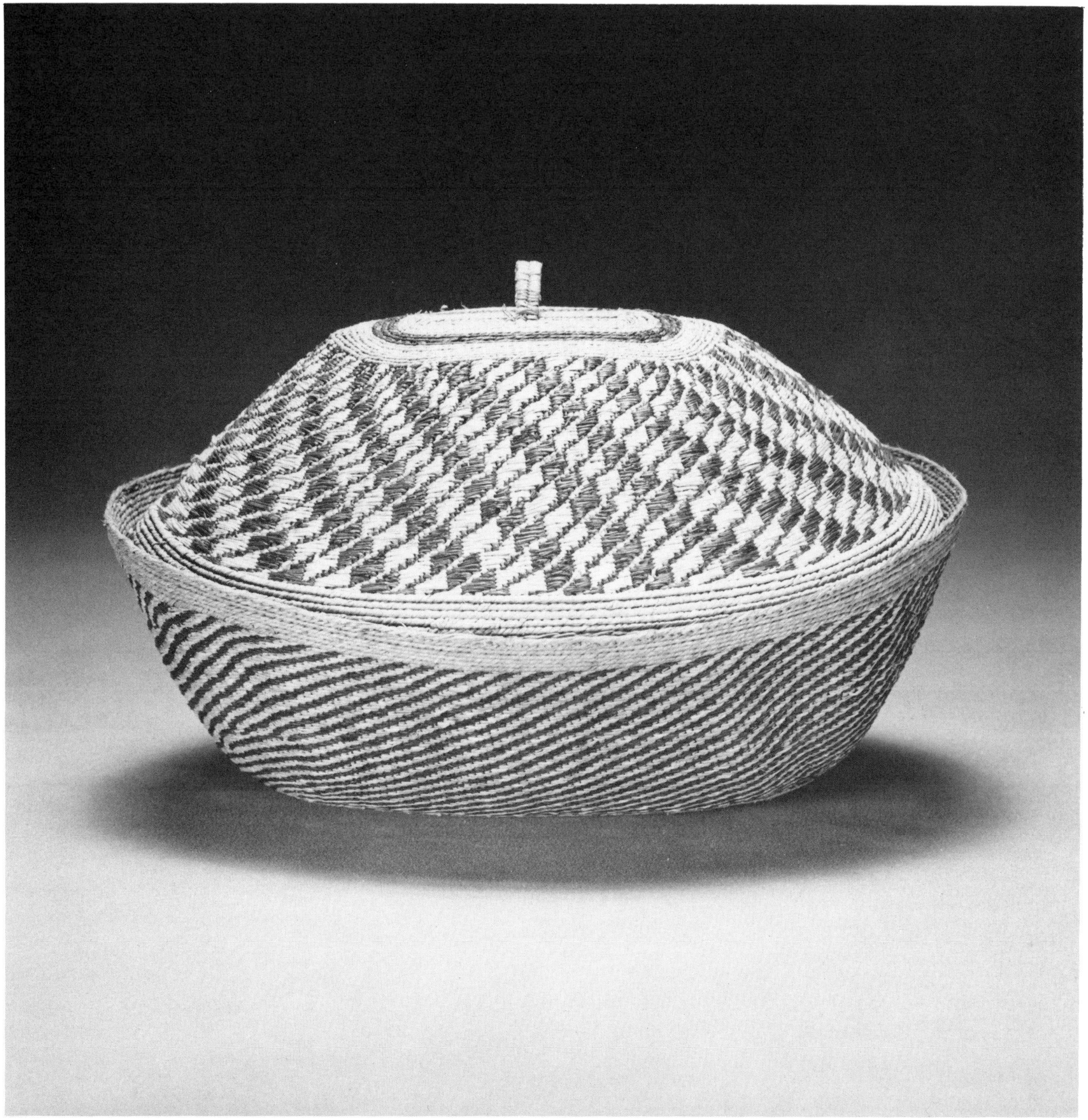

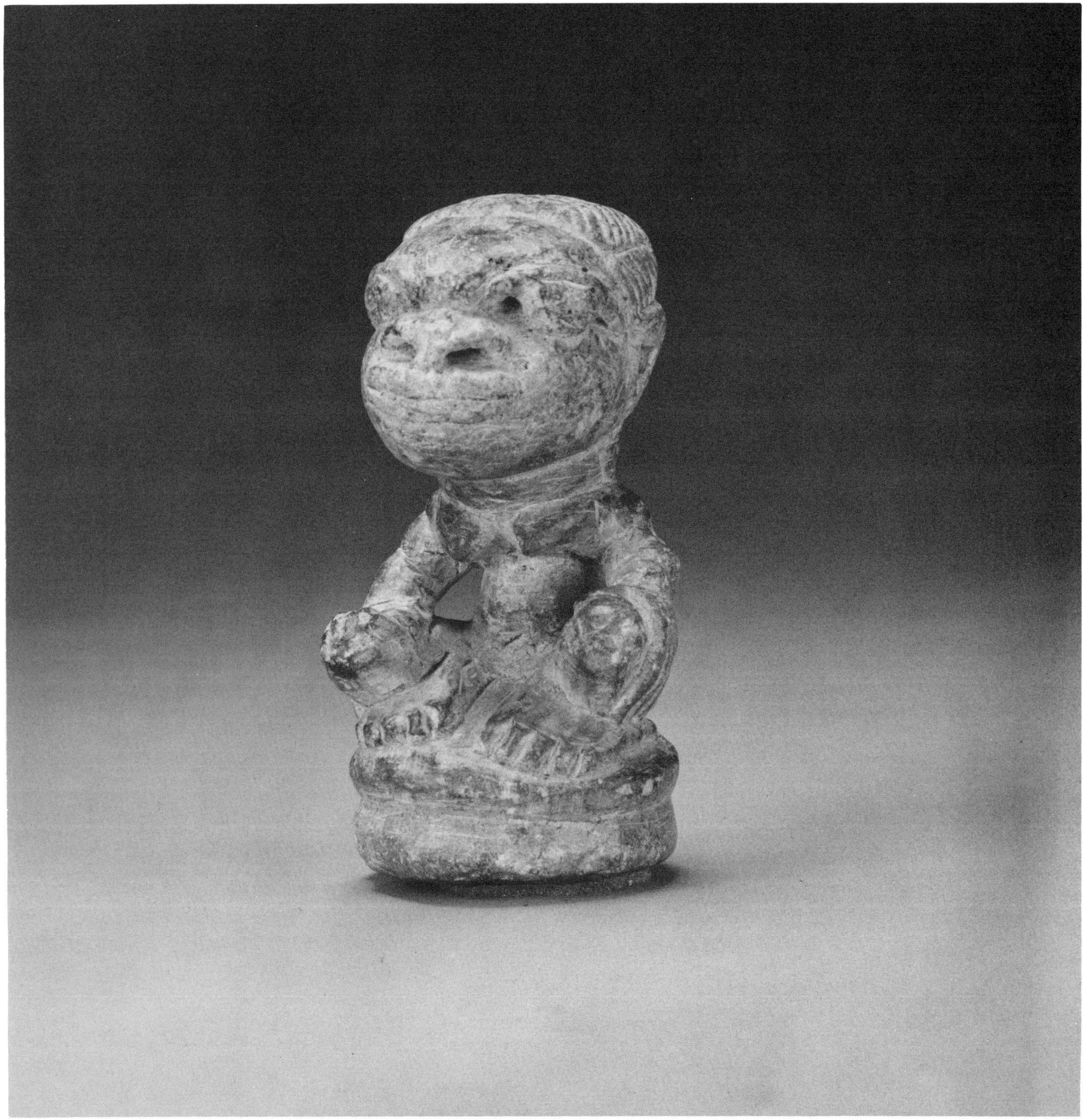

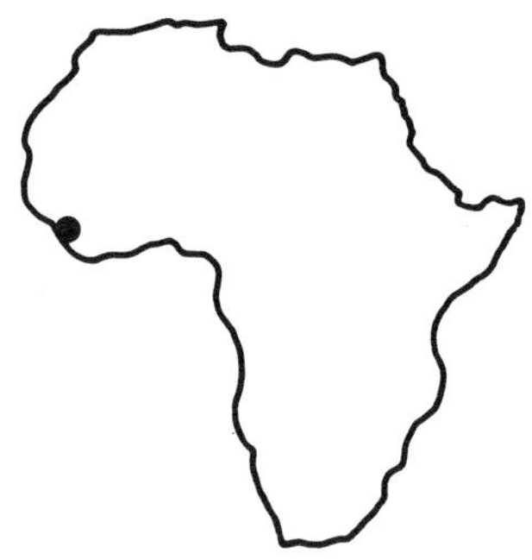

Figure (E72,091)

Sherbro, Sierra Leone

Steatite

H. 15 cm.

Little is known of these small steatite figures, which are periodically unearthed in the Sherbro country in Sierra Leone. They would seem to predate European contact, since there is no account of their manufacture by contemporary natives. The Sherbro regard them as magical beings, *nomoli*, who are consulted as oracles or set up in small shrines to serve as field protectors. *Anonymous gift, 1981.*

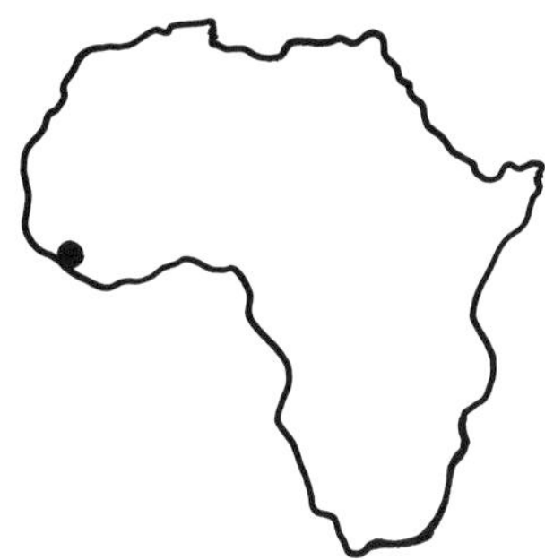

Mask (E28,249)

Mende, Sierra Leone

Wood, pigment

H. 43 cm.

Women maintain an important political presence among the Mende. This power is embodied in the *Bundu* society, an exclusively female organization which enforces standards for behavior and controls initiation ceremonies marking the transition to womanhood. *Bundu* society masks incorporate the ideal of feminine beauty, with high forehead, serene expression, and elaborate hairstyle. The fleshy folds at the base of the mask signify wealth. *Gift of the estate of I. Anderson, 1949.*

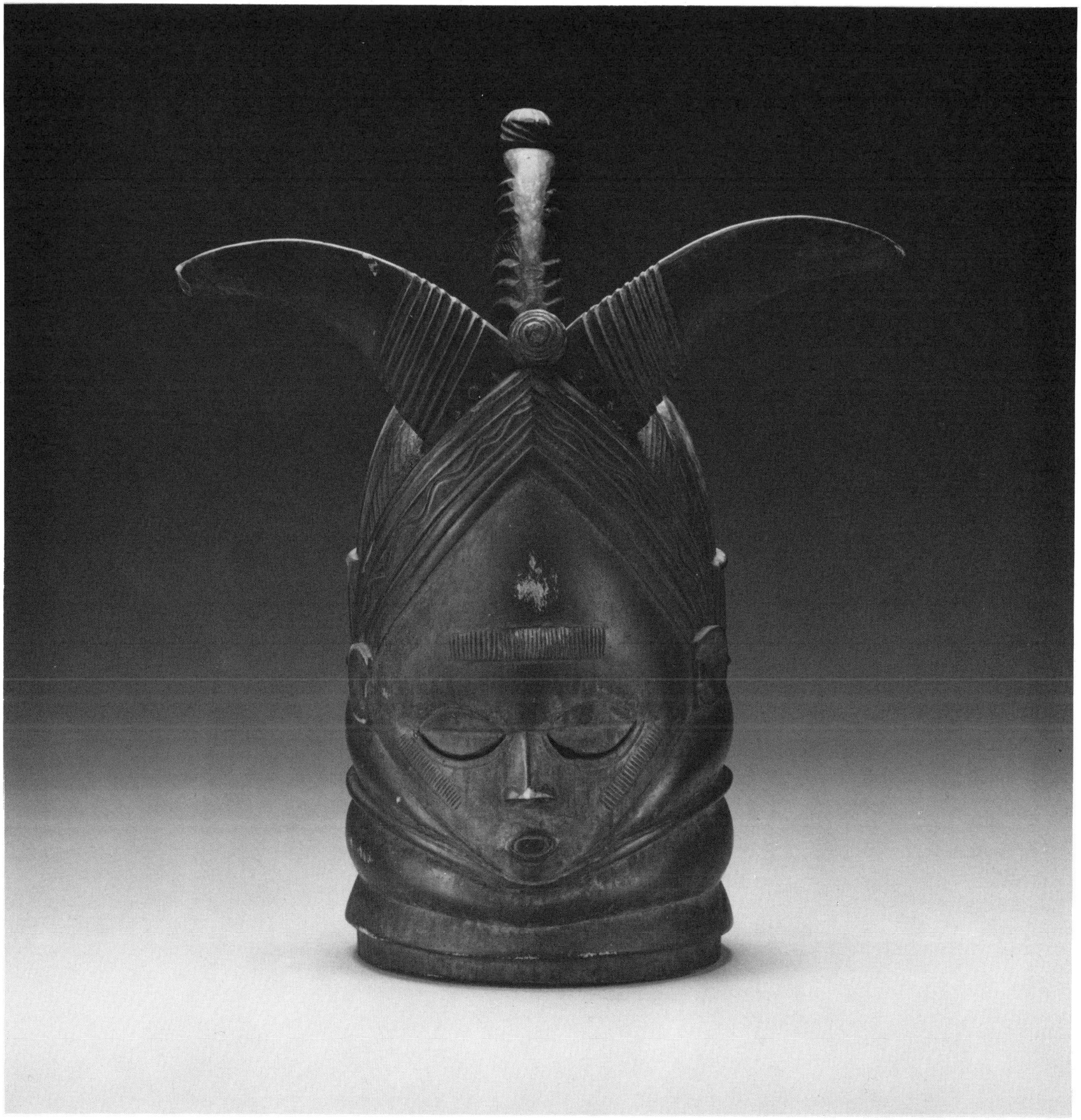

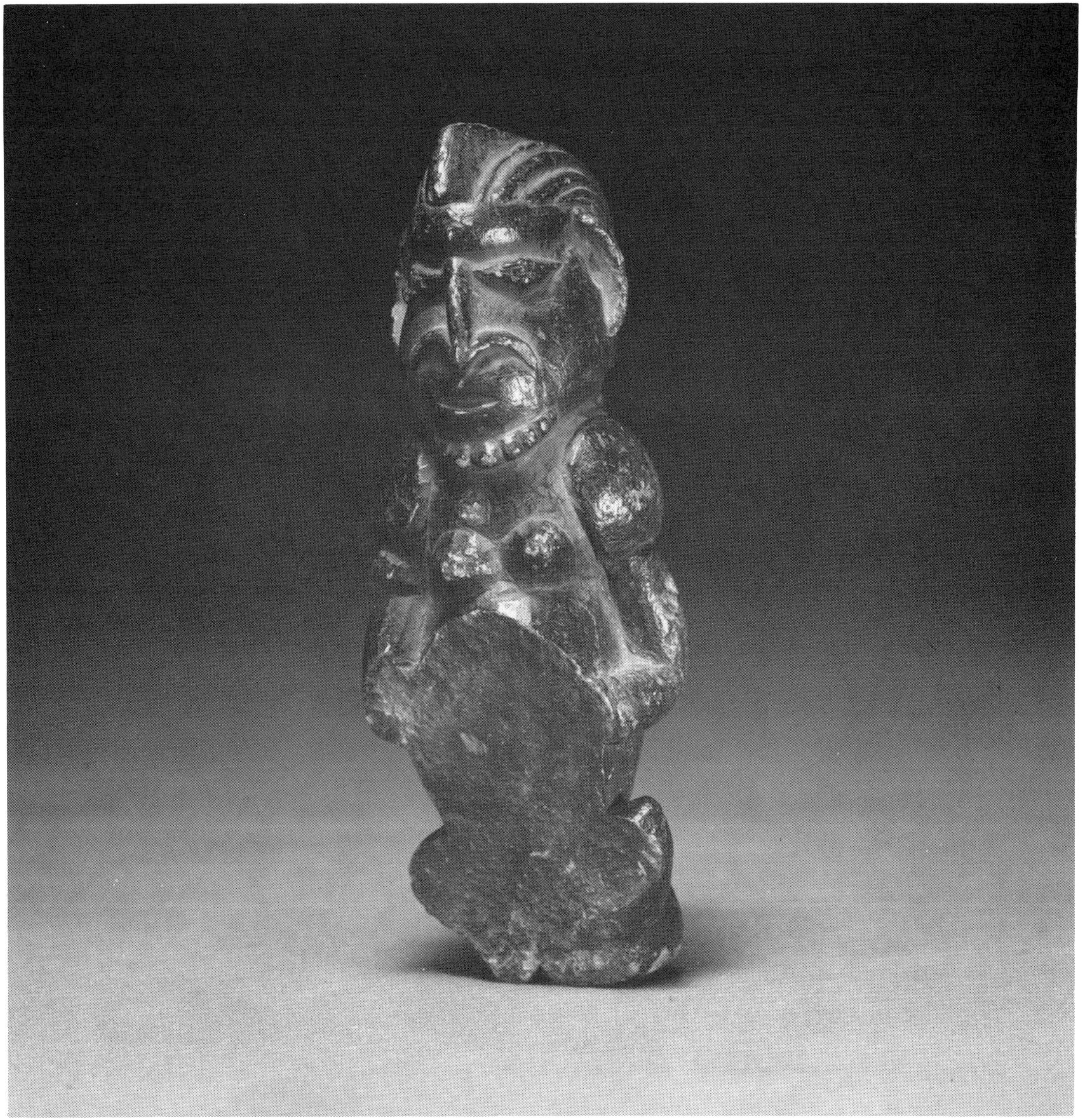

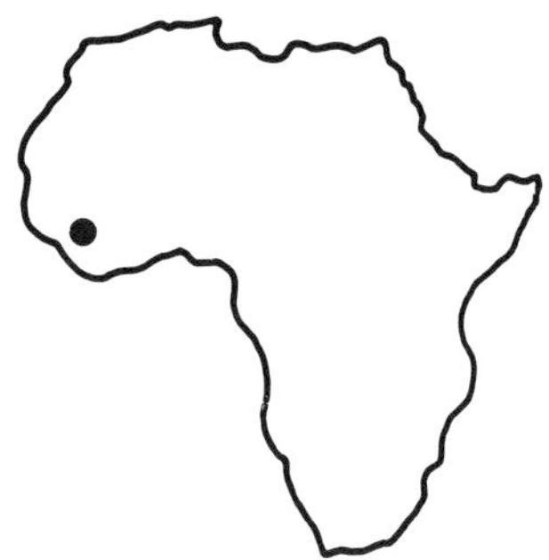

Figure (E48,592)

Kissi, Guinea

Steatite

H. 18 cm.

The Kissi do not presently practice carving, but like the Sherbro they occasionally find archaeological stone figures in their fields. Called *pomtan*, these figures are believed to embody the spirits of ancestors, whose identity can be revealed in dreams. *Gift of Dr. Enoch Ware, 1972.*

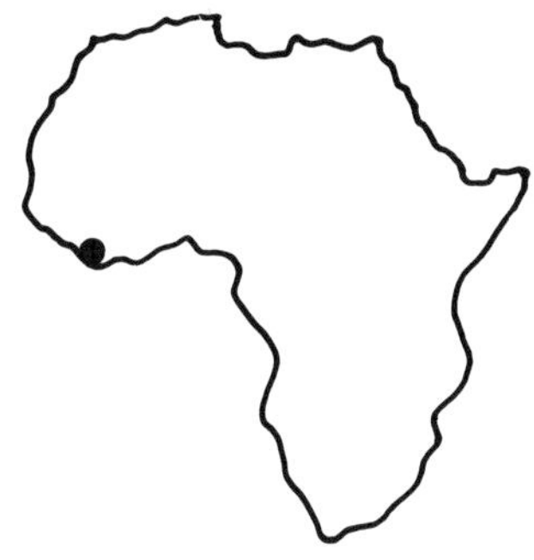

Mask (E6,764)

Probably Grebo, Liberia

Wood, ceramic, iron nails, pigment

H. 46 cm.

This mask was collected by a Salem physician, George A. Perkins, while acting as a secular agent for the Episcopal Mission at Cape Palmas. Stylistically, it is similar to those of the Grebo, who live in the Cape Palmas vicinity. The limbs protruding from the forehead are unusual, however, and may represent an early type, since this is one of the oldest masks known from the area. *Ex Essex Institute collection, 1867. Collected by George A. Perkins, ca. 1839-1849.*

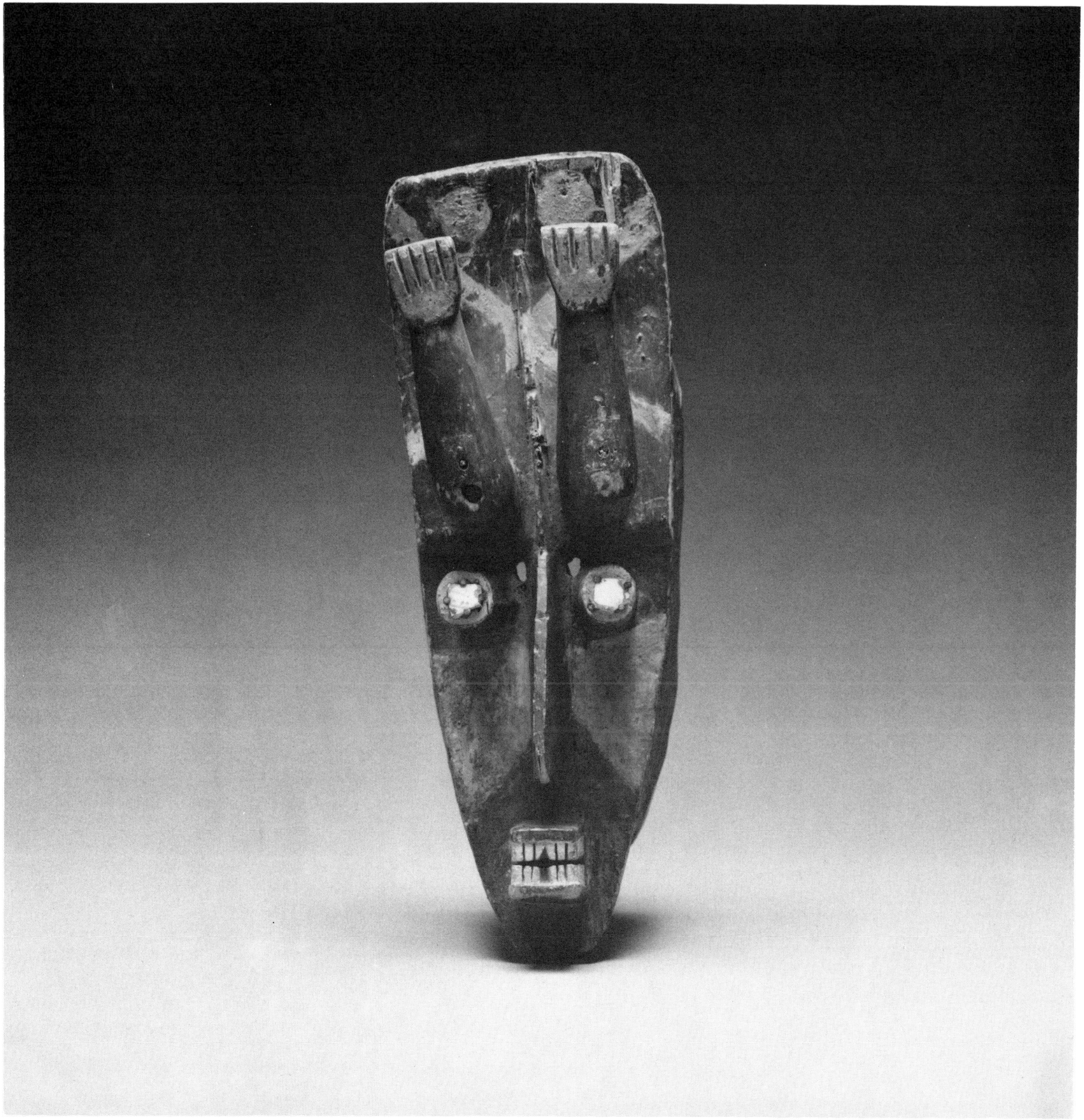

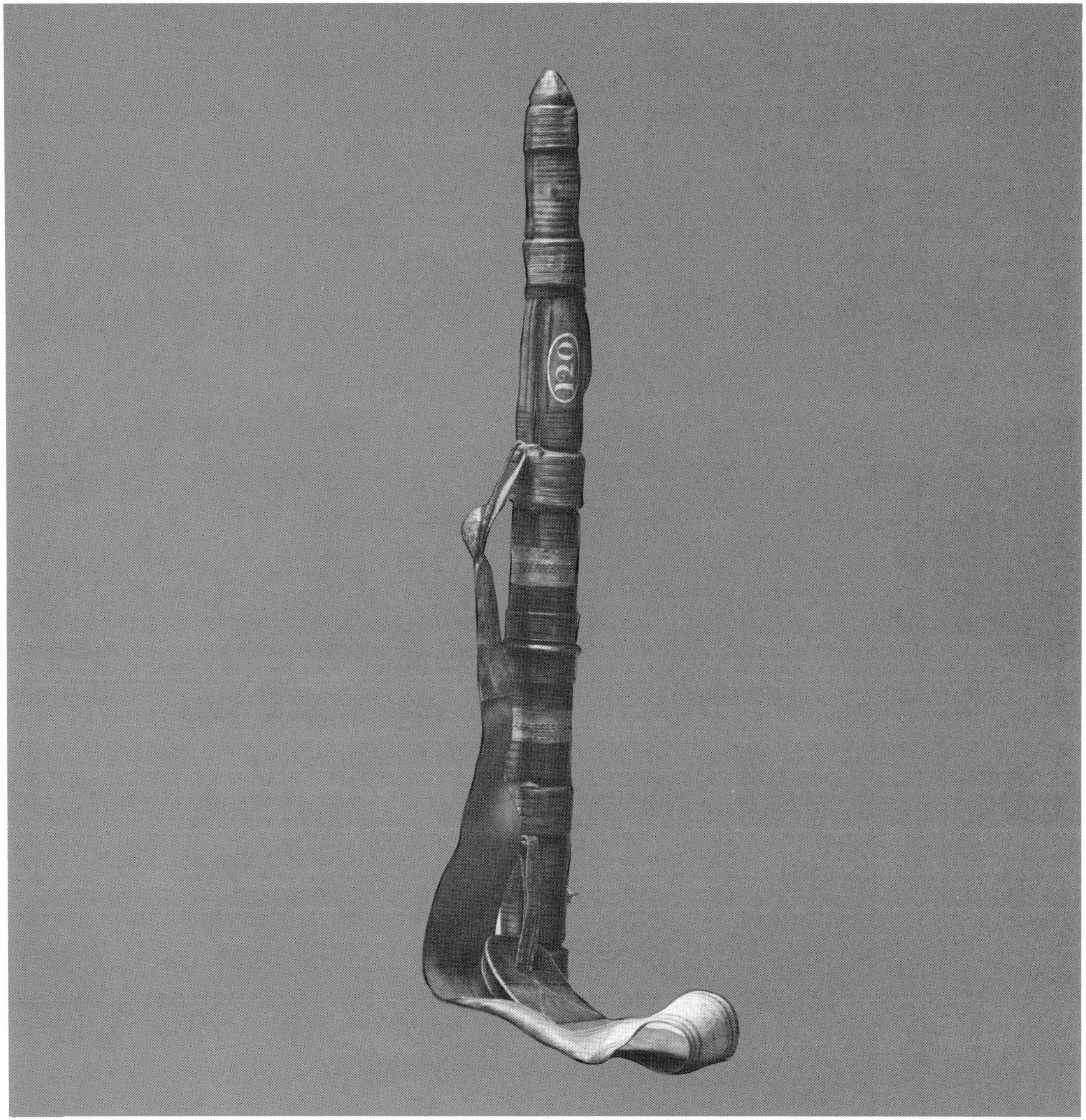

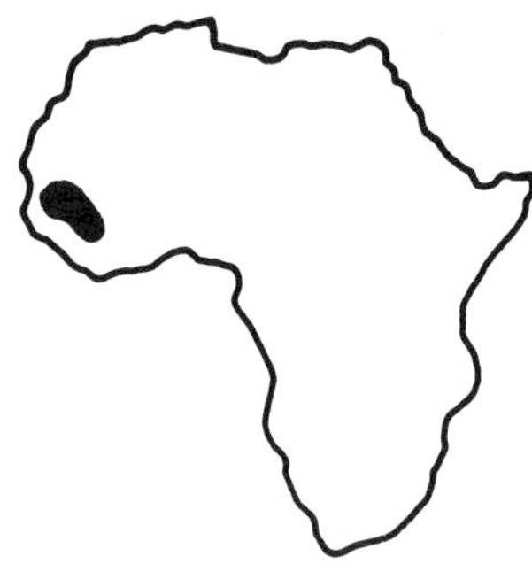

Quiver (E9,966)

Malinke, Guinea - Mali
-Ivory Coast

Leather

L. (quiver only) 67 cm.

The Malinke, or Mandingo, inhabit a large area of the western
Sudan, where they have for centuries been in contact with Arab
traders. This quiver, one of the
earliest African objects acquired
by the East India Marine Society,
displays Muslim influence in
manufacture and decoration. *Gift
of Capt. Francis Sevens, prior to
1821.*

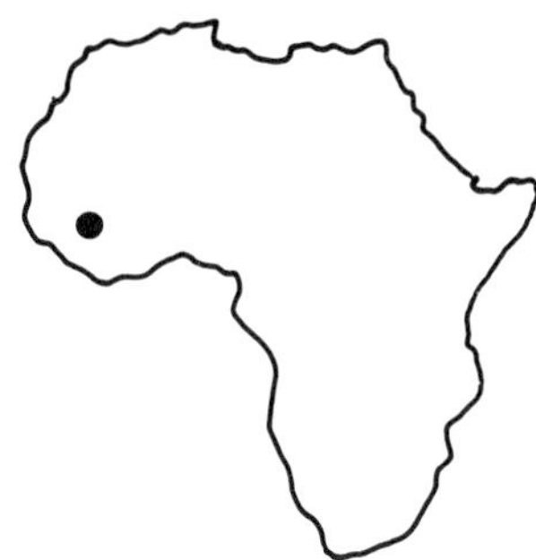

Headdress (E72,094)

Bambara, Mali

Wood

H. 66 cm.

Prior to the return of the rainy season, and during rites associated with the establishment of new fields, young male initiates among the Bambara, or Bamana, perform dances with pairs of such headdresses, known as *chi wara*, to evoke agricultural fertility. The form represents an eland, and the pairs represent the male and female principle which are evoked to insure fertility. This is the male *minianka* type with vertical curved neck and openwork mane. *Anonymous gift, 1981.*

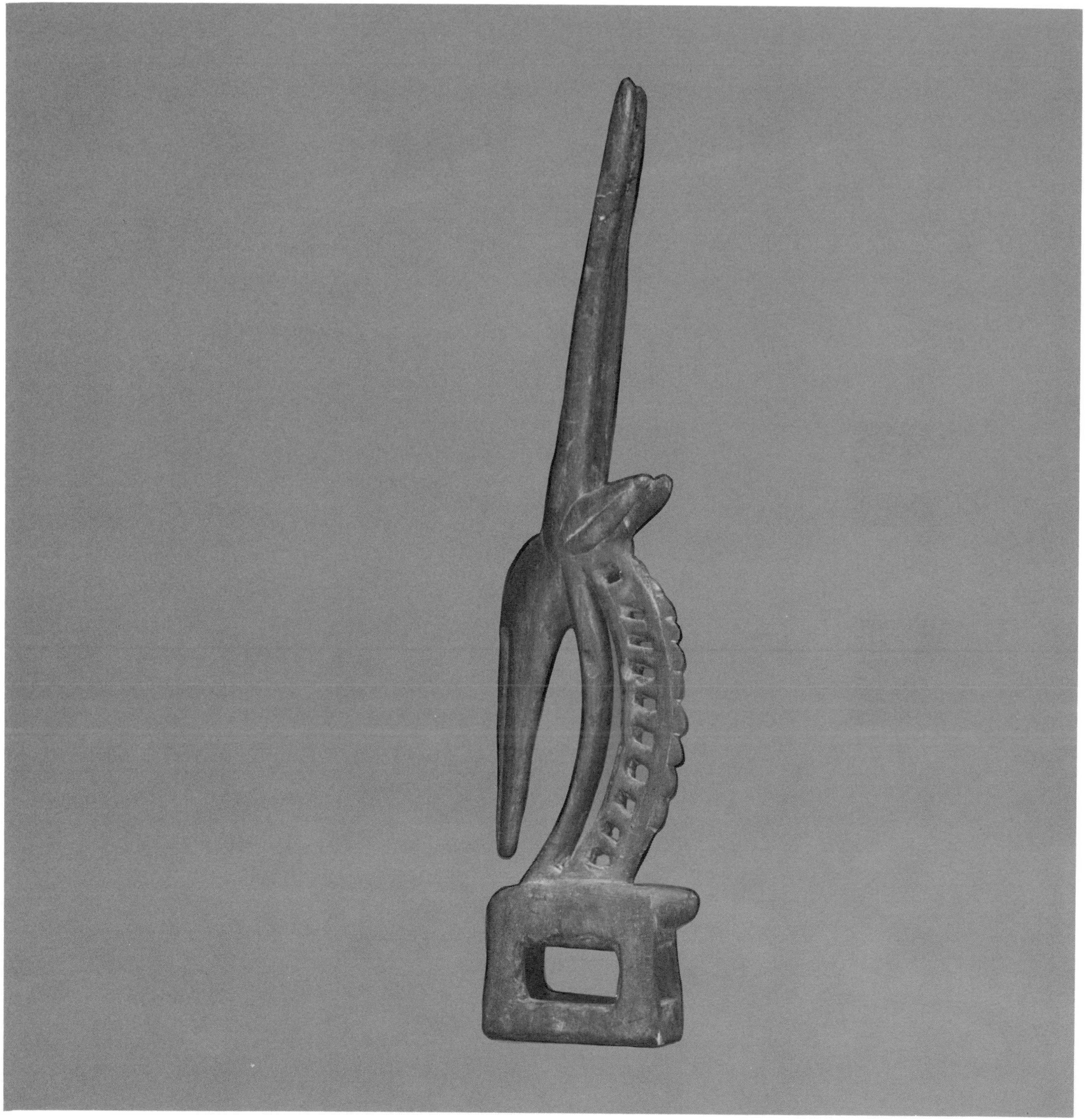

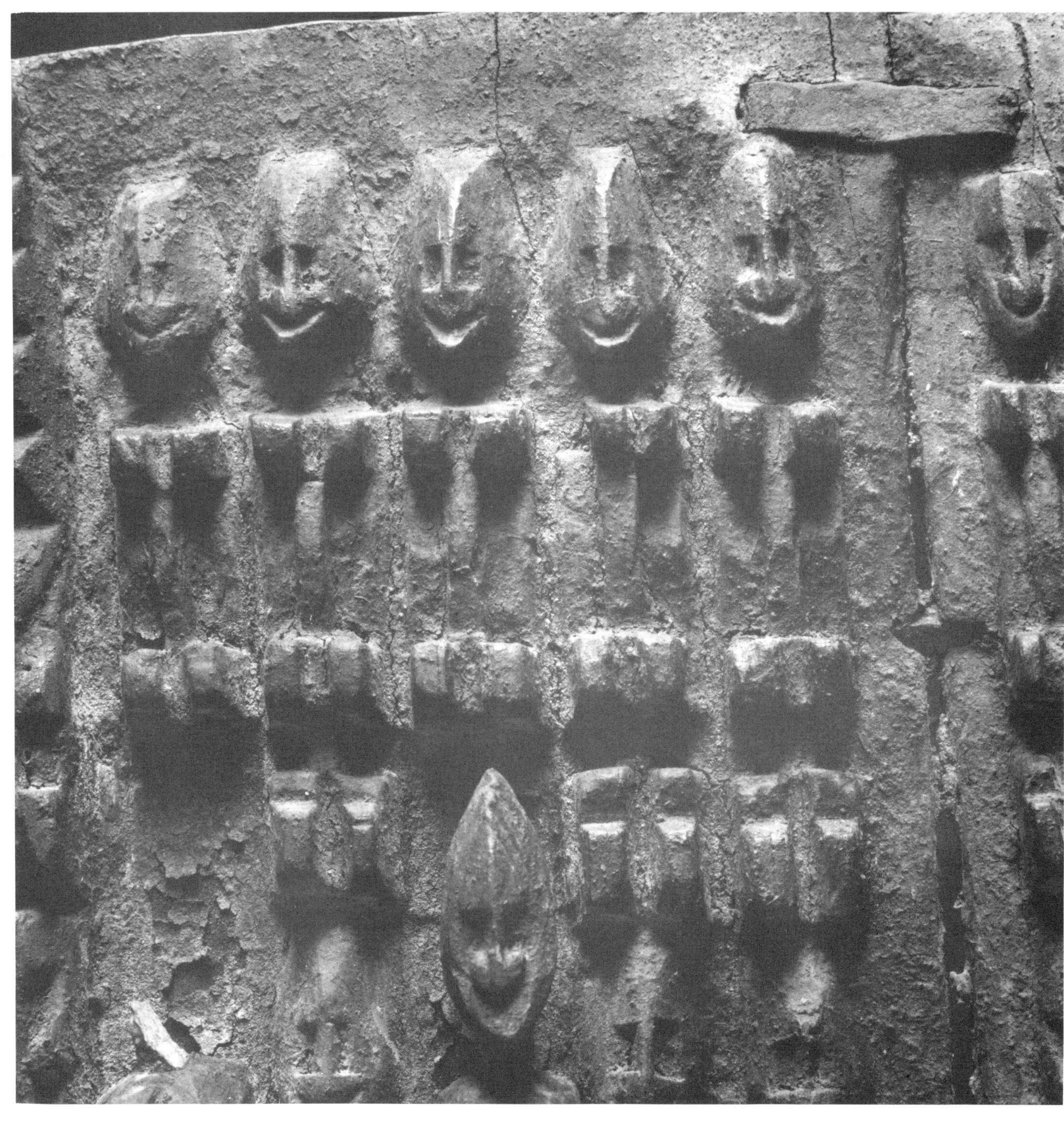

Detail of Dogon granary shutter (opposite).

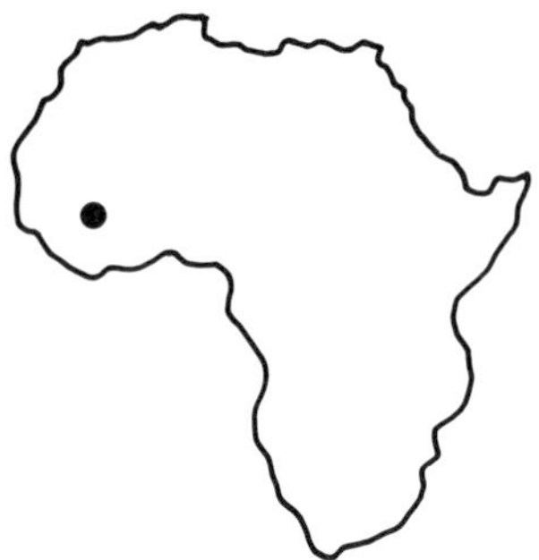

Granary Shutter (E72,097)

Dogon, Mali

Wood, iron

H. 74 cm.

The Dogon inhabit the irregular sandstone escarpment of southern Mali, at the point where the northeasterly flowing Niger River begins a wide curve toward the southeast. The rugged geometry of the countryside is mirrored in Dogon life by a pervasive symmetry, in which the elements of home and village are laid out according to a plan which likens them to members of the human body. An important part of the household complex is the small, mud-walled millet storehouses, equipped with wooden shutters and locks to protect their contents from intruders. Typically, the shutters are heavily carved with forms representing mythological ancestors. This shutter is carved with 44 figures, alluding to the 44 groups which the Dogon believe descended from the ancestral homeland, *Mande. Anonymous gift, 1981.*

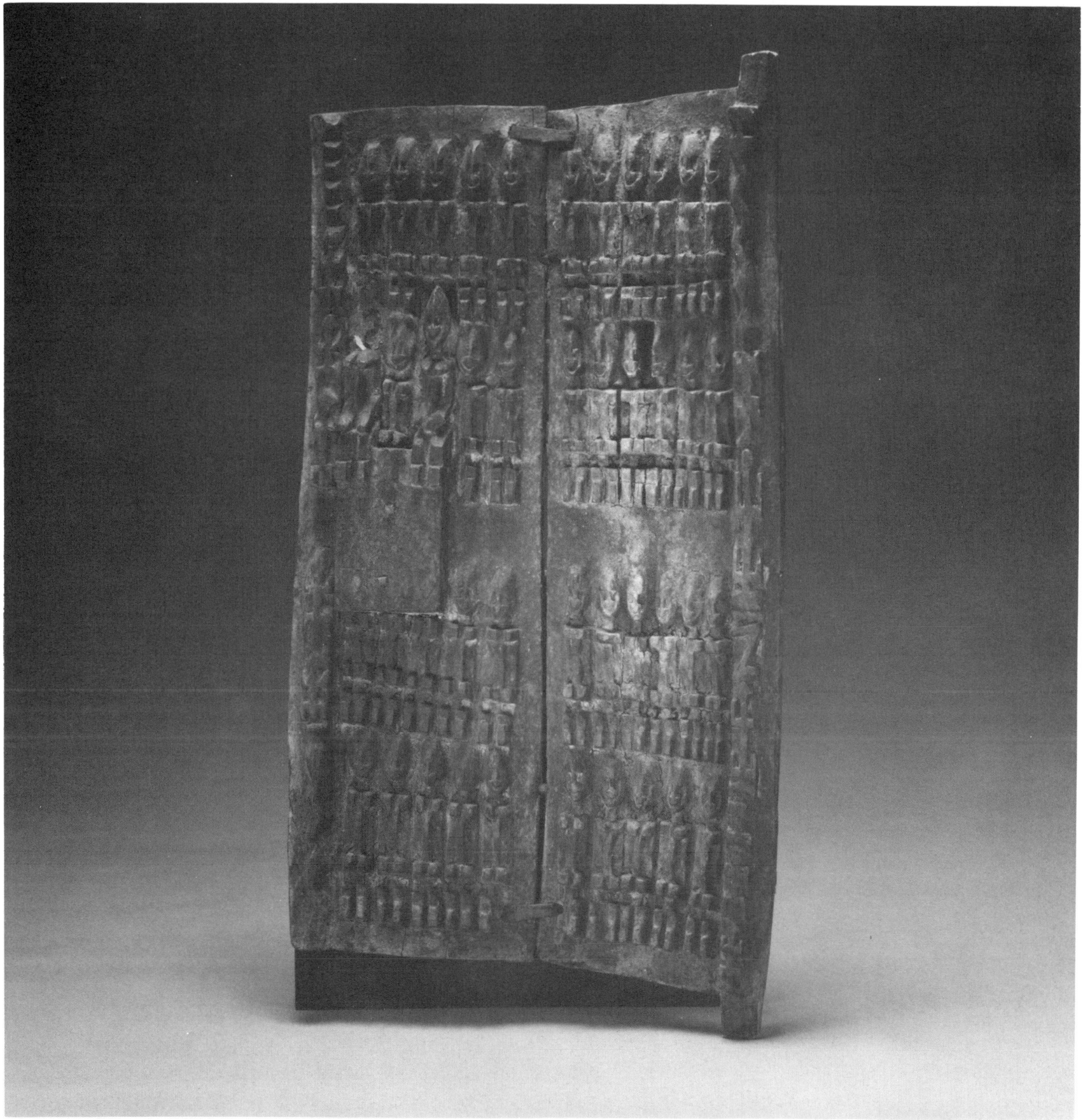

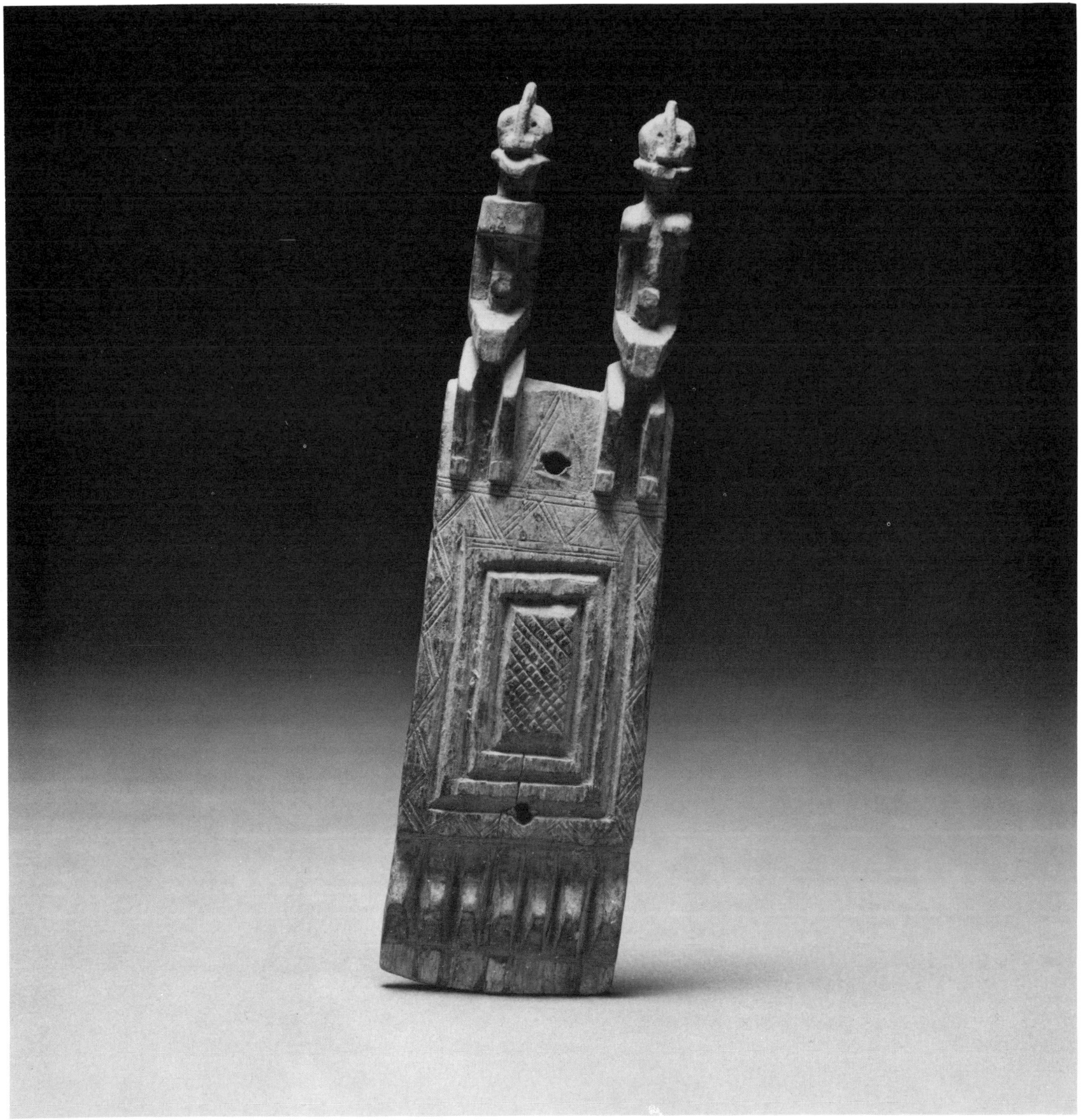

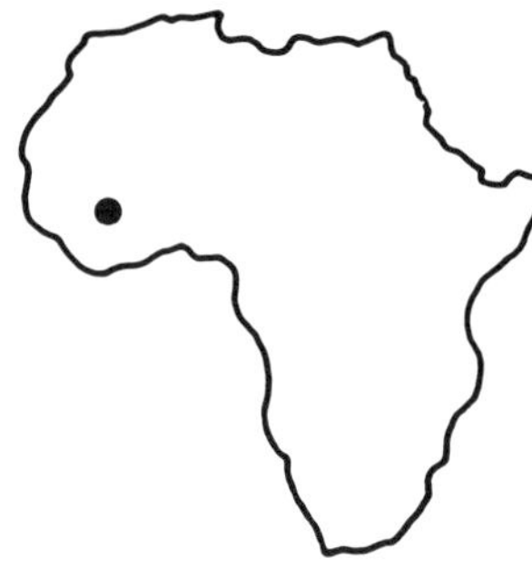

Granary Shutter Lock
(E34,473)

Dogon, Mali

Wood, iron

H. 30 cm.

Dogon granary shutter locks are often surmounted by a pair of figures representing the Primordial Couple. The geometric designs on the face of the lock are associated with the individual owner of the storehouse. *Gift of Mr. Stanley Marcus, 1958.*

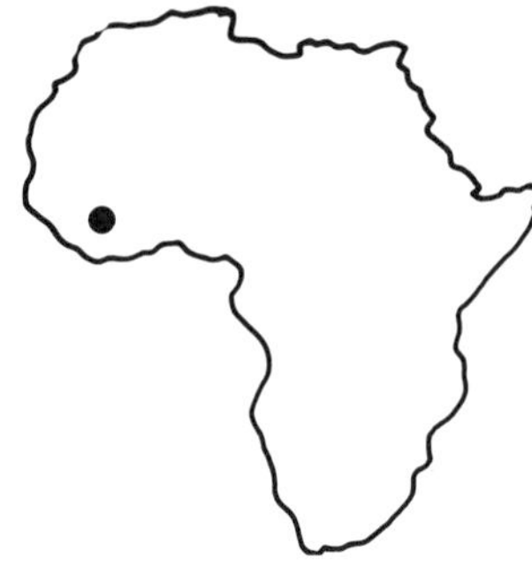

Figure Pair (E72,096)

Senufo, Mali-Ivory Coast

Wood

H. 75 cm.

Situated between the peoples of the western Sudan and those of the Guinea Coast, the Senufo, or Siena, produce art which incorporates attributes of both stylistic areas. Senufo sacred carvings are kept in secluded clearings and huts; this carving represents an ancestoral couple, and served in a protective capacity or for divination. *Anonymous gift , 1981.*

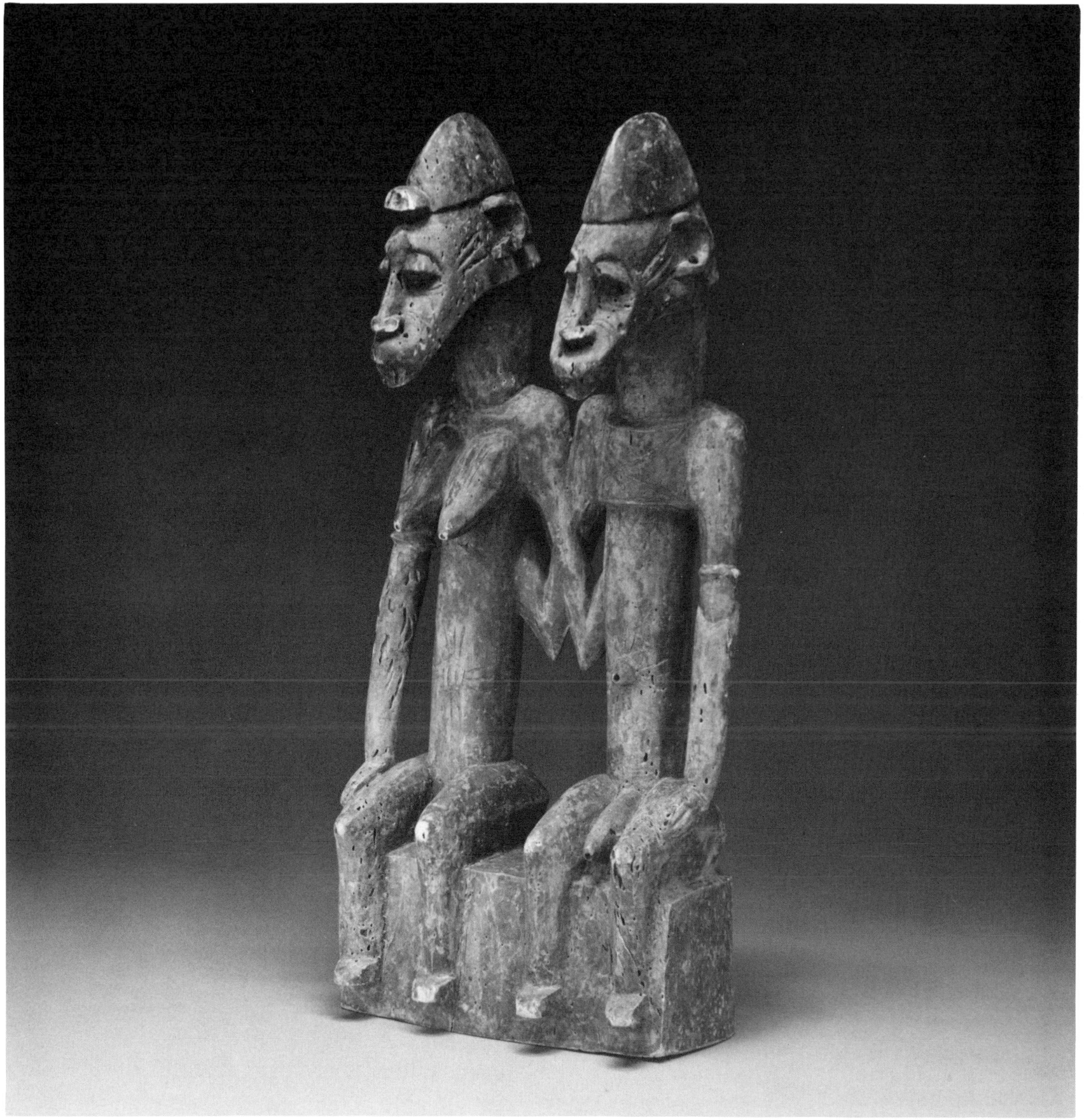

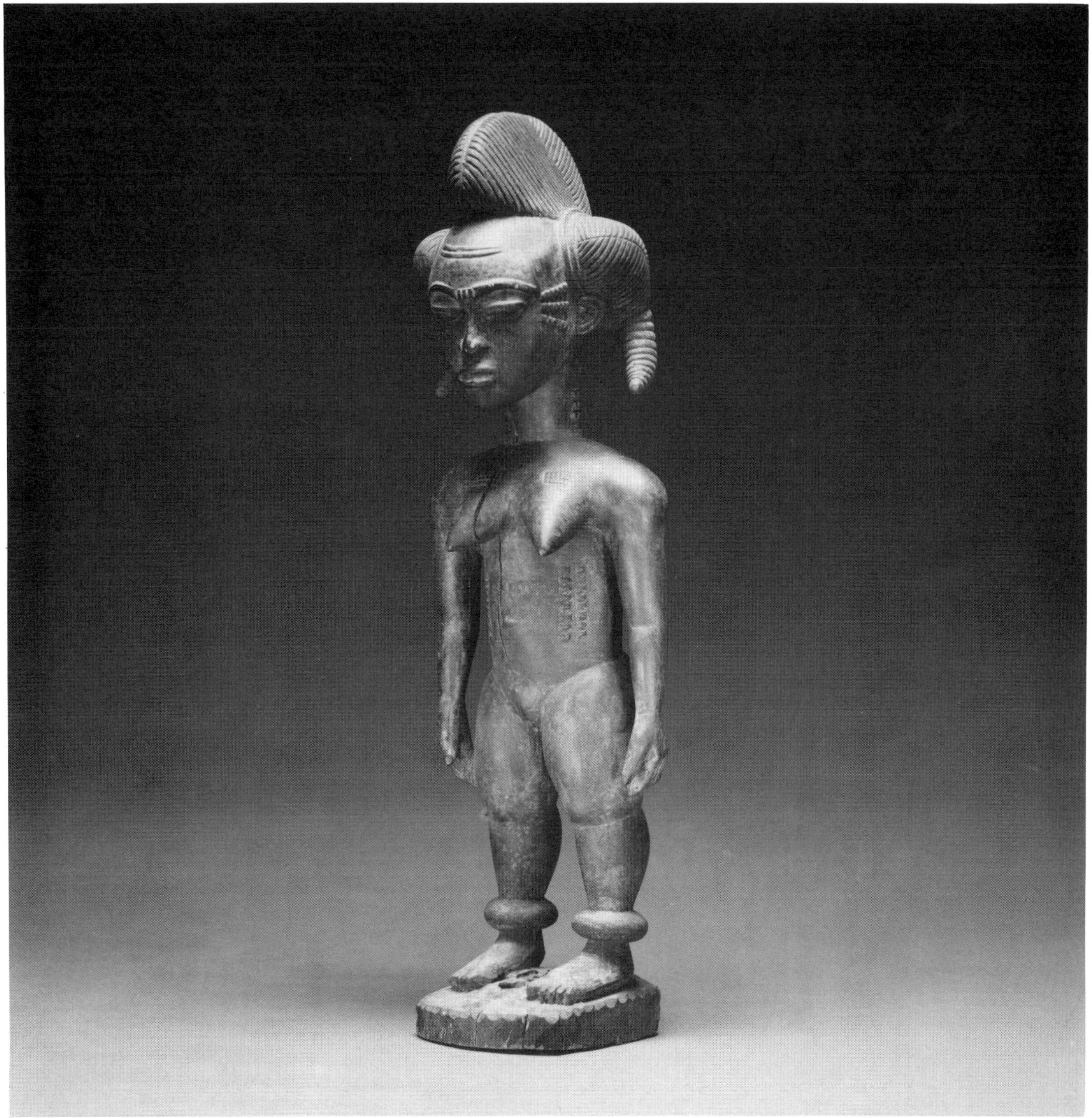

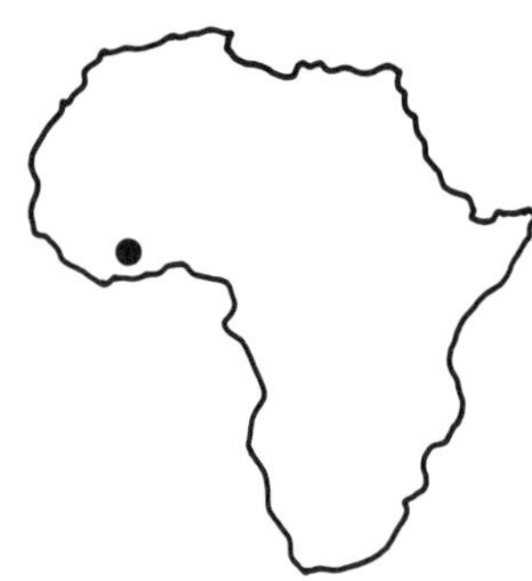

Figure (E72,098)

Baule, Ivory Coast

Wood

H. 68 cm.

The Baule are culturally and linguistically closely related to the Ashanti, who live further to the east in Ghana. This standing female figure, probably representing an ancestor, is typical of Baule carving, with rounded, naturalistic features, polished surface and complex hairstyle. *Anonymous gift, 1981.*

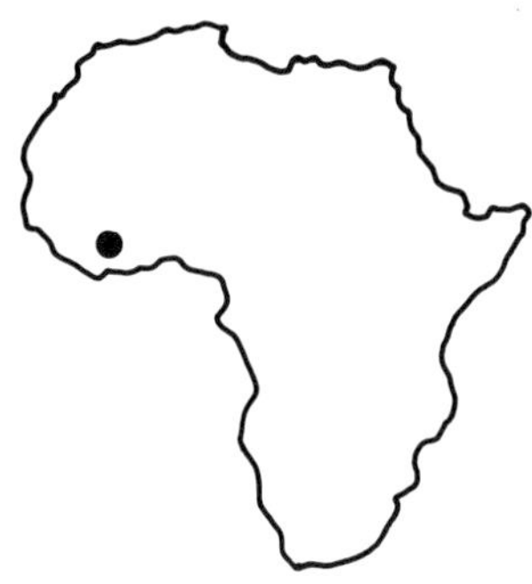

Sword and Scabbard
(E20,769)

Baule, Ivory Coast

Iron, wood, leather, brass, shells, human maxilla

L. (Sword) 51 cm.

Although the Baule are not noted for being particularly war-like, their metal workers produce a variety of edged weapons. This sword must have belonged to an individual of considerable wealth and power as it is accompanied by an unusually ornate scabbard. Since the Baule are not known to have practiced cannibalism, the human maxilla which decorate the scabbard are probably derived from slain enemies. *Museum purchase, 1931.*

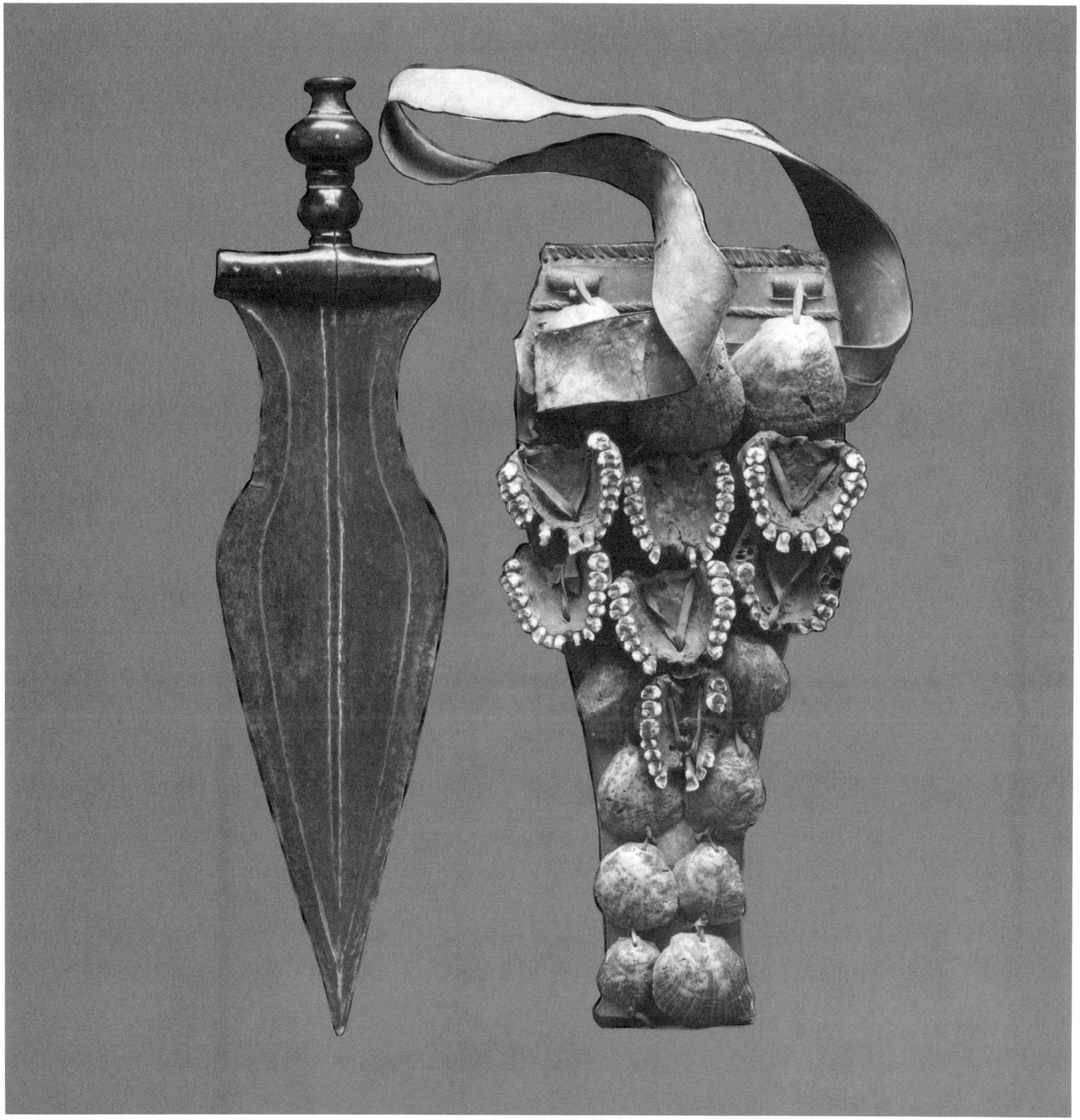

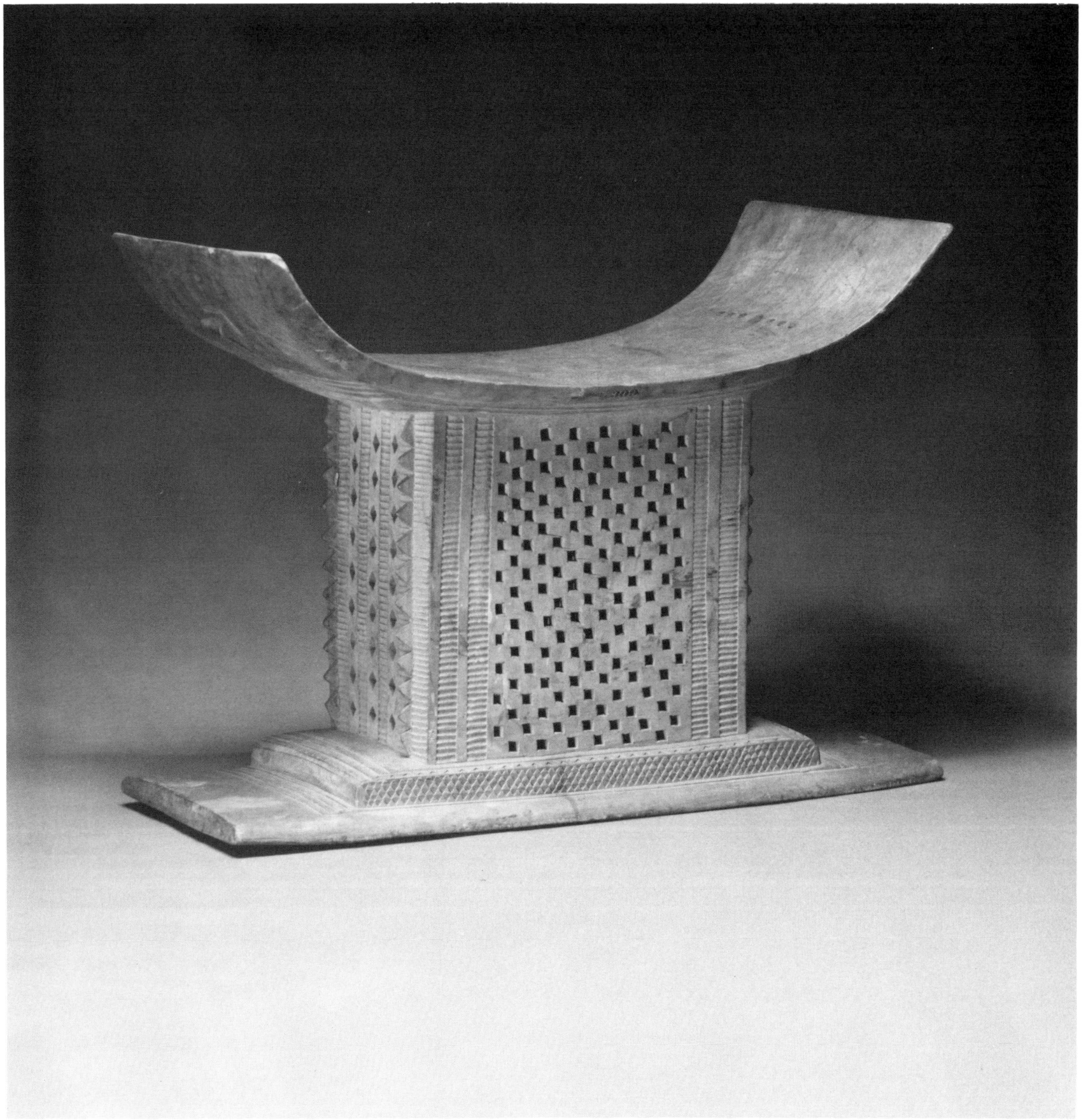

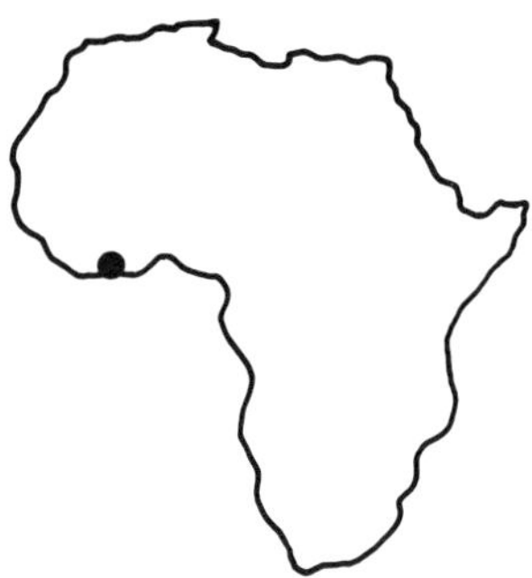

Stool (E8,682)

Akan (Ashanti), Ghana

Wood

H. 28 cm

This type of low stool, carved from a single piece of wood, has a variety of associations for the Ashanti. Traditionally, the culmination of Ashanti unification of the Akan peoples in the early eighteenth century was heralded by the appearance from heaven of the Golden Stool, *Kofi.* The stool represented the embodiment of the Ashanti state and was a critical symbol of authority for the *Asantehene,* or king. *Ex Essex Institute collection, 1867.*

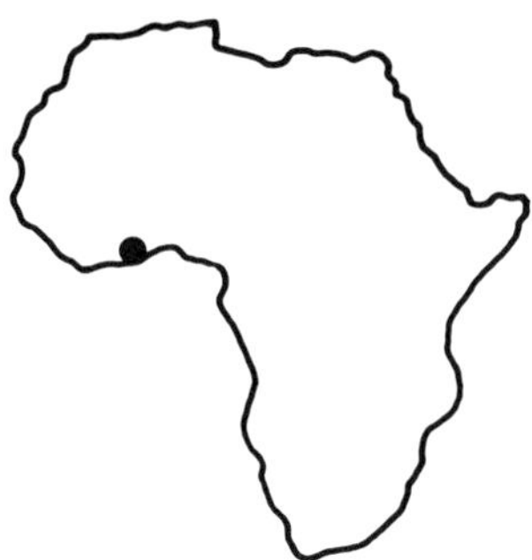

Stool (E8,681)

Akan (Ashanti), Ghana

Wood

H. 41 cm.

Ashanti personal stools, such as this and the previous example, were believed to house the spirit of the owner and were regularly scrubbed to ensure spiritual purity. Upon the death of an important individual, his stool would often be blackened and kept in a sanctuary with those of other ancestors. *Donor unknown, 1826.*

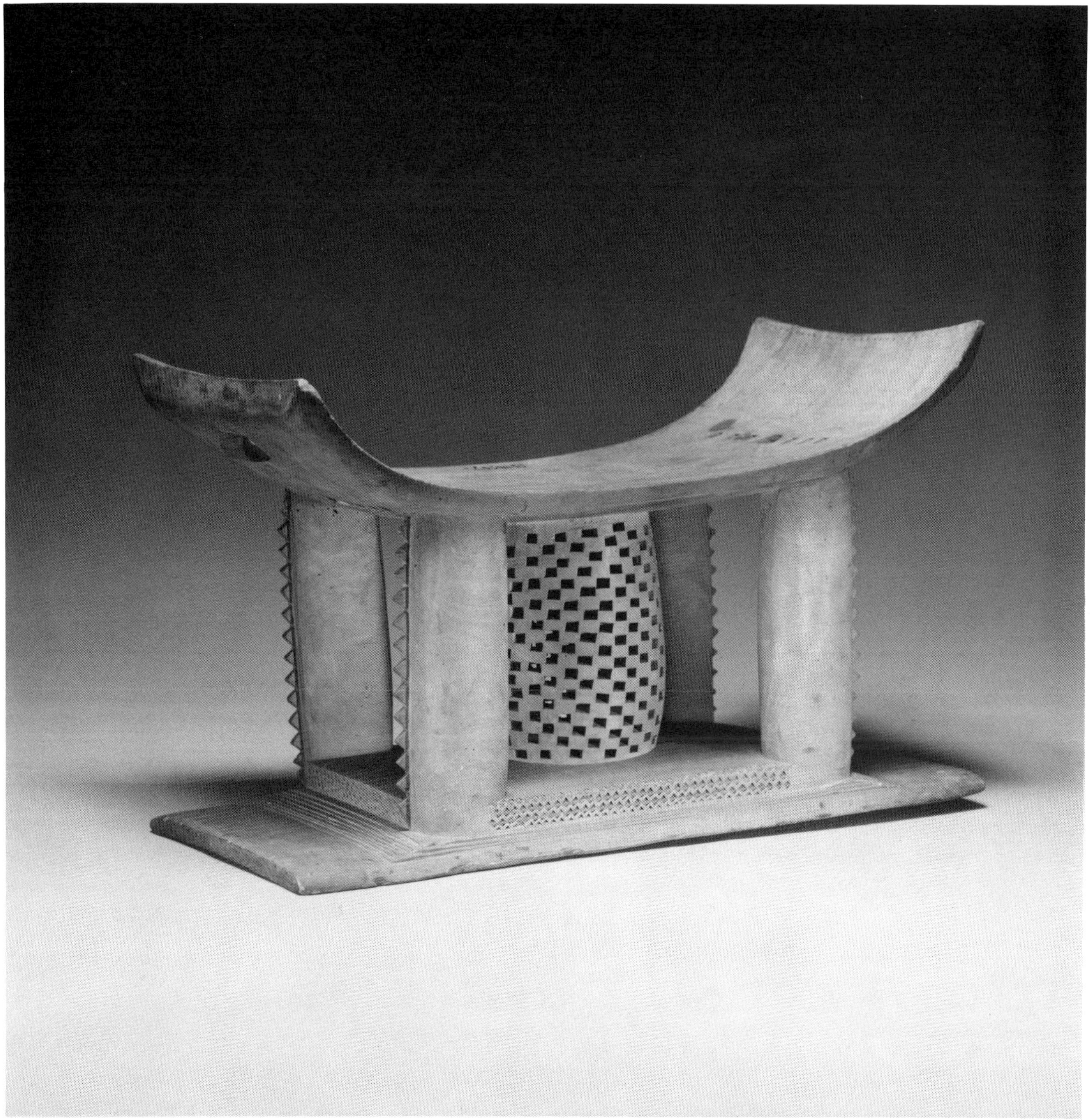

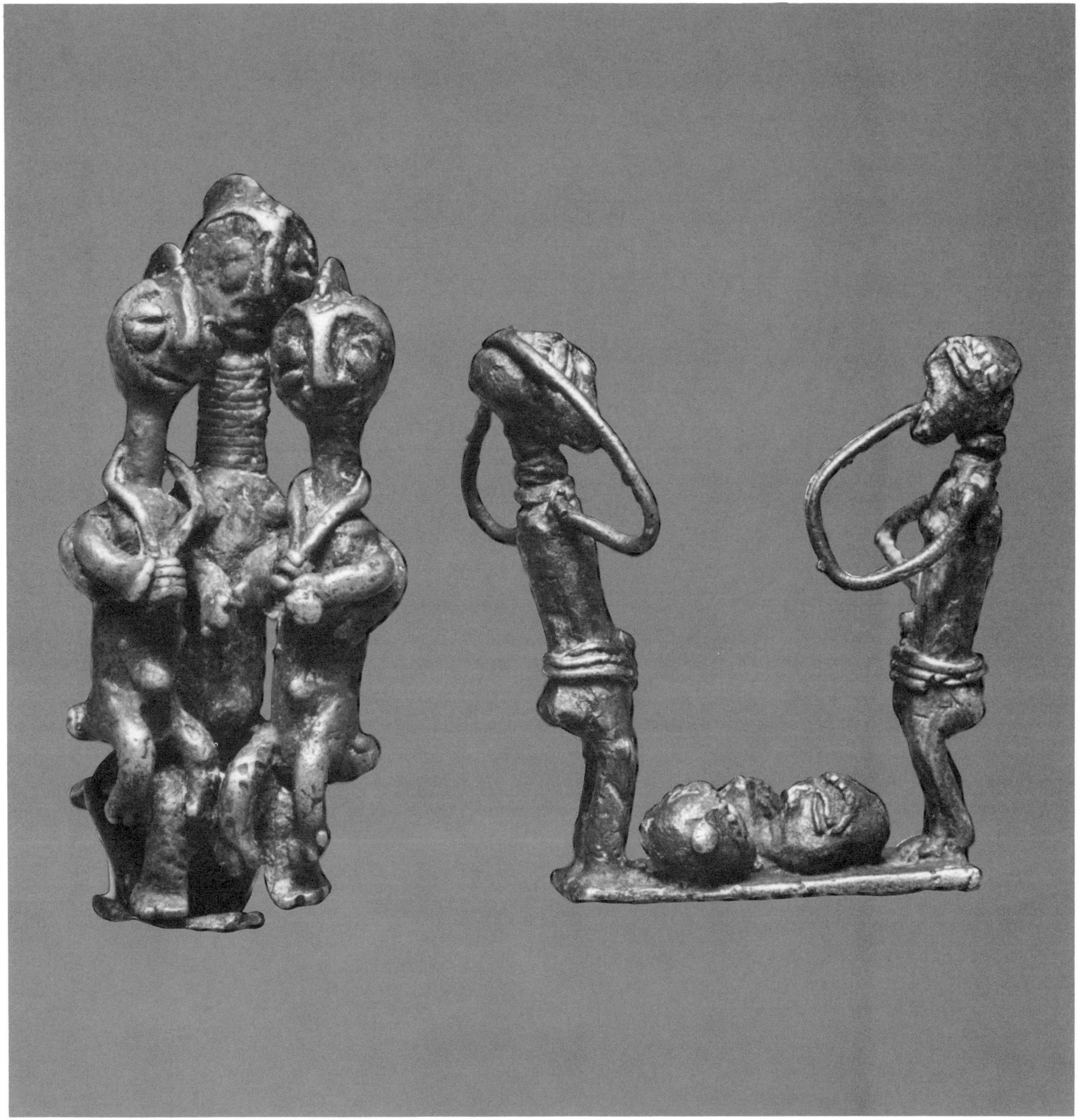

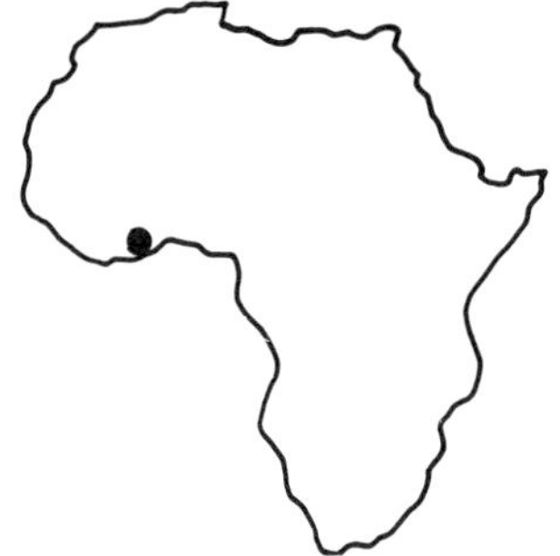

Left

Gold Weight (E29.126)

Akan (Ashanti), Ghana

Brass

H. 6 cm.

Right

Gold Weight (E14,391)

Akan (Ashanti), Ghana

Brass

H. 5 cm.

The Ashanti used gold dust routinely as currency, apportioning it with small scales and brass counterweights called *mrammuo*. *E29,126, gift of Mr. Lawrence W. Jenkins. Collected by John J. Coker, 1867; E14,391, gift of Dr. Charles G. Weld, 1910*

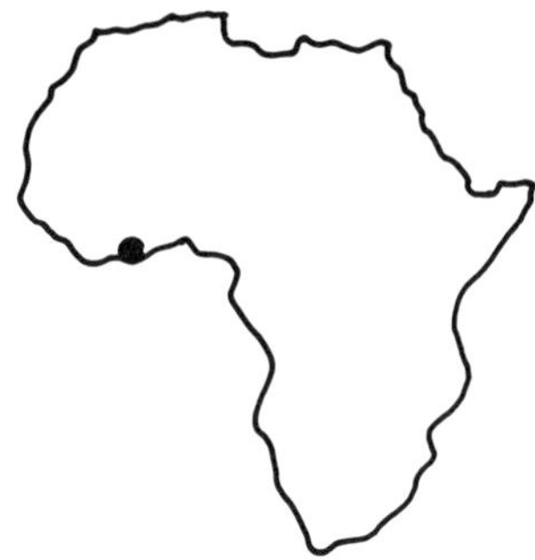

Doll (E72,093)

Akan (Ashanti), Ghana

Wood, paint, glass beads

H. 31 cm.

Children, particularly females, are highly desired among the Ashanti since descent is traced matrilineally. Dolls, called *akua'mma* (singular *akua'ba*) are obtained by women fearing infertility and worn strapped on the back like an infant in order to magically assist in conception. In some cases, they were given to female children to insure fertility in adulthood. *Anonymous gift, 1981.*

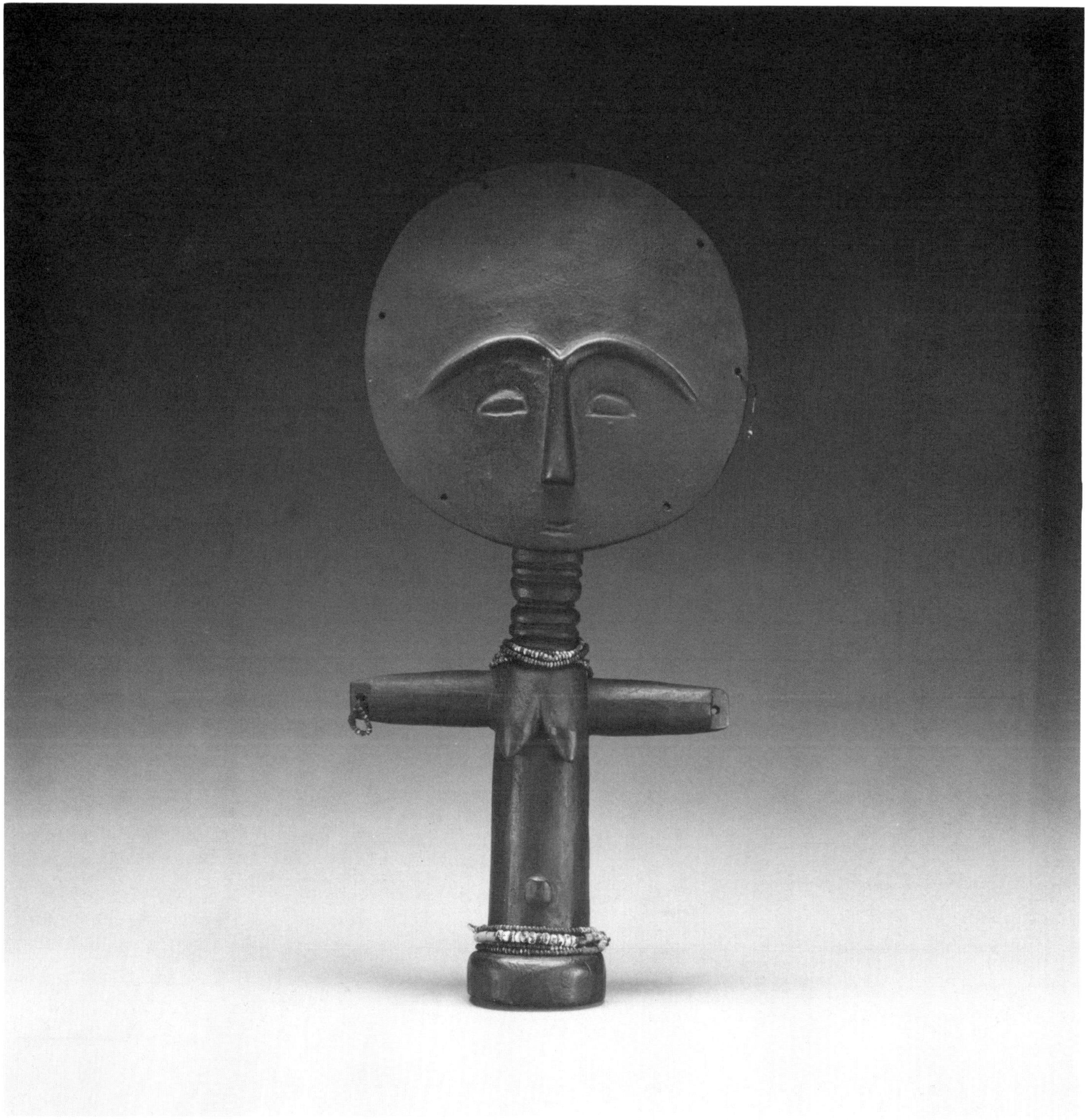

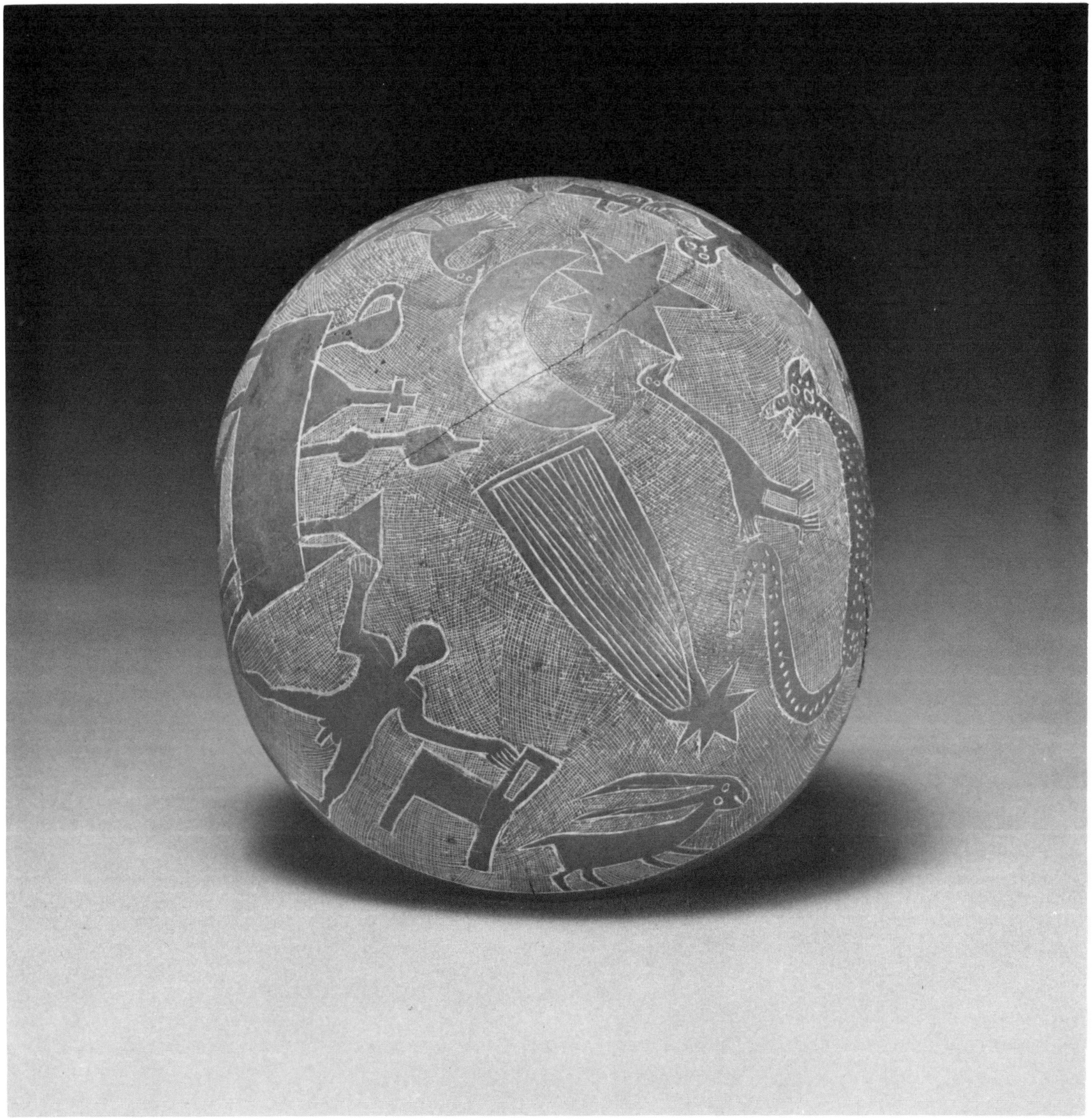

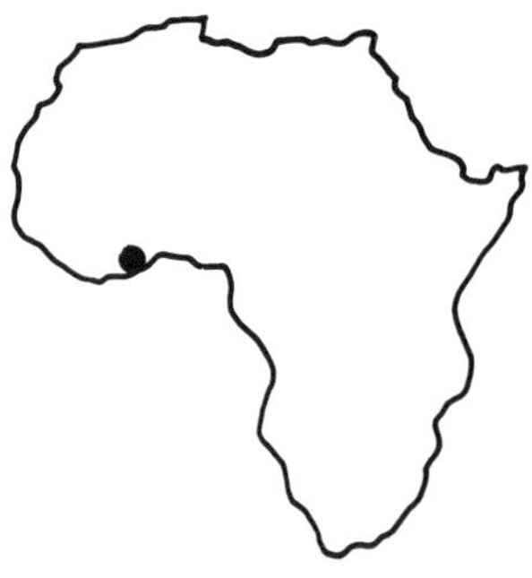

Container (E24,847)

Akan (Ashanti), Ghana

Gourd, pigment

D. 19 cm.

Containers made from gourds are widespread in Africa. This example from the Ashanti is engraved with an allegorical scene whose meaning is unclear. Inside the gourd is a pencil notation which reads, "Gourd from Ashanti War," which may refer to either the British expedition of 1874 or the Ashanti uprising of 1900-1901. The design may represent a battle scene, or some form of mythological imagery. *Gift of Dr. E.A. Rushford, 1945. Collected ca. 1874-1901.*

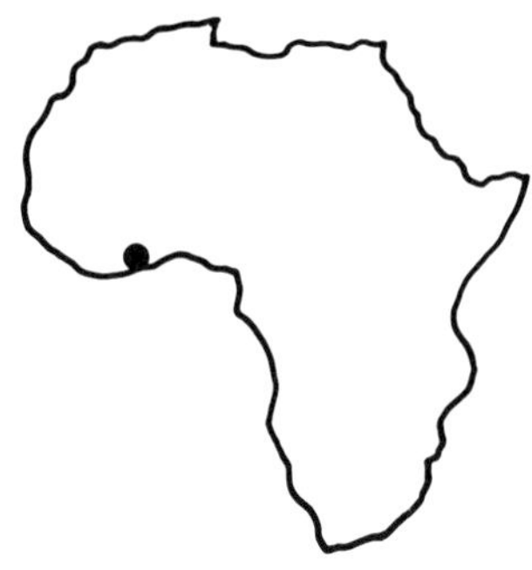

Pipe Bowl (E38,905)

Akan (Ashanti), Ghana

Earthenware, pigment

H. 13 cm.

Ashanti ceramics, made for a variety of purposes, often include embossed or applied figures of animals and humans. Although both sexes engage in ceramic manufacture, only Ashanti men produce pipe bowls. Tobacco, *nicotiana*, is a New World plant introduced to Africa by Europeans sometime after the 16th century. *Gift of Mrs. Albert Hanscom, 1956.*

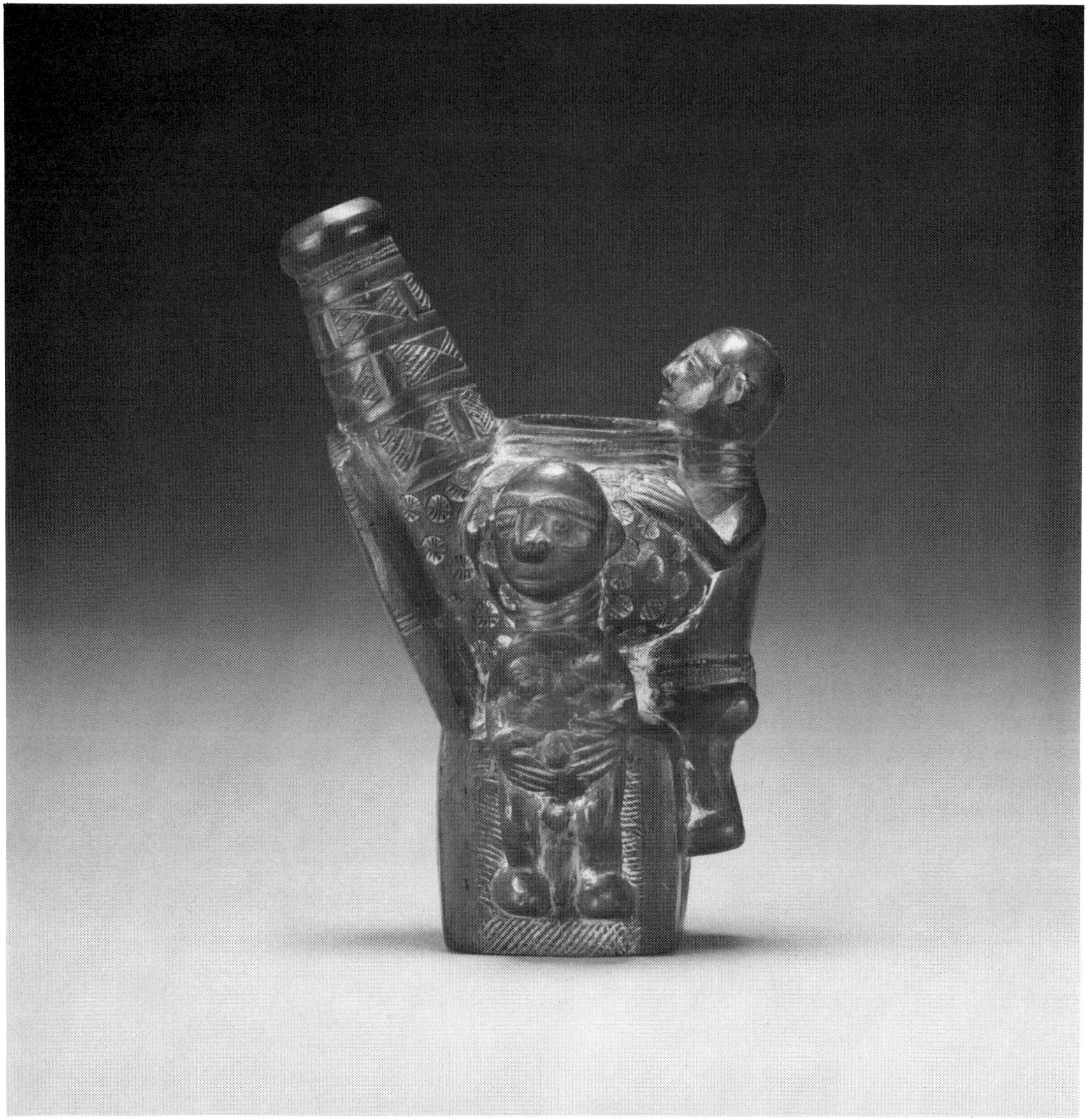

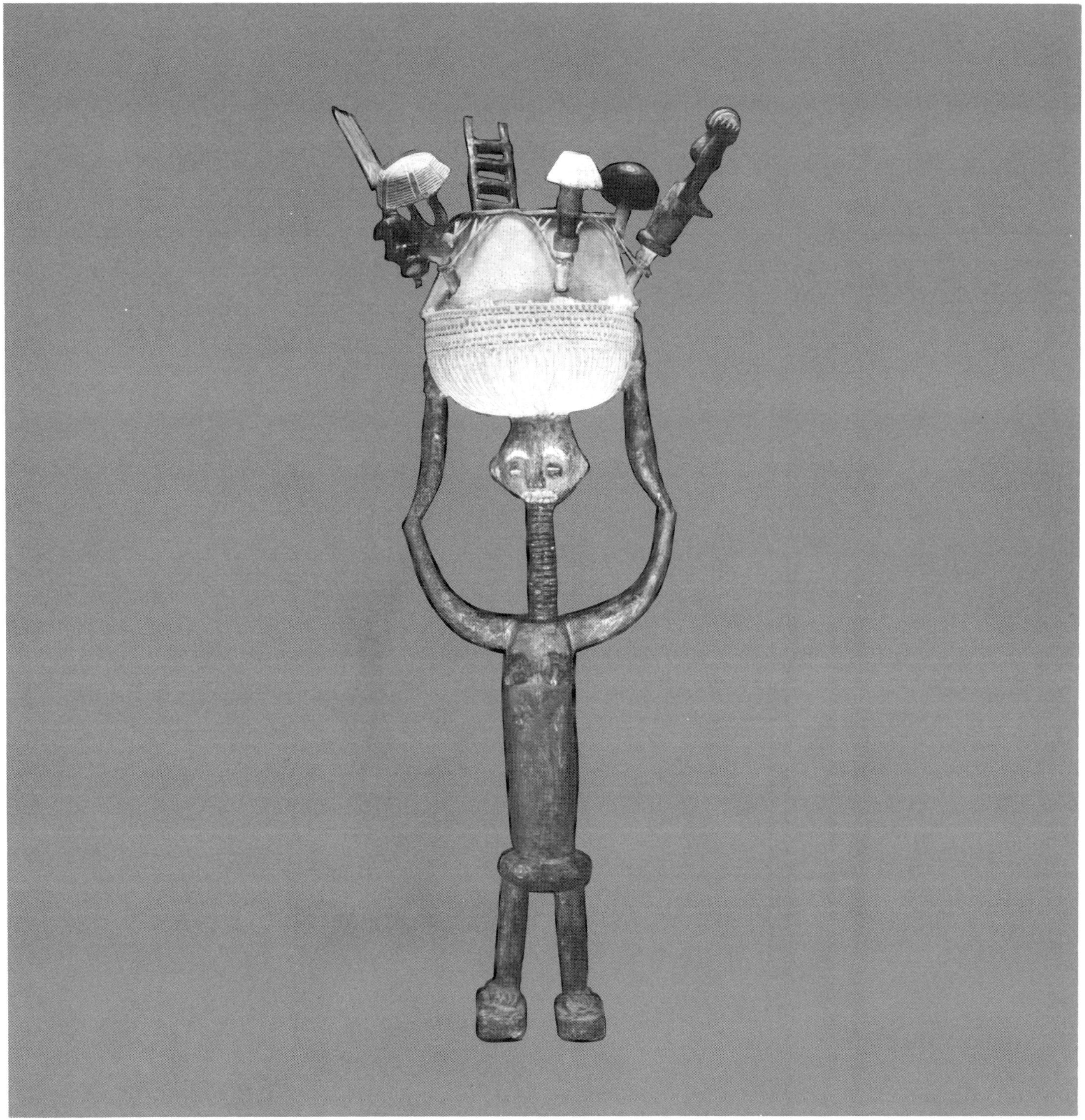

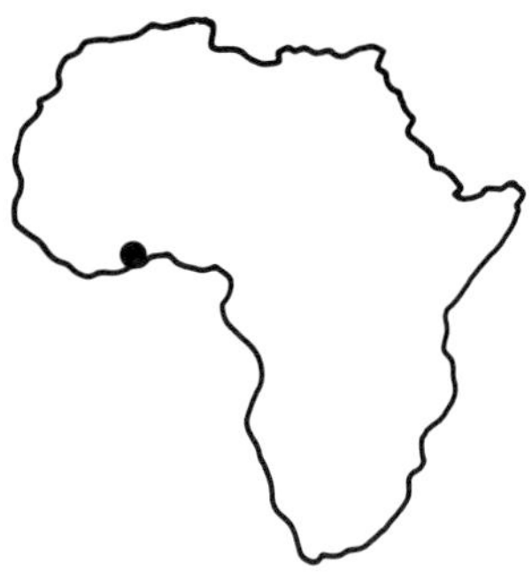

Drum (E6,756)

Ga, Ghana

Wood, pigment, animal skin

H. 102 cm.

The Ga inhabit the coast to the east of the Akan peoples, including the Ashanti, with whom they have close cultural ties. This drum is apparently the Ga equivalent of an Ashanti type known as *atumpan*, a state drum used to send messages, accompany certain dances, and call upon ancestors. According to the donor, the stretchers represent chiefs' umbrellas, a ladder, comb, rum keg, and water gourd. The donor also stated that the drum was loaned by several Ga chiefs for a British colonial exhibition in London prior to its acquisition by the Museum. *Gift of Mr. T.C.W. Nash, 1890.*

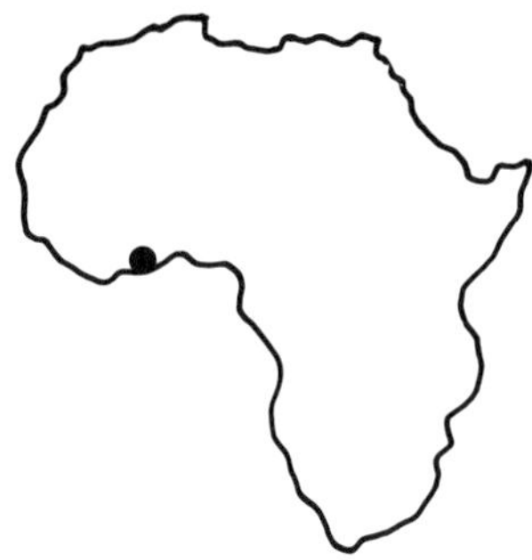

Cap (E7,010)

Ga, Ghana

Cloth, wood, paper

H. 47 cm.

A Ga military leader would have worn this hat in combination with a similarly ornamented shirt. The attachments are actually talismans, including wrapped bits of wood and inscribed paper (often Koranic texts purchased from Muslims), which were believed to protect the wearer from enemy weapons. *Gift of Mr. T.C.W. Nash, 1890.*

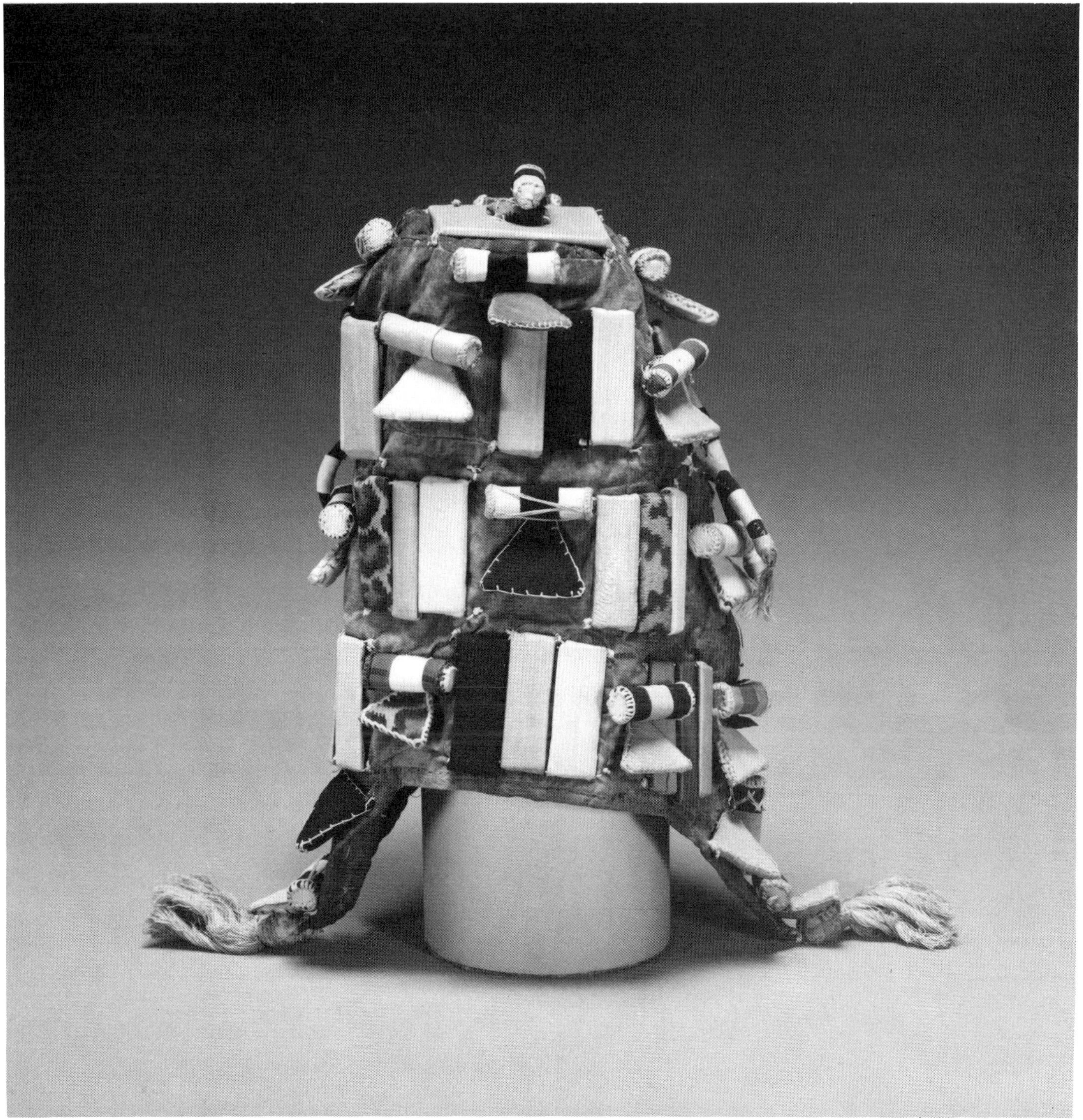

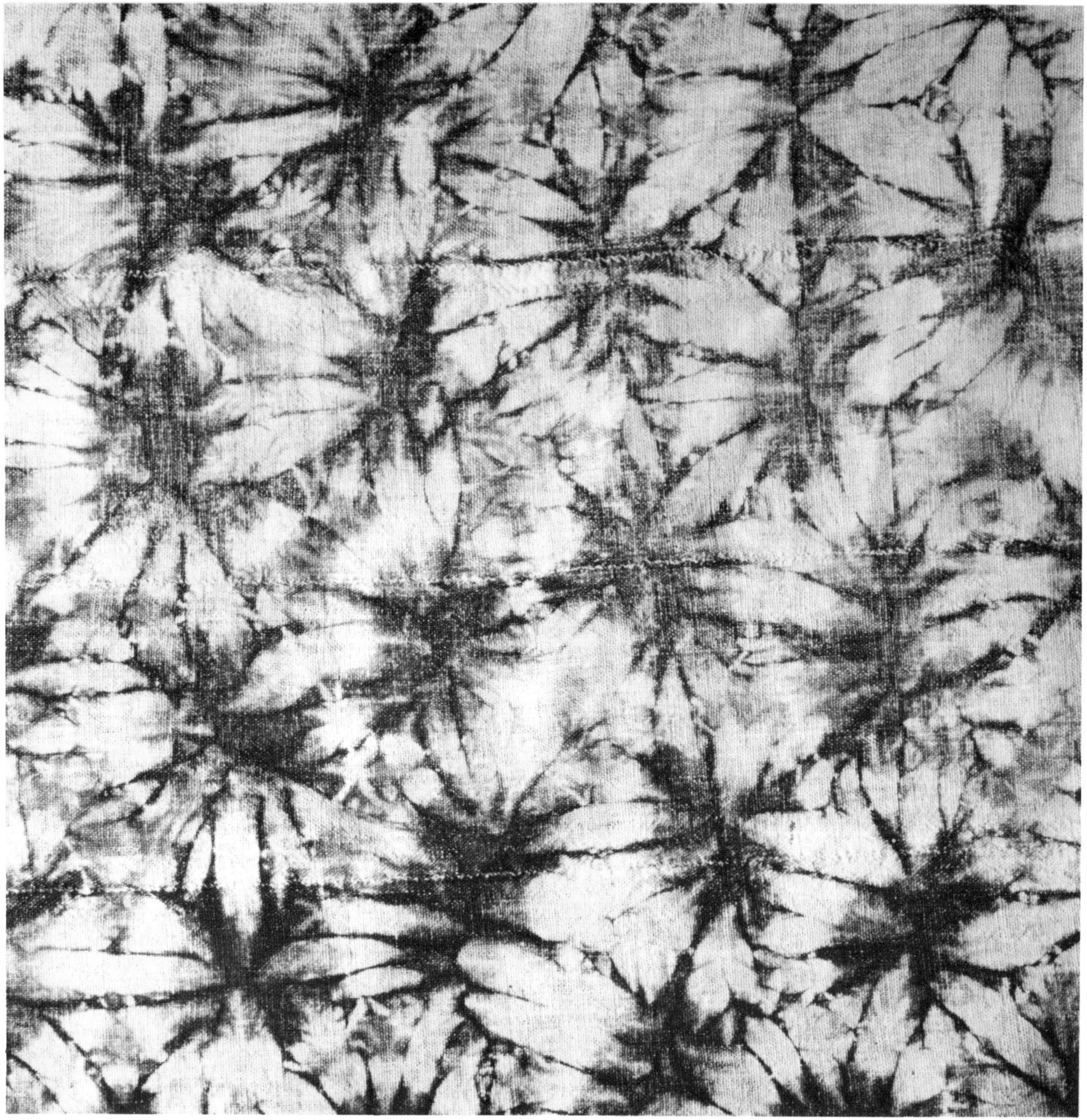

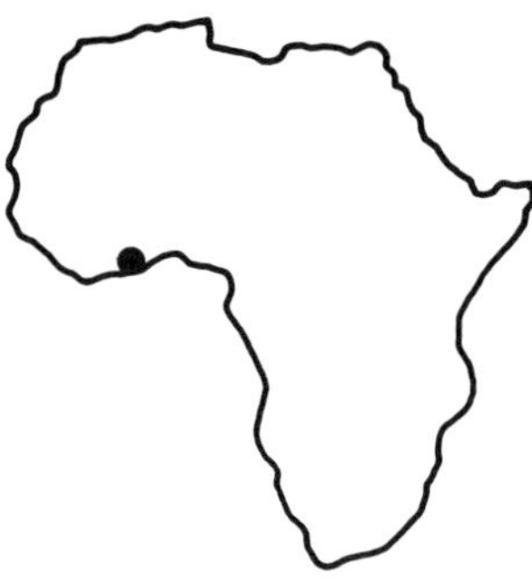

Garment (E20,169)

Group uncertain, Ghana

Cotton, indigo

L. 225 cm. *Detail*

Traditionally, indigo has been one of the favorite dyes for the manufacture of African loom-woven textiles. It is obtained from the leaves of various plants, including *Lonchocarpus cyanescens*, which are mashed, formed into balls and combined with a wood-ash mordant in the dyeing vats. The striking pattern of this garment was produced by tightly wrapping sections of it prior to immersion in the dye. *Gift of Miss Mary B. Perkins, 1927.*

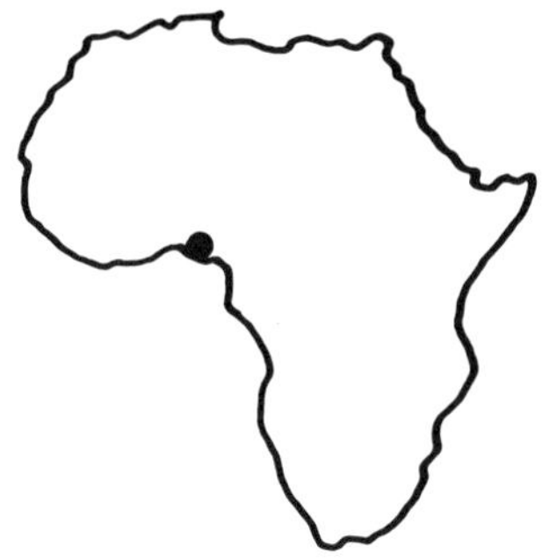

Garment (E15,158)

Group uncertain, Nigeria

Cotton, dyes

L. 250 cm. *Detail*

West African textiles are
characteristically woven in narrow
strips which are sewn together for
a finished garment, usually worn
draped over one shoulder, toga-
style. *Gift of Miss Harriet Phillips,
1912.*

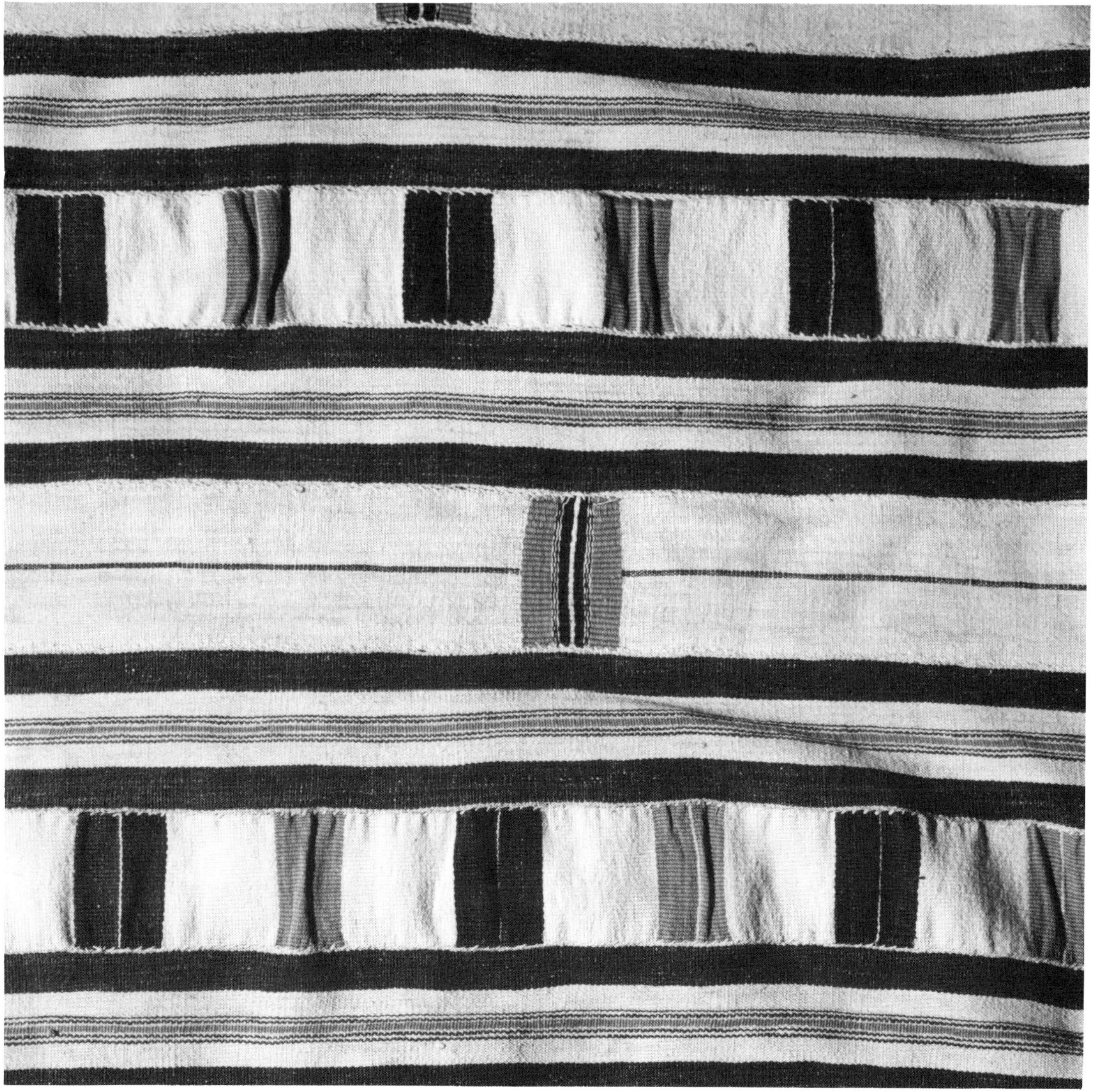

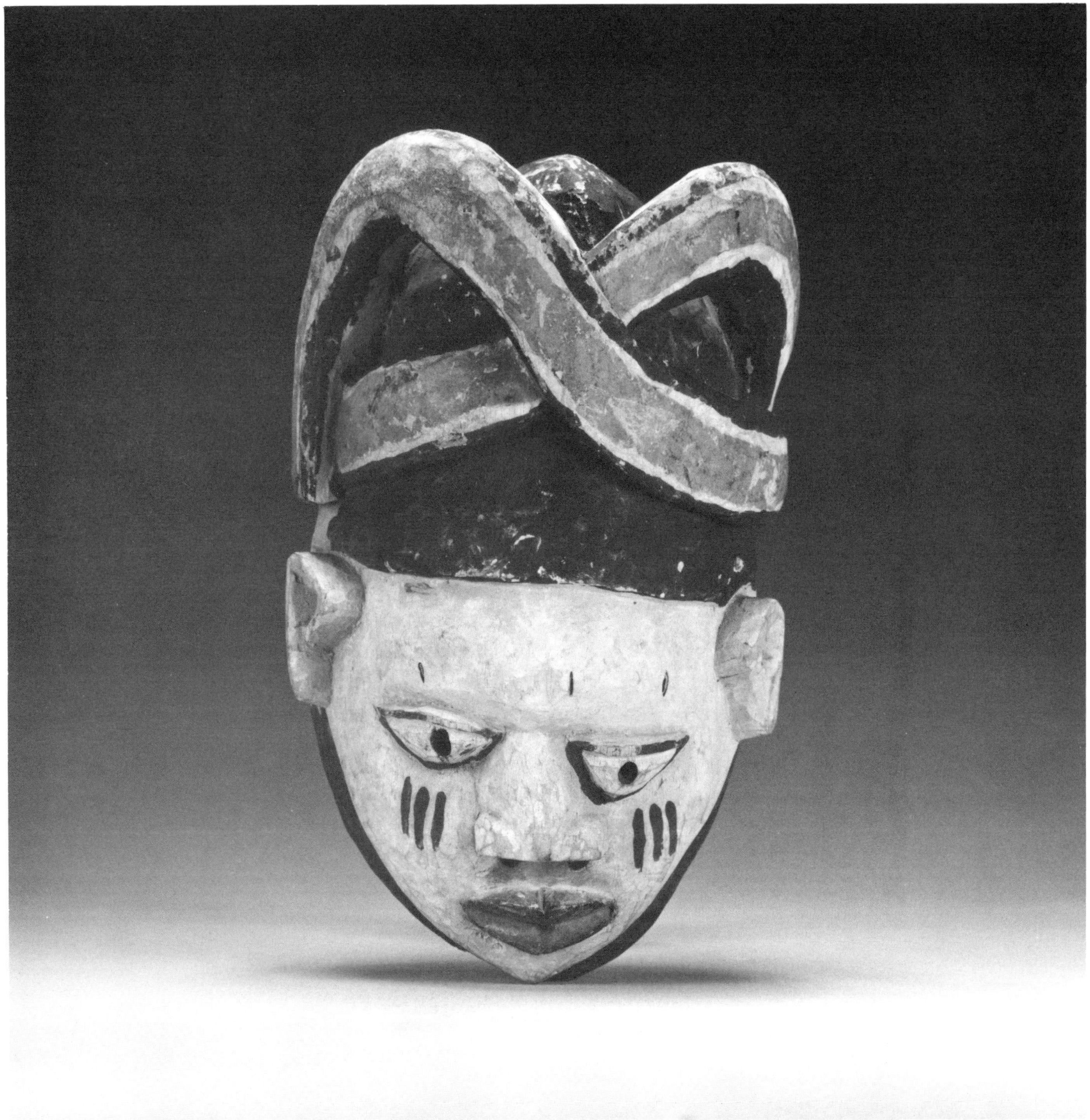

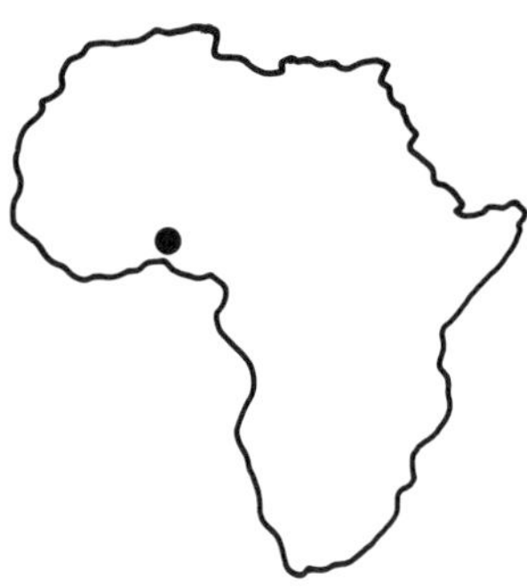

Mask (E14,383)

Yoruba, Nigeria

Wood, pigment

H. 30 cm.

The Yoruba of southern Nigeria are among the most prolific carvers in Africa producing a wide variety of figures, masks, and other articles to fulfill the requirements of their complex religious system. Some of the best known Yoruba masks are those involved in the annual *geleda* masquerade, performed by men impersonating women, intended to propitiate witches. This mask represents *Pansaga*, the prostitute. *Gift of Dr. Charles G. Weld, 1910.*

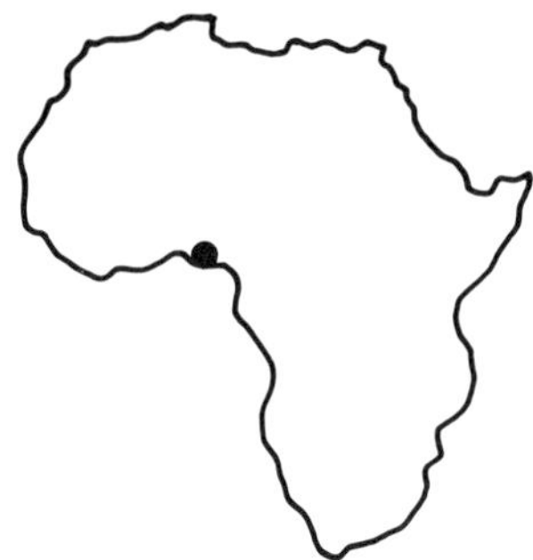

Mask (E14,379)

Ijaw, Nigeria

Wood, feathers, stain

H. 54 cm.

The Ijaw inhabit the area adjoining the creeks and swamps of the Niger delta. Water spirits are an important component of Ijaw mythology, and masks dedicated to water spirits are prominent among their art. Ijaw carving in general is characterized by its pronounced geometry and has been likened to cubism. This example, which has twin-faced figures projecting from a conical headpiece, is unusual in that Ijaw masks are typically made to be viewed from above, with the face pointing skyward during use. *Gift of Dr. Charles G. Weld, 1910.*

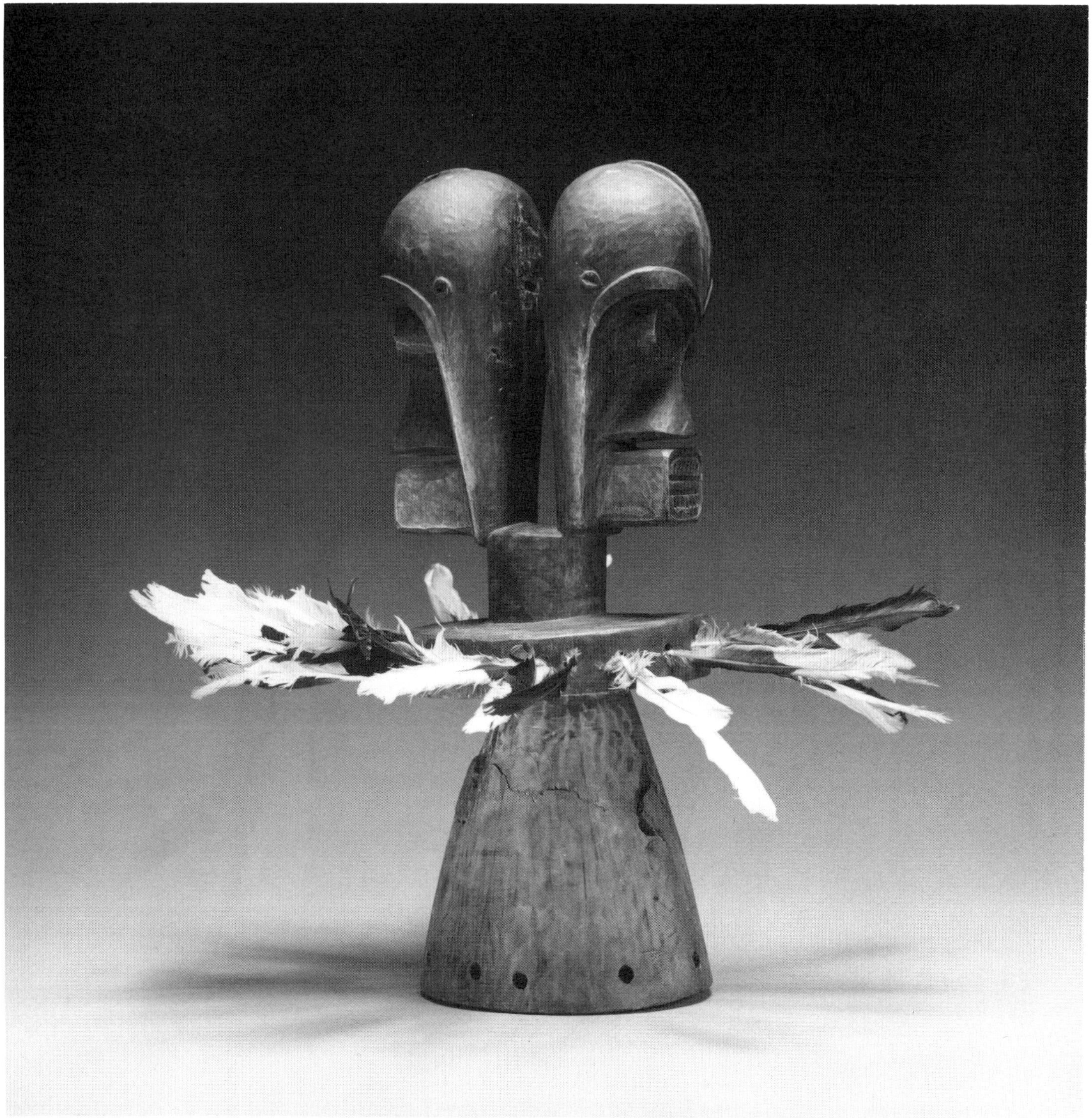

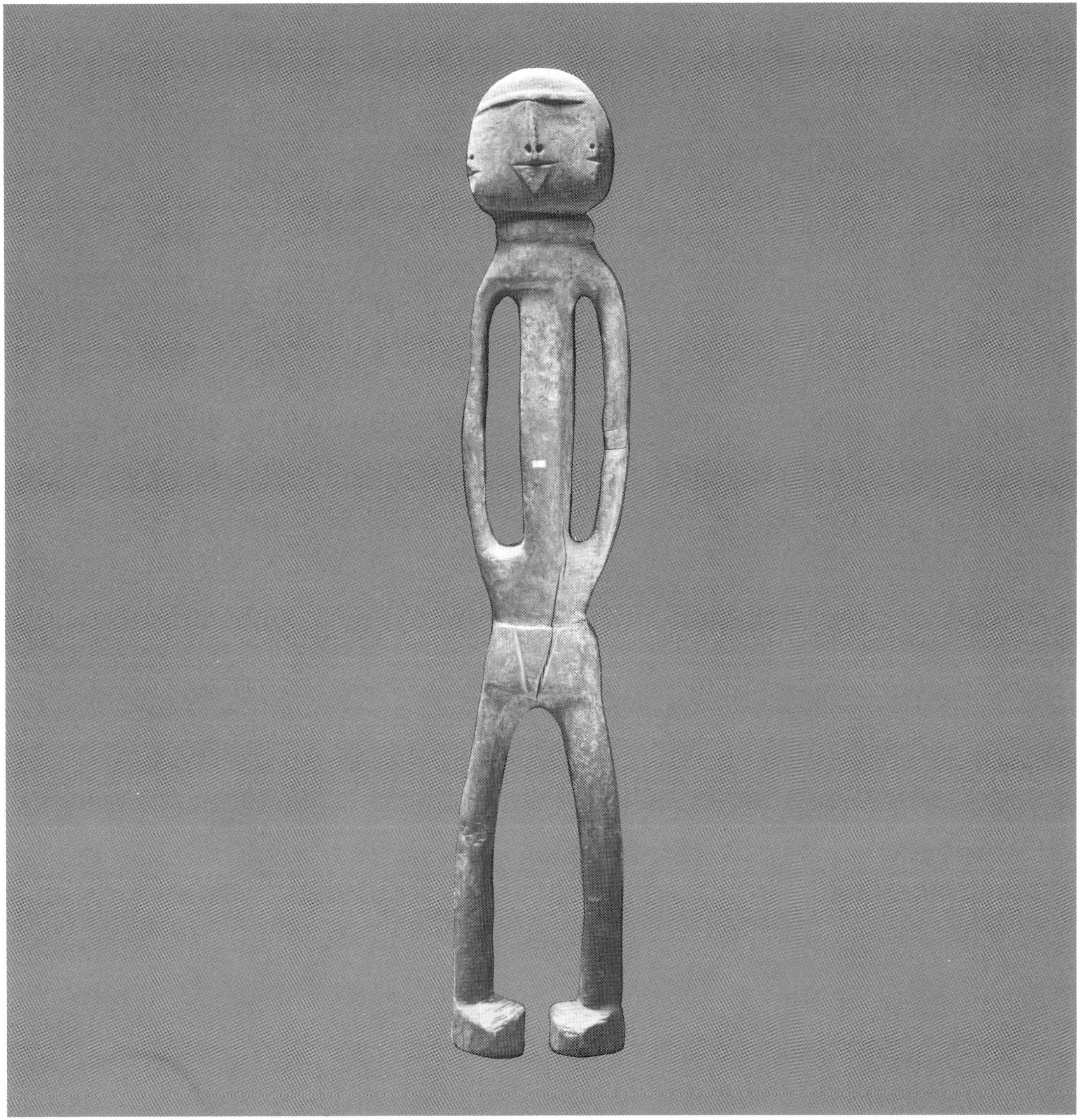

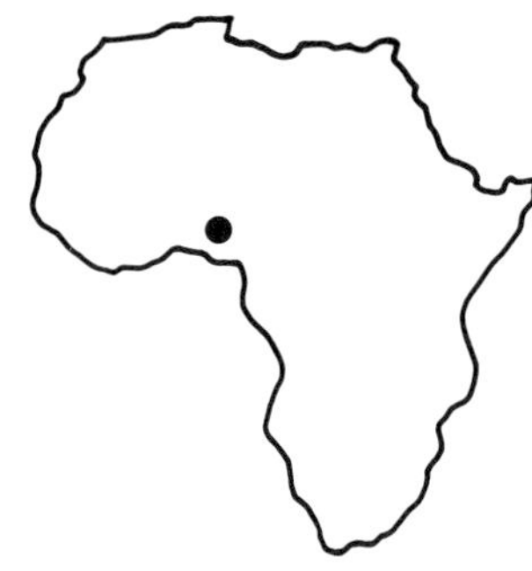

Figure (E54,415)

Group uncertain, Nigeria

Wood

H. 64 cm.

Simple pole-like figures are produced in several areas of Africa, including the western Sudan, upper Volta and Nile Rivers, and Nigeria. This example, collected by an American missionary in the second quarter of the 19th century, is stylistically related to figures produced in the Benue River-Lake Chad area. *Ex American Board of Commissioners for Foreign Missions Collection, 1976. Collected prior to 1850.*

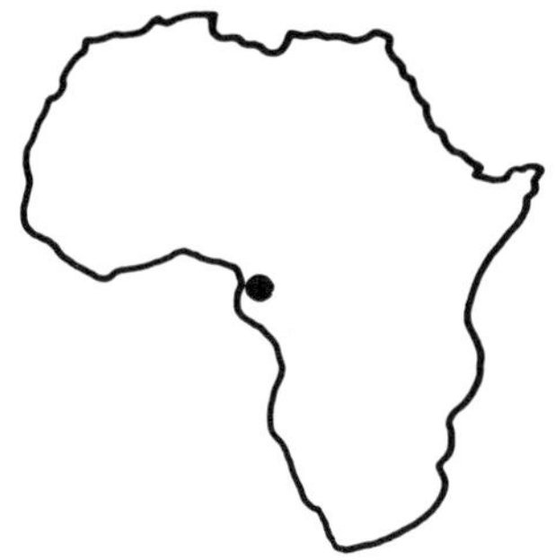

Gaming Pieces (E26,309)

Fang, Gabon

Nutshell

L. 3.4 - 4.3 cm.

The Fang play a game called *abia*
with gaming pieces such as these.
The reverse sides are blank, and
players bet on how the pieces will
land when emptied on the ground
from a basket. *Gift of Dr. Frank
G. Speck, 1946. Collected ca.
1938.*

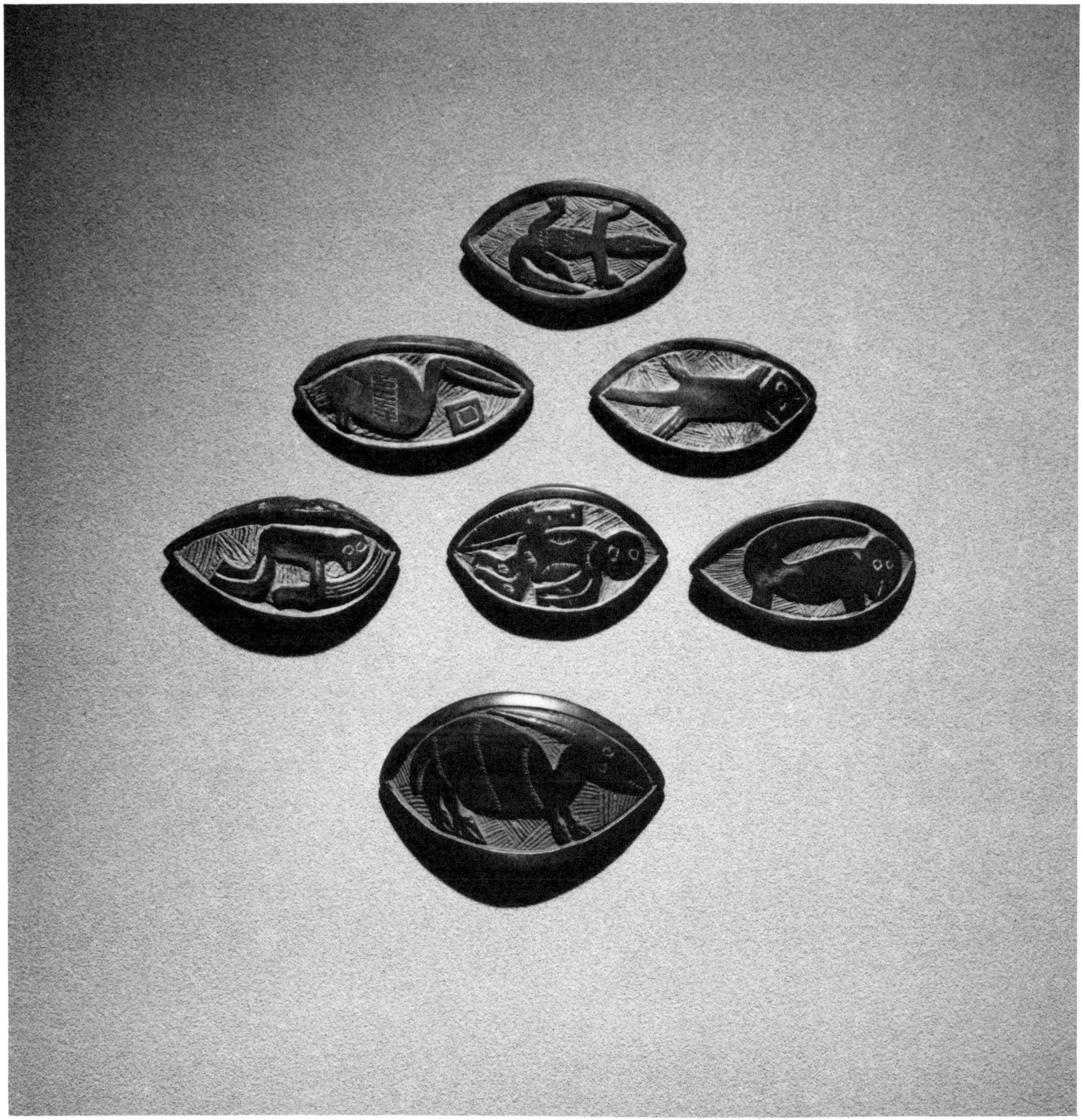

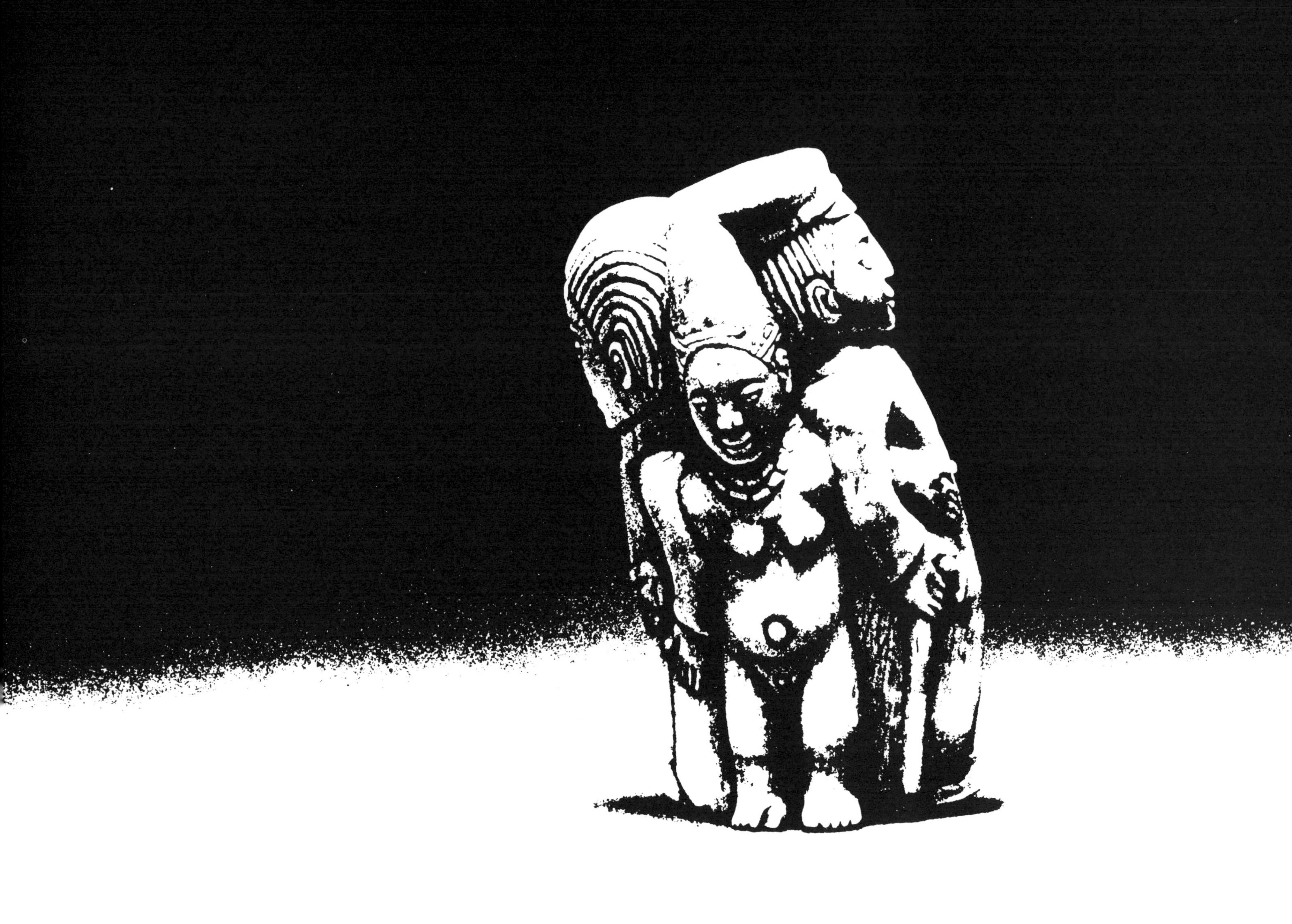

The Congo River Basin

The Congo River, together with its numerous tributaries, comprises the most extensive river system in Africa. Flowing nearly 3,000 miles from its source in southern Zaire to the Atlantic Ocean, the Congo drains the immense rain forest which extends over much of central equatorial Africa west of the Mitumba Mountains.

Aside from isolated groups of Pygmies, and pockets of Negritic and Sudanic speakers, the Congo River basin is inhabited by Bantu-speaking peoples whose primary means of subsistence is shifting agriculture. Major crops in the region include bananas, yams, manioc, maize and peanuts. Most groups supplement their diet through hunting and fishing and by raising small livestock such as goats and chickens. The Pygmies are hunters and gatherers who live in a dependent relationship with neighboring agricultural peoples.

Many homogeneous tribal groups with different social structures flourished within the reaches of the Congo River at different times. Some chiefdoms grew into centralized states comparable to those of West Africa, their kings reigning as divine embodiments of the wealth and power of their peoples. The coastal Kongo and Loando kingdoms sustained active trading partnerships with Europeans after the Portuguese arrival in 1482. Oral history of the Kuba federation of central Zaire, renowned for its court-sponsored arts, traces some 124 kings from about the year 500. Written accounts of the region appear much later, since Islamic inroads are less evident than Christian, especially among the coastal trading tribes.

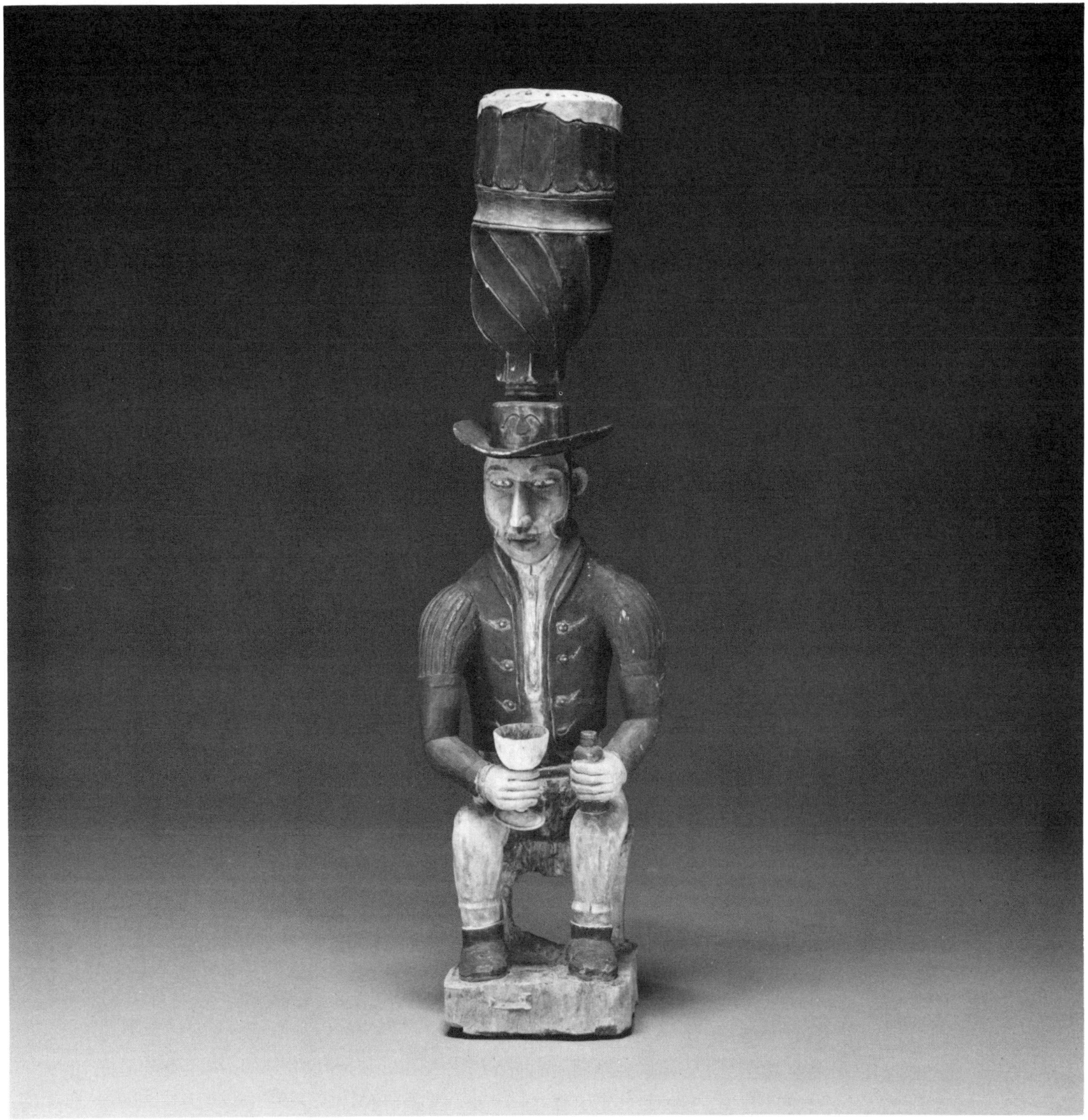

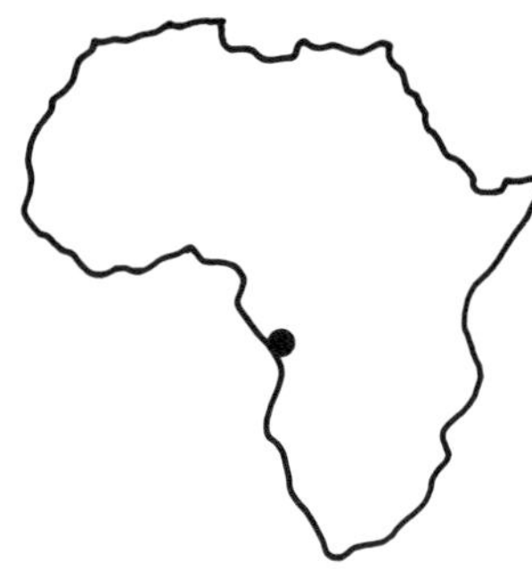

Drum (E6,754)

Kongo or Vili, Congo-Zaire

Wood, animal skin, pigment, glass

H. 99 cm.

The Portuguese were an important political presence in the Congo-Zaire area, beginning as early as 1482 when the explorer Diego Cao visited the mouth of the Nzadi River, which he renamed the Zaire. This impressive figurative drum probably depicts a Portuguese sailor of the early 19th century, when the area was still an important center for the slave trade. *Gift of Capt. William T. Julio, 1843.*

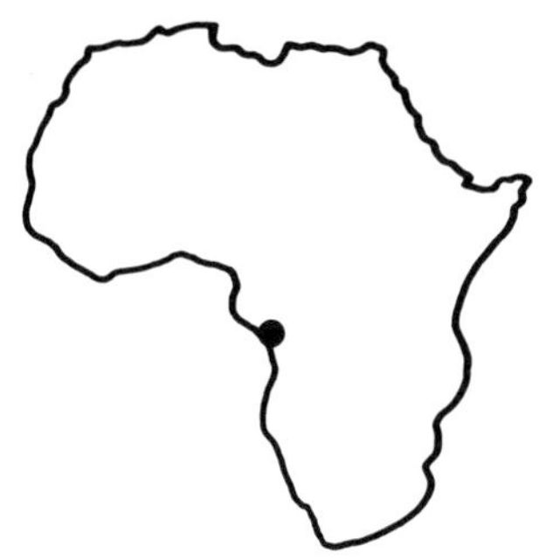

Figure Group (E16,924)

Kongo or Vili, Congo-Zaire

Ivory

H. 10 cm.

Beginning in the 19th century, native artists living in the vicinity of the European trading settlement of Loango began to produce carved ivory tusks and figures intended for the foreign market. This group of three figures depicts a native man and woman, together with a European. *Museum purchase, 1917. Collected by John J. Coker, 1848.*

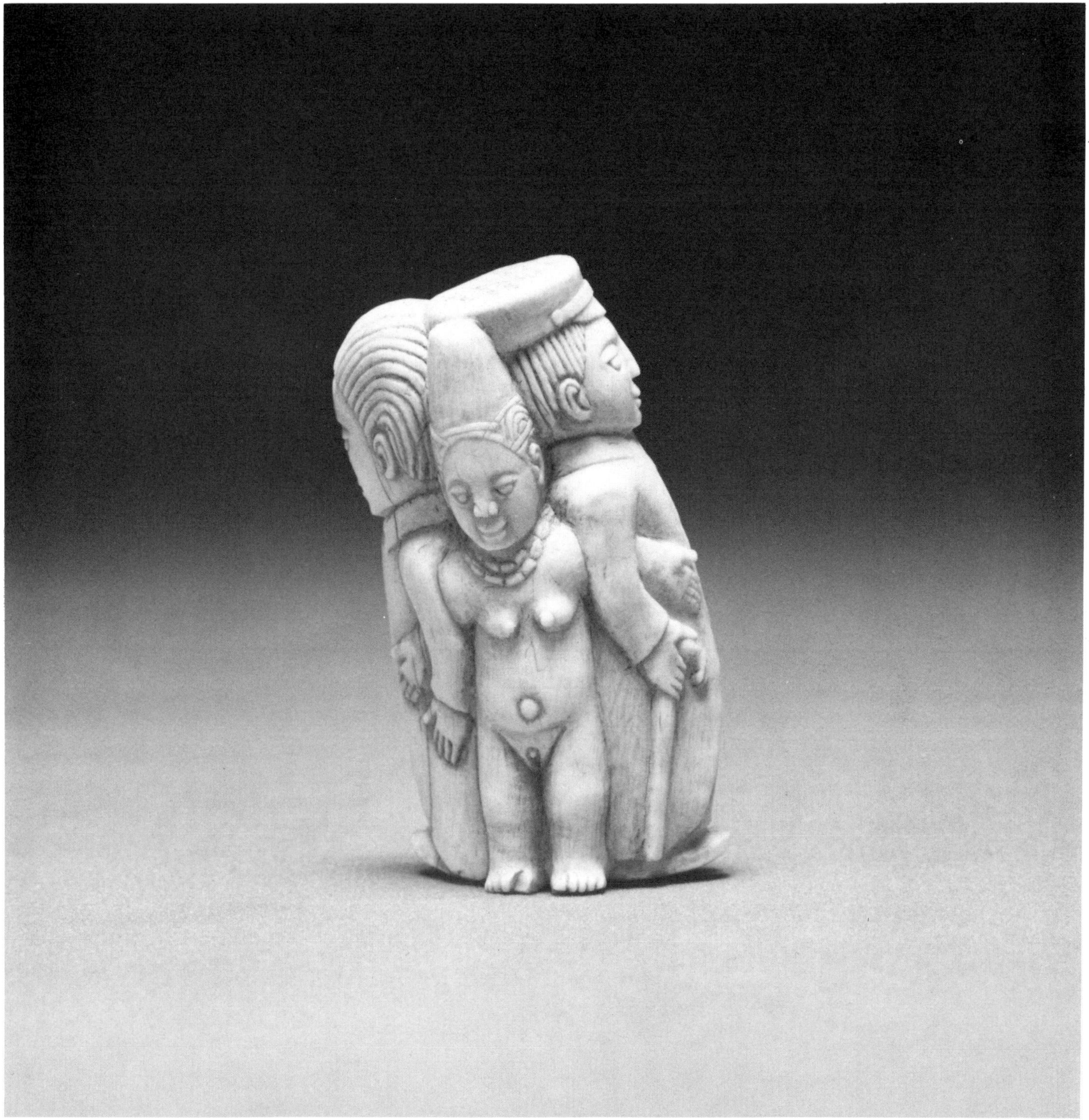

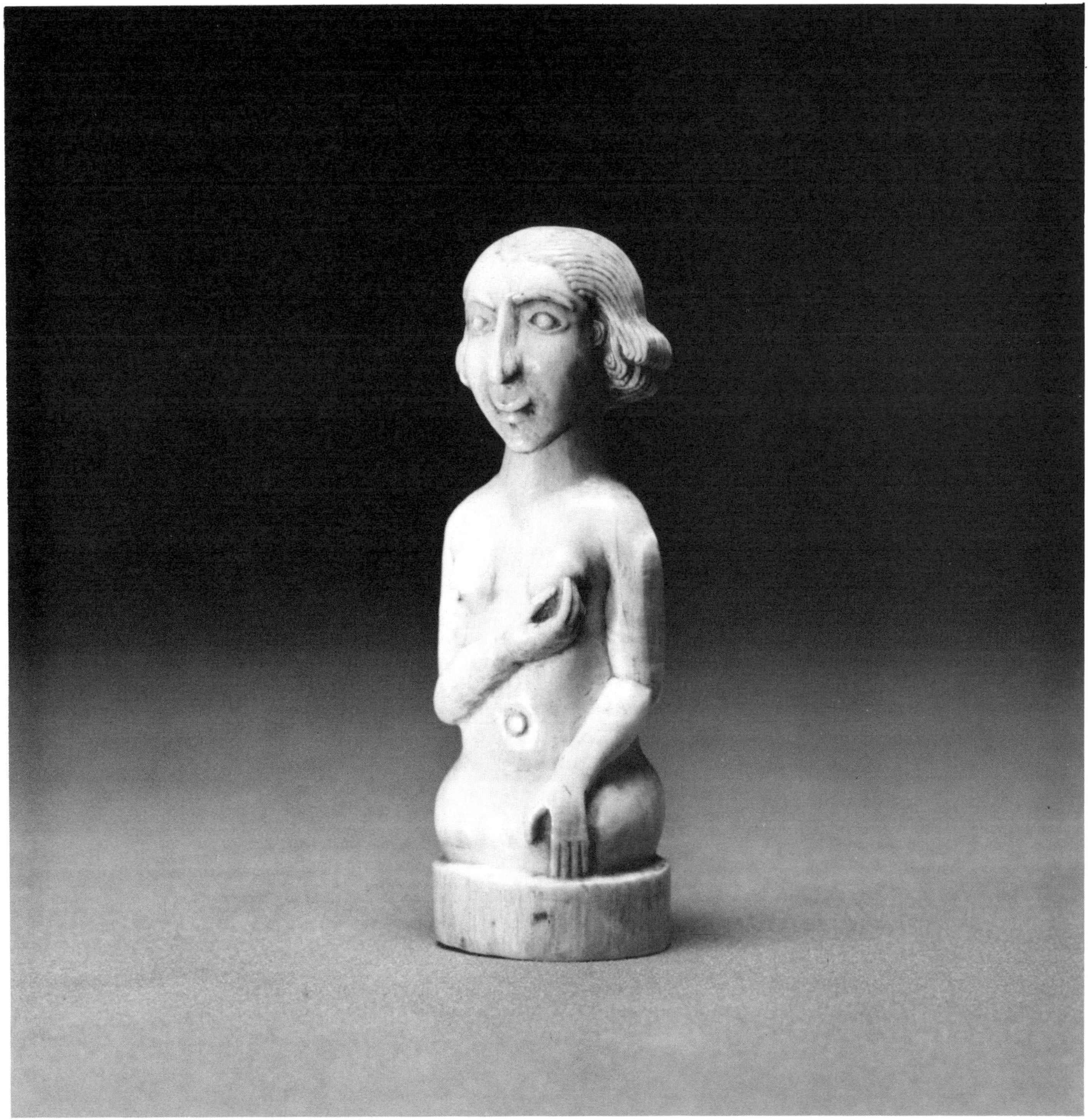

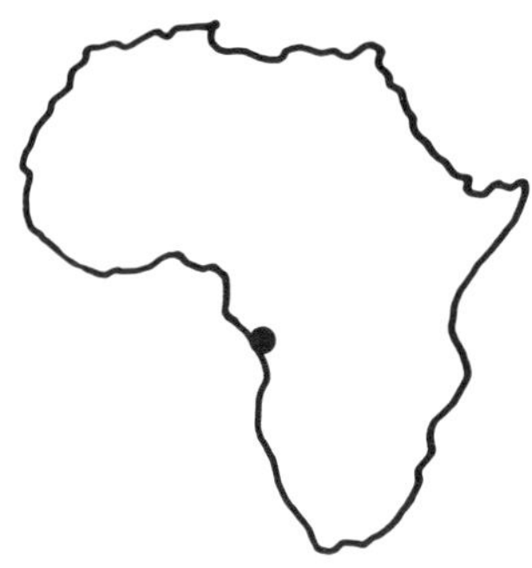

Figure (E6,757)

Kongo or Vili, Congo-Zaire

Ivory

H. 13 cm.

The subject of this Loango carving is obviously a European woman, but her posture, with one hand placed on the breast, is one that is found in more traditional sculpture. *Ex Essex Institute collection, 1867. Collected by George Goldthwait, prior to 1859.*

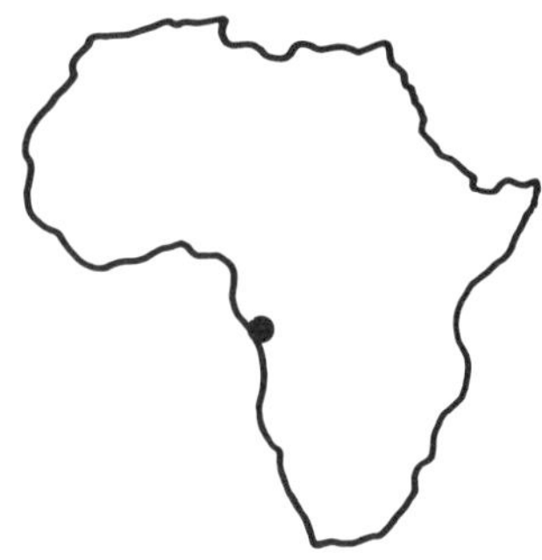

Drum (E6,753)

Kongo, Zaire

Wood, snake or lizard
skin, pigment, metal

H. 102 cm.

The Kongo are actually a group of
related cultures inhabiting the
large area around the mouth of
the Congo River. During the 15th
and 16th centuries, these cultures
were united in a powerful political
state, and the term "Kongo" is still
used to describe the large body of
art produced in the area. Kongo
sculpture is noted for its
naturalism, as in this early drum.
*Ex Essex Institute collection,
1867. Collected by H.F. Shepard,
1859.*

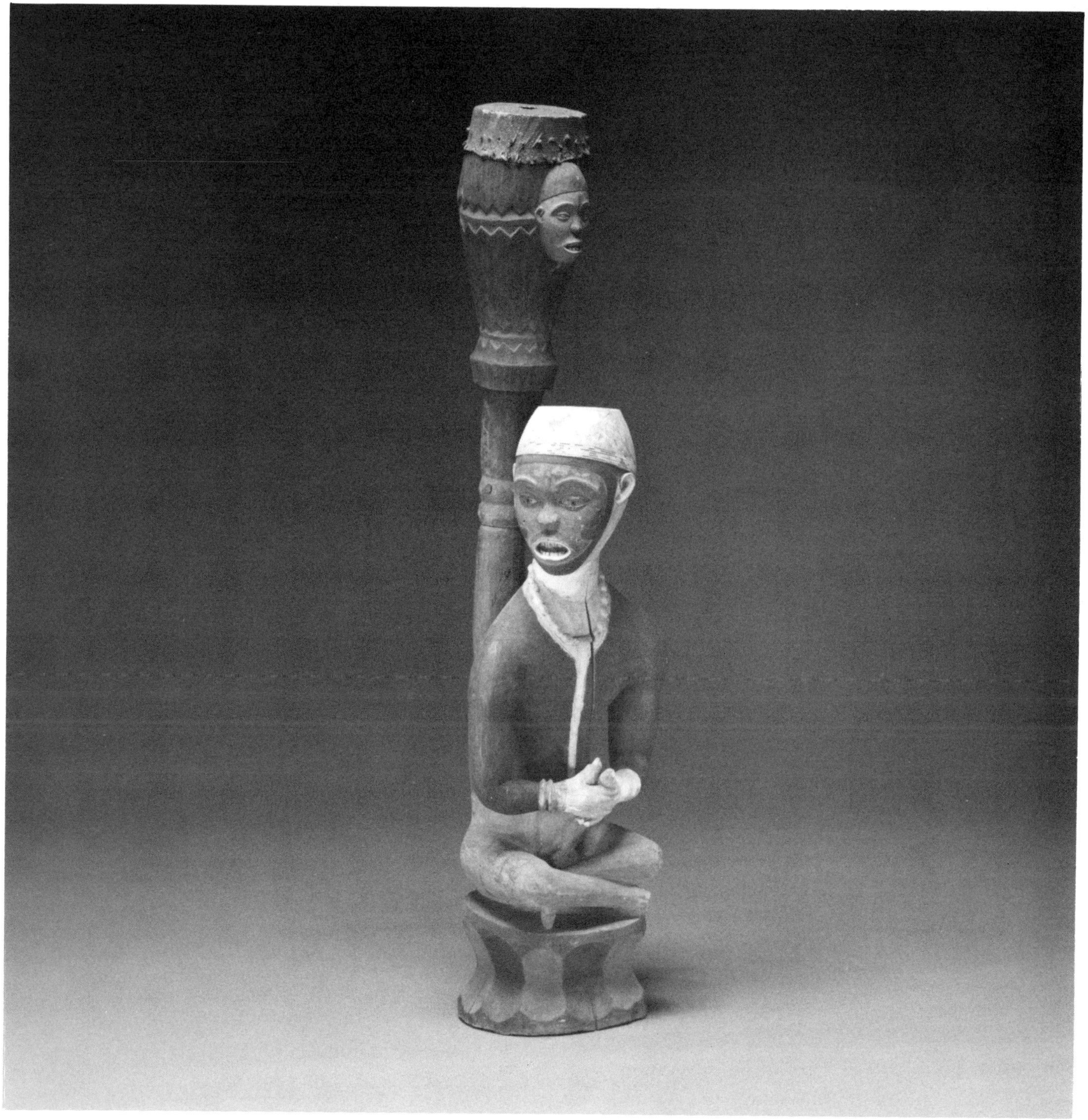

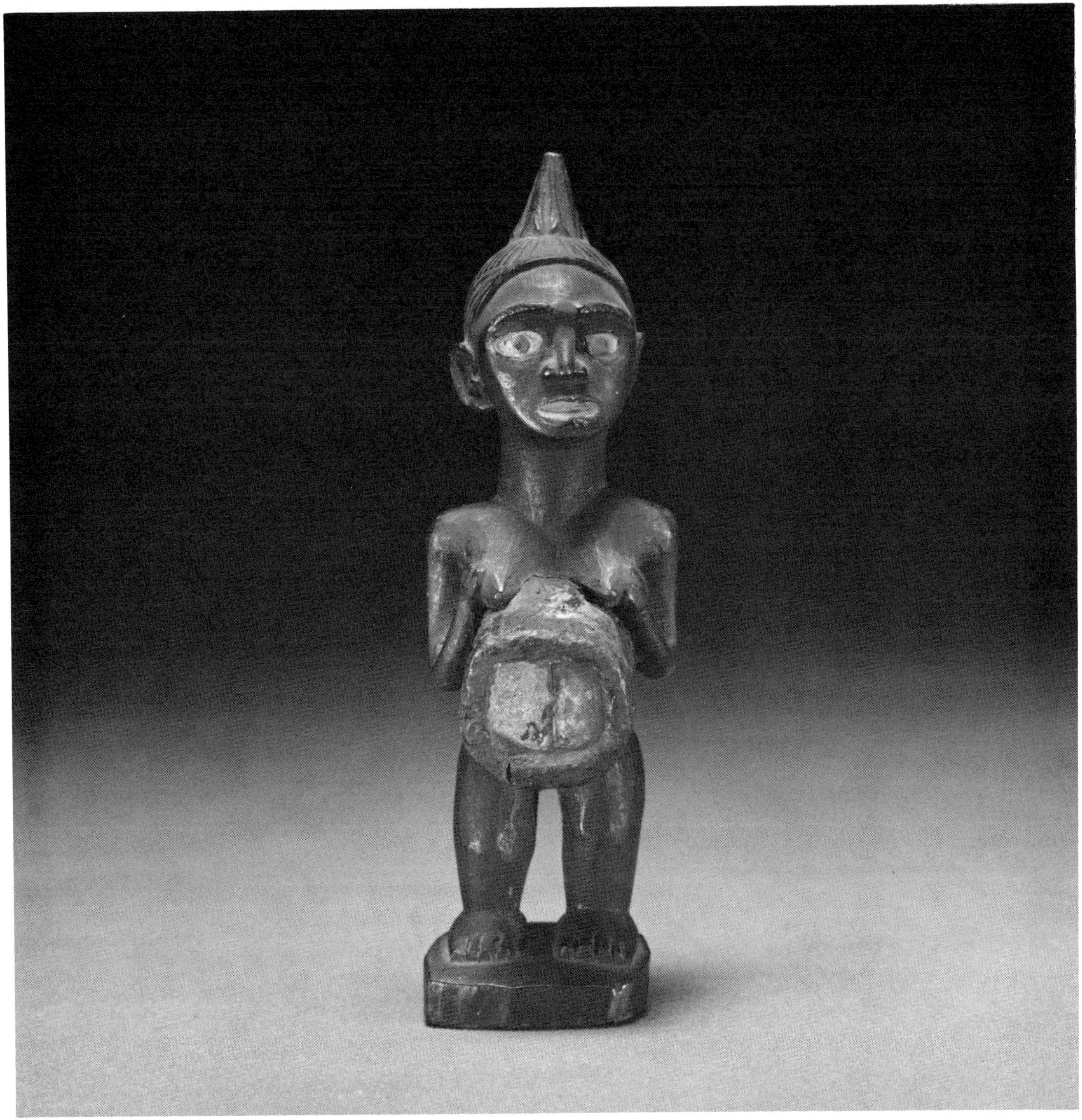

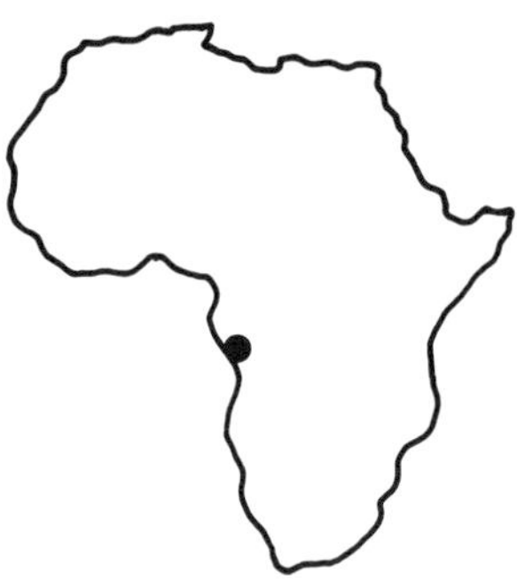

Figure (E8,952)

Kongo, Zaire

Wood, resin, magic
substances, mirrored
glass, pigment

H. 18 cm.

The Kongo make extensive use of
magical figures, called *nkisi* or
n'konde, which achieve their
power through the addition of
special substances, such as nails,
bits of cloth, herbs, etc. In this example, these substances are con-
cealed in a mirror-capped compartment on the abdomen. In other in-
stances, magic substances are tied
onto the figure, driven into it, or
wrapped around it. *Gift of Dr.
Charles G. Weld, 1906.*

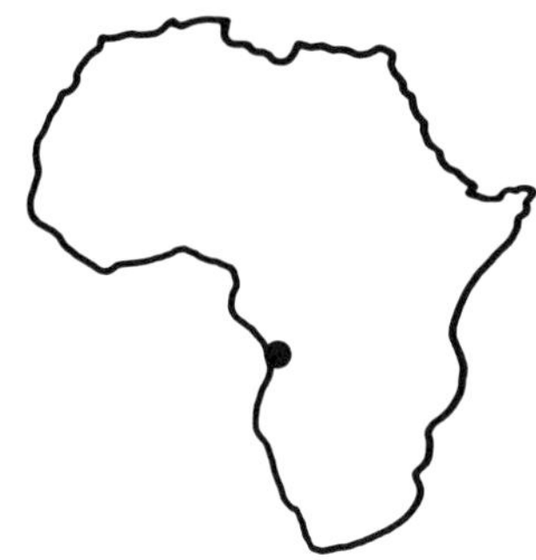

Crucifix (E6,762)

Kongo, Zaire

Wood, pigment

L. 36 cm.

In 1491, the king of Kongo, Nz-
inga Nkuwu, converted to Chris-
tianity creating the first Christian
state in black Africa. During the
next few decades, Catholicism, introduced by the Portuguese,
achieved a brief florescence, but it
was gradually eclipsed by a
resurgence of native beliefs. Christian iconography remained fixed in
Kongo art, however, even though
the original meanings were often
blurred. This striking crucifix is
true to the European prototype,
but may not have functioned in a
Christian context at all. Instead, it
may have been used as a cult object. *Gift of Mr. Emmanuel Curtis,
1893.*

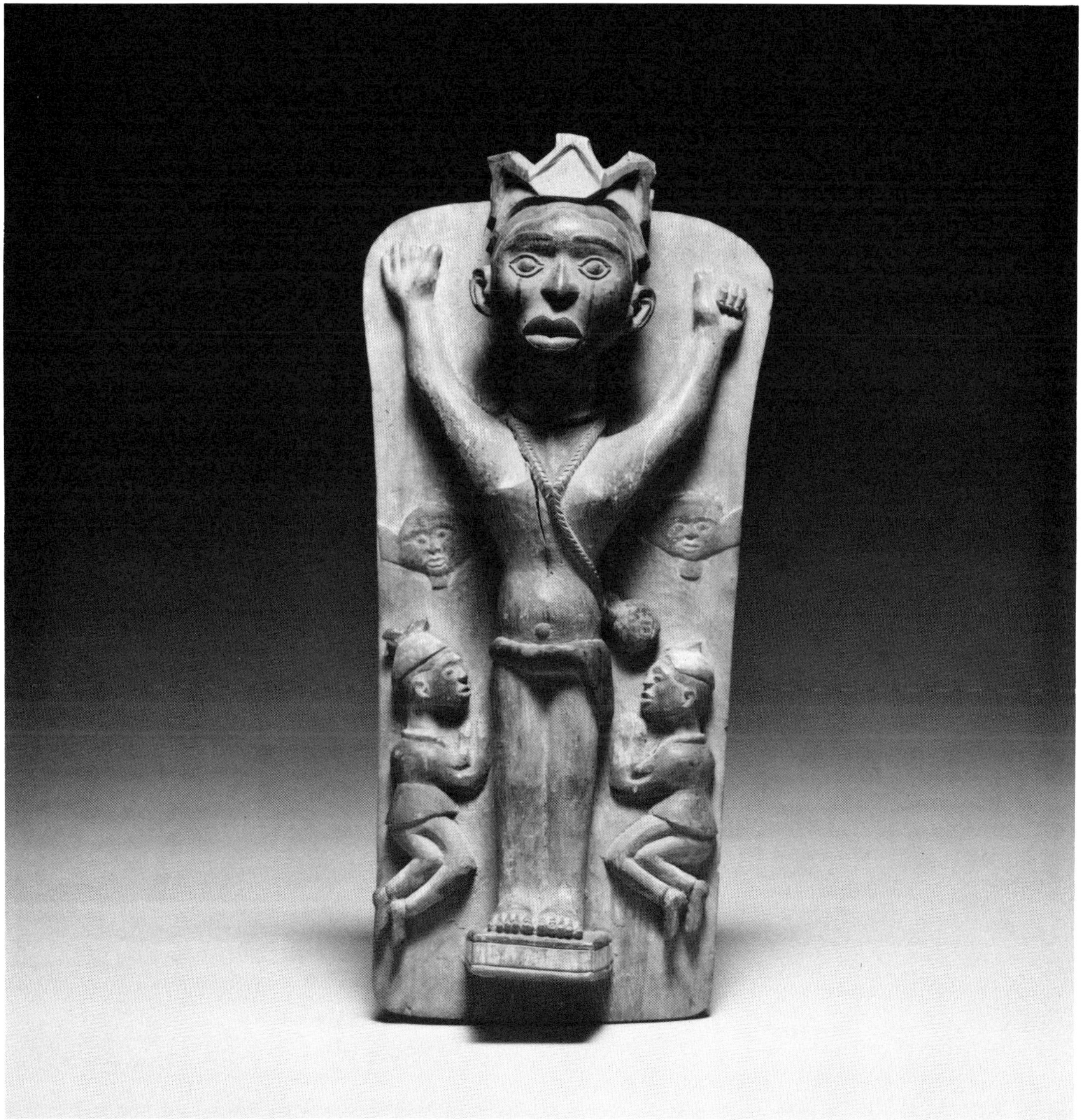

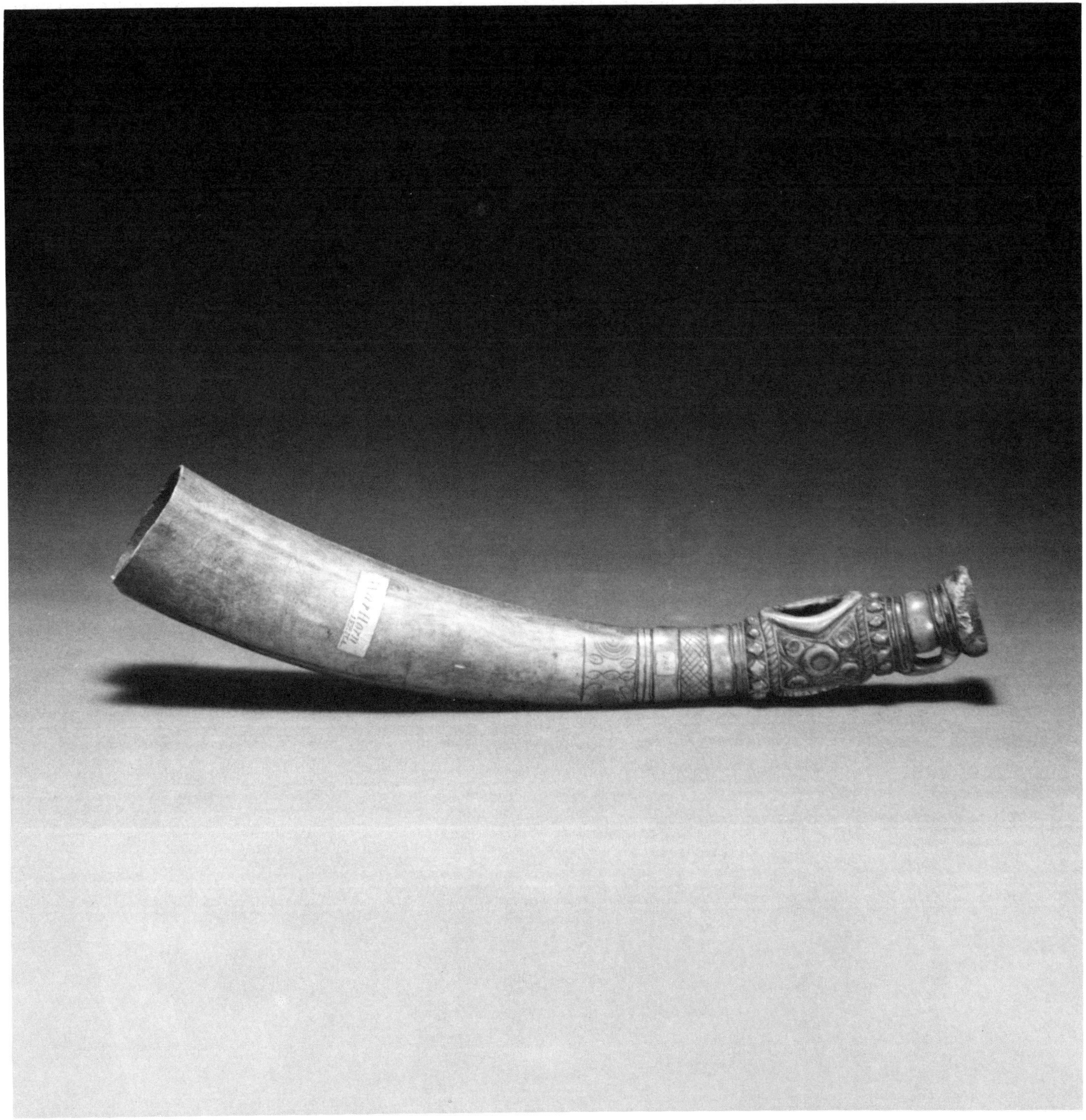

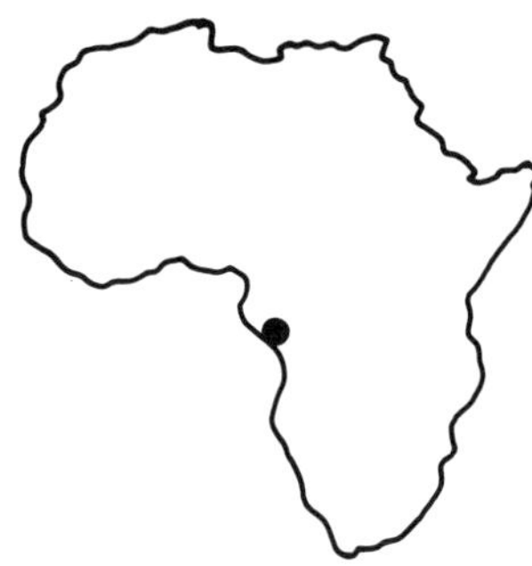

Trumpet (E53,567)

Possibly Kongo, Zaire

Ivory

L. 46 cm.

Trumpets made from elephant tusks occur in many parts of Africa. This beautifully carved and patinated example was collected by an American missionary in the middle of the 19th century. *Ex American Board of Commissioners for Foreign Missions collection, 1976. Collected prior to 1850.*

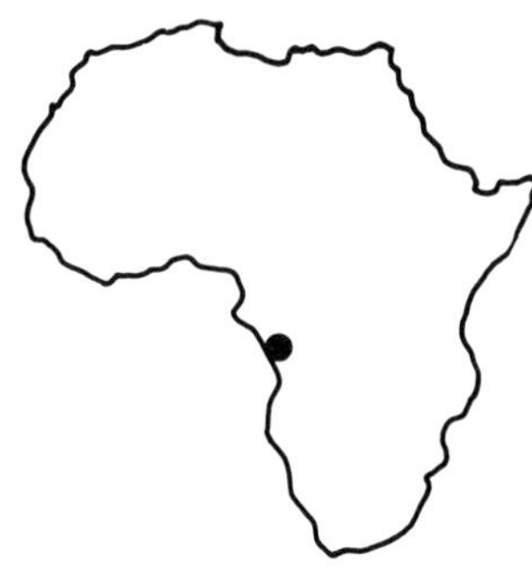

Powder Horn (E16,194)

Possibly Kongo, Zaire

Ivory

L. 41 cm.

Firearms were an important European trade item in Africa, particularly during the slave trading years. *Gift of H.J. Lane, 1915.*

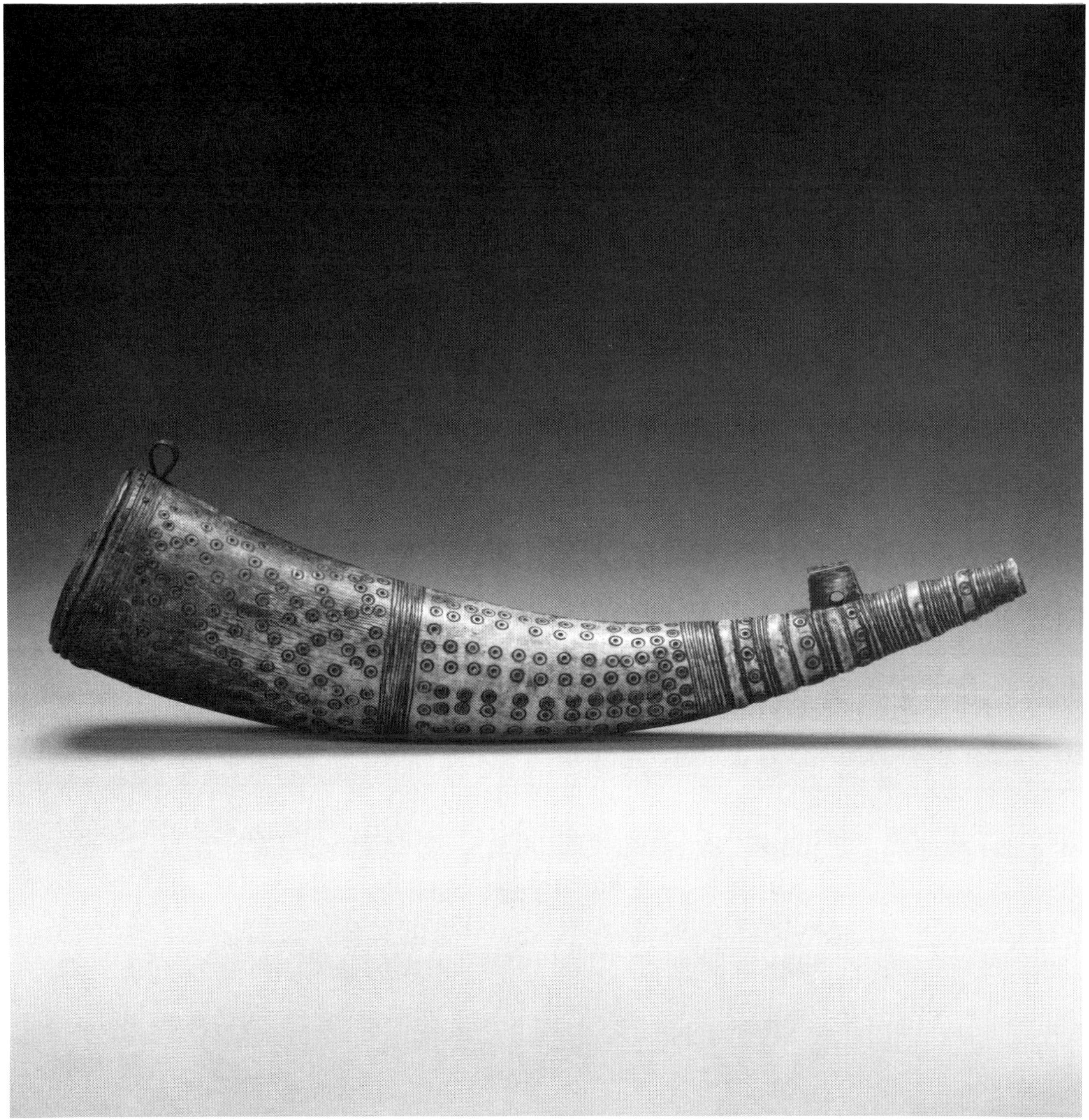

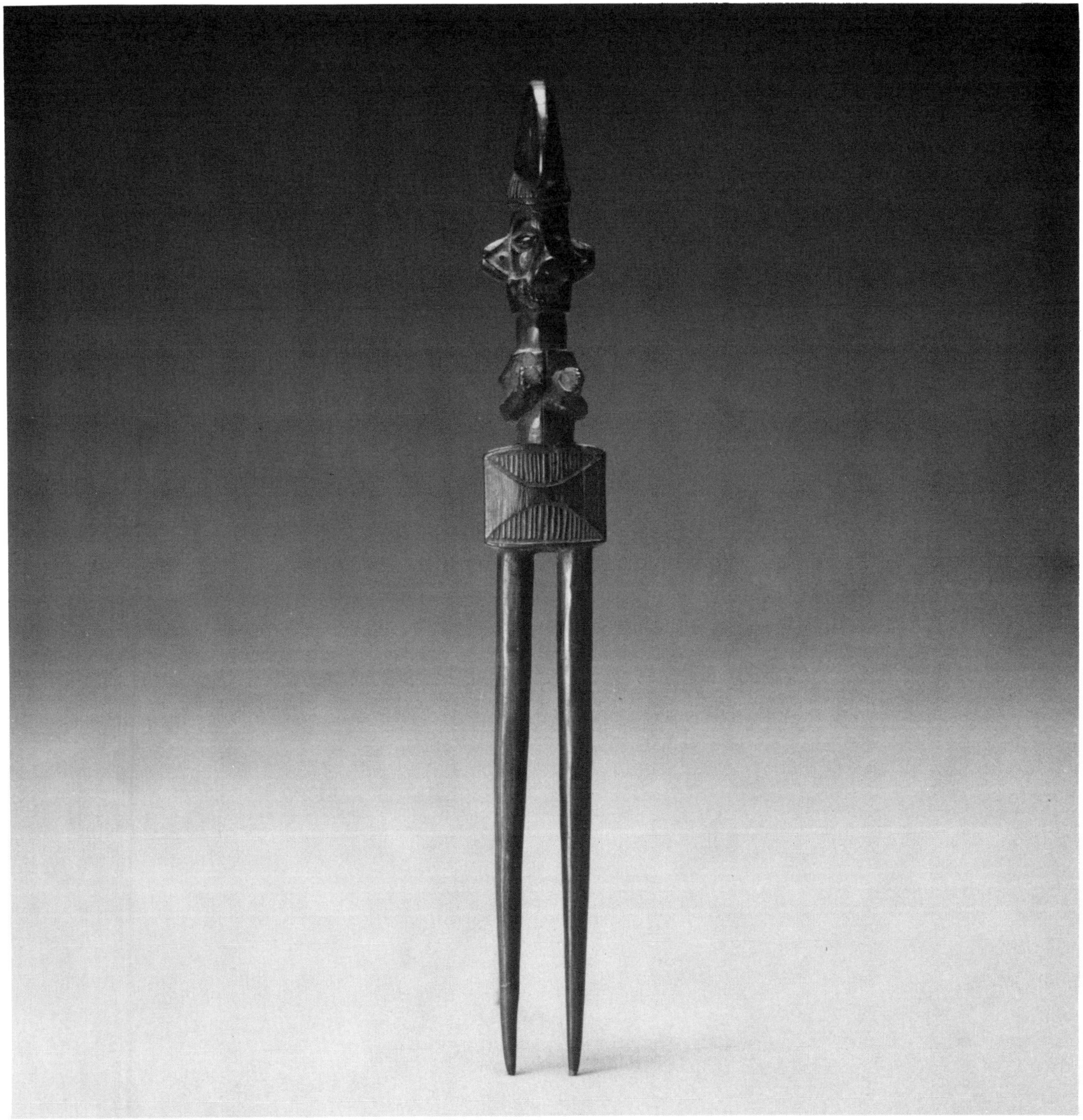

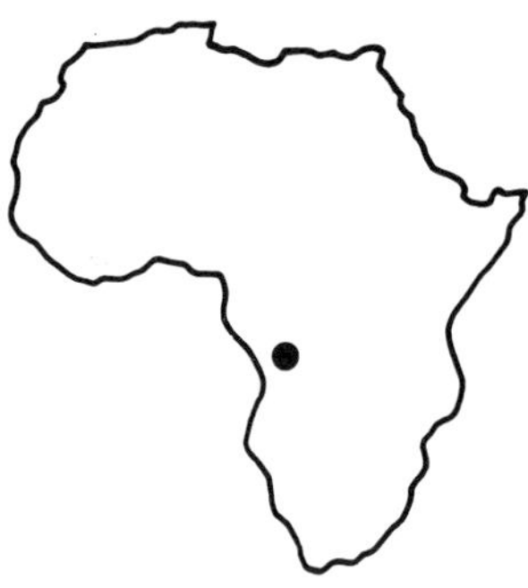

Comb (E18,805)

Yaka, Zaire

Wood

L. 20 cm.

The Yaka inhabit the area east of the Kwango River, a major tributary of the Congo. Renowned warriors, they produce a variety of masks and figurative sculpture, many characterized by prominent, upturned noses. This comb is a hair ornament for a man. *Gift of Mr. William A. Northey, 1922.*

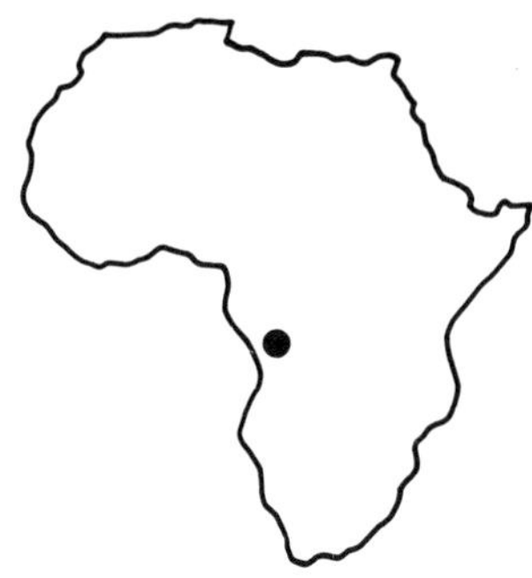

Figure (E22,427)

Sundi, Zaire

Wood, shell

H. 15 cm.

The Sundi, better known as the Bembe, live north of the Kongo area and were part of the Kongo kingdom prior to 1569. Small figures such as this are among the most common of Sundi sculpture. This example originally served as a fetish and has an anal compartment for the inclusion of magic substances. *Gift of Stephen W. Phillips, 1936.*

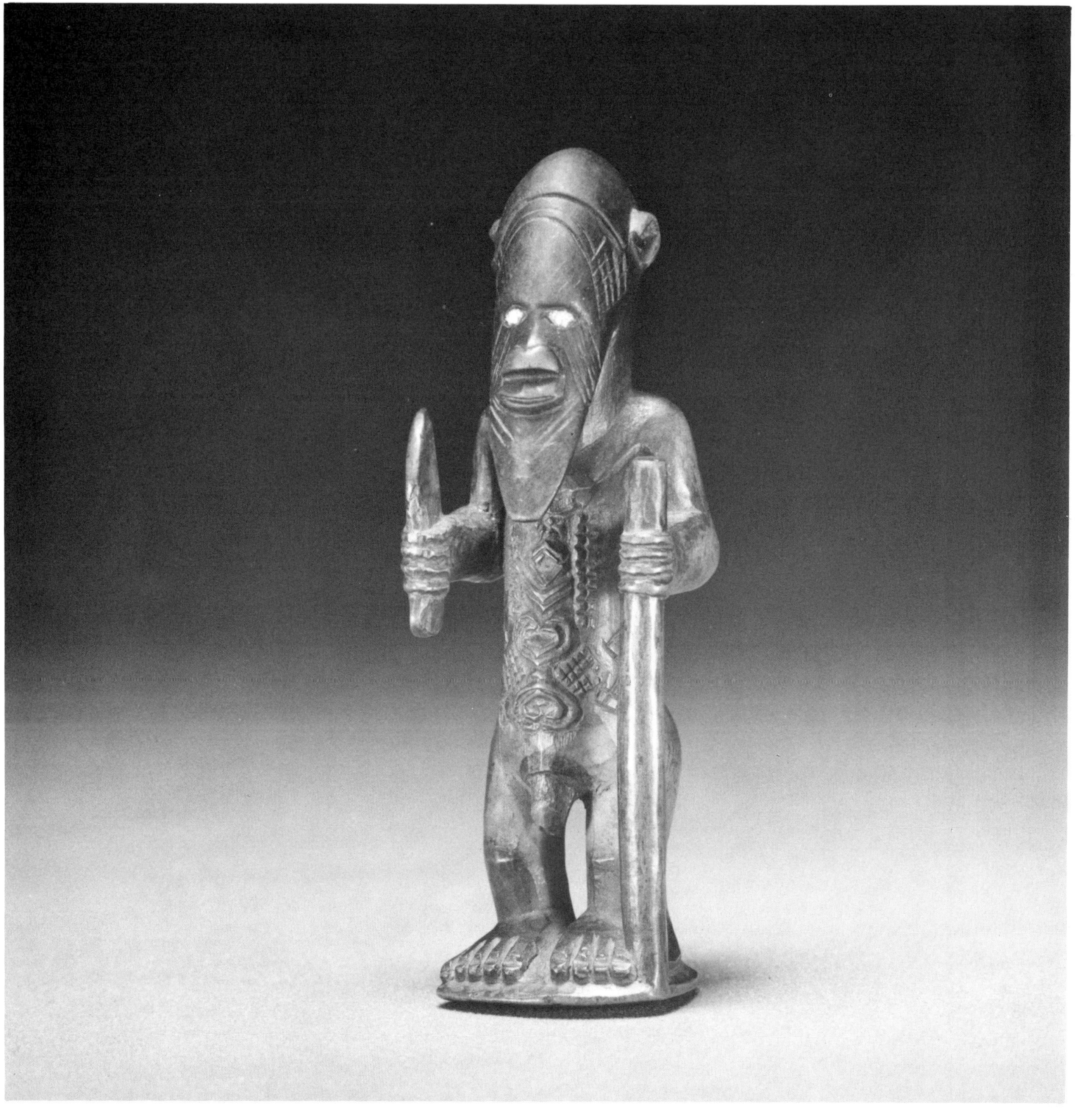

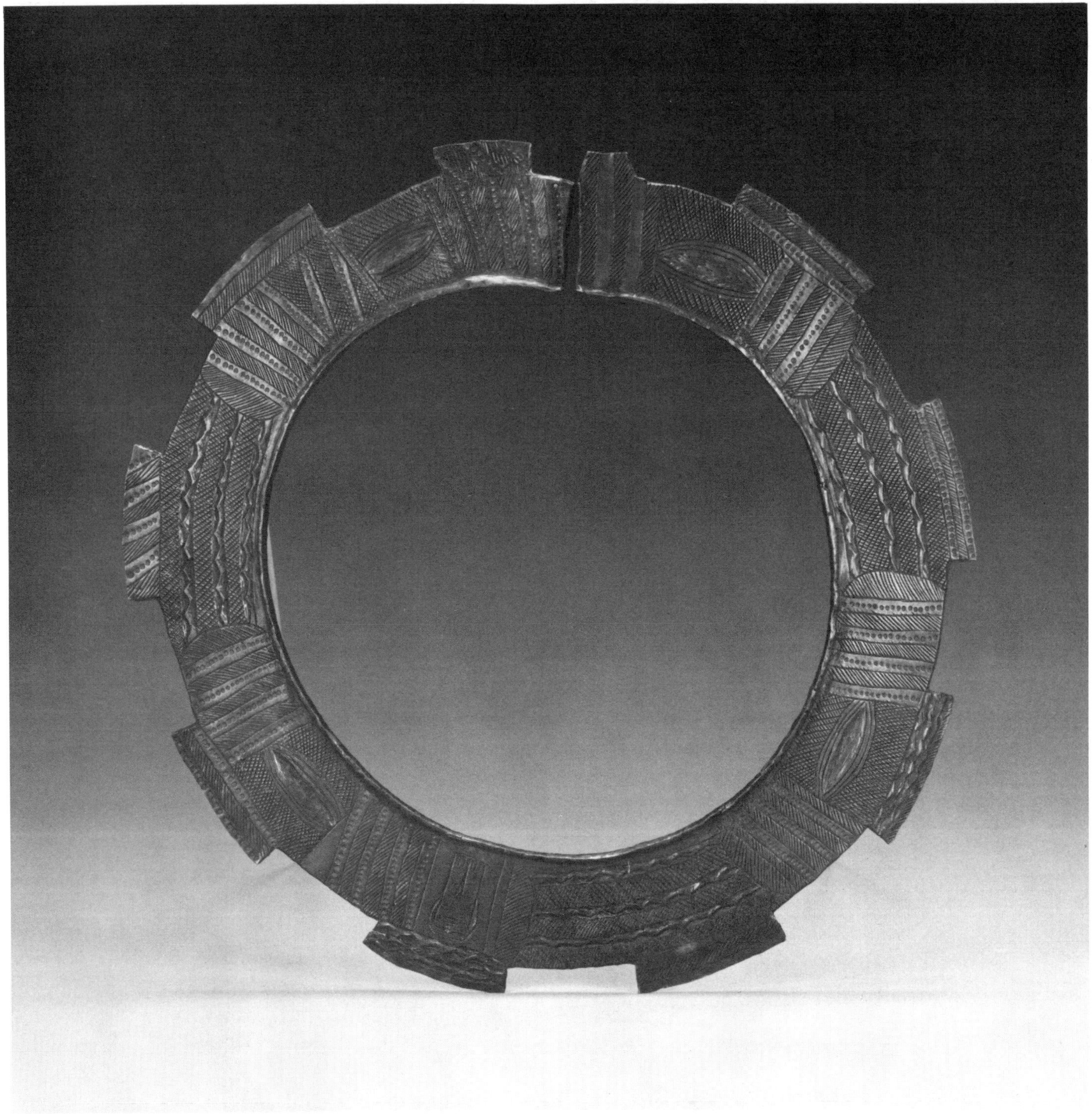

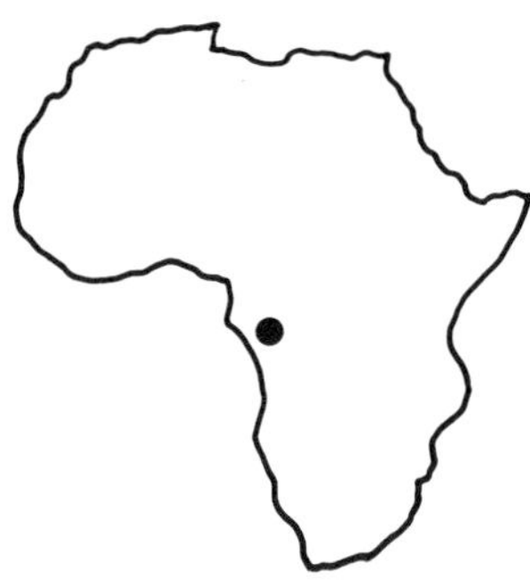

Collar (E2,337)

Teke, Zaire

Brass

D. 34 cm.

"Teke" means figure in one of the
Kongo dialects; an allusion to the
many skillfully carved fetish
figures made by the Teke. They
also produce cast brass or-
naments, such as this collar with
engraved geometric designs. This
piece, together with several others
to follow, was collected by E.J.
Glave, a member of H.M. Stanley's
field crew in Africa from
1883-1889. *Gift of Mr. William C.
Endicott, 1892. Collected by E.J.
Glave, 1883-1889.*

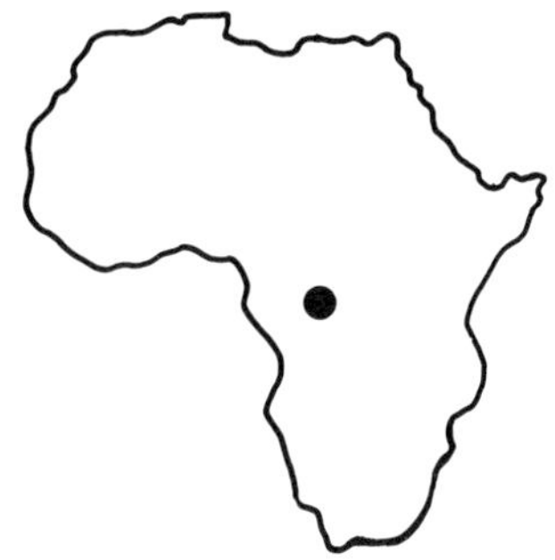

Pot (E12,770)

Possibly Ekonda, Zaire

Earthenware

D. 11 cm.

Neither the potter's wheel nor the kiln existed in sub-Saharan Africa before their introduction by Europeans. Traditionally, pots were formed by coiling or pinching and fired *en masse* in the open air. This finely made pot from the Lake Tumba region of Zaire has an incised and fluted collar. The high polish is the result of burnishing the pot with a smooth object, such as a pebble, prior to firing. *Ex Philadelphia Museum collection, 1909.*

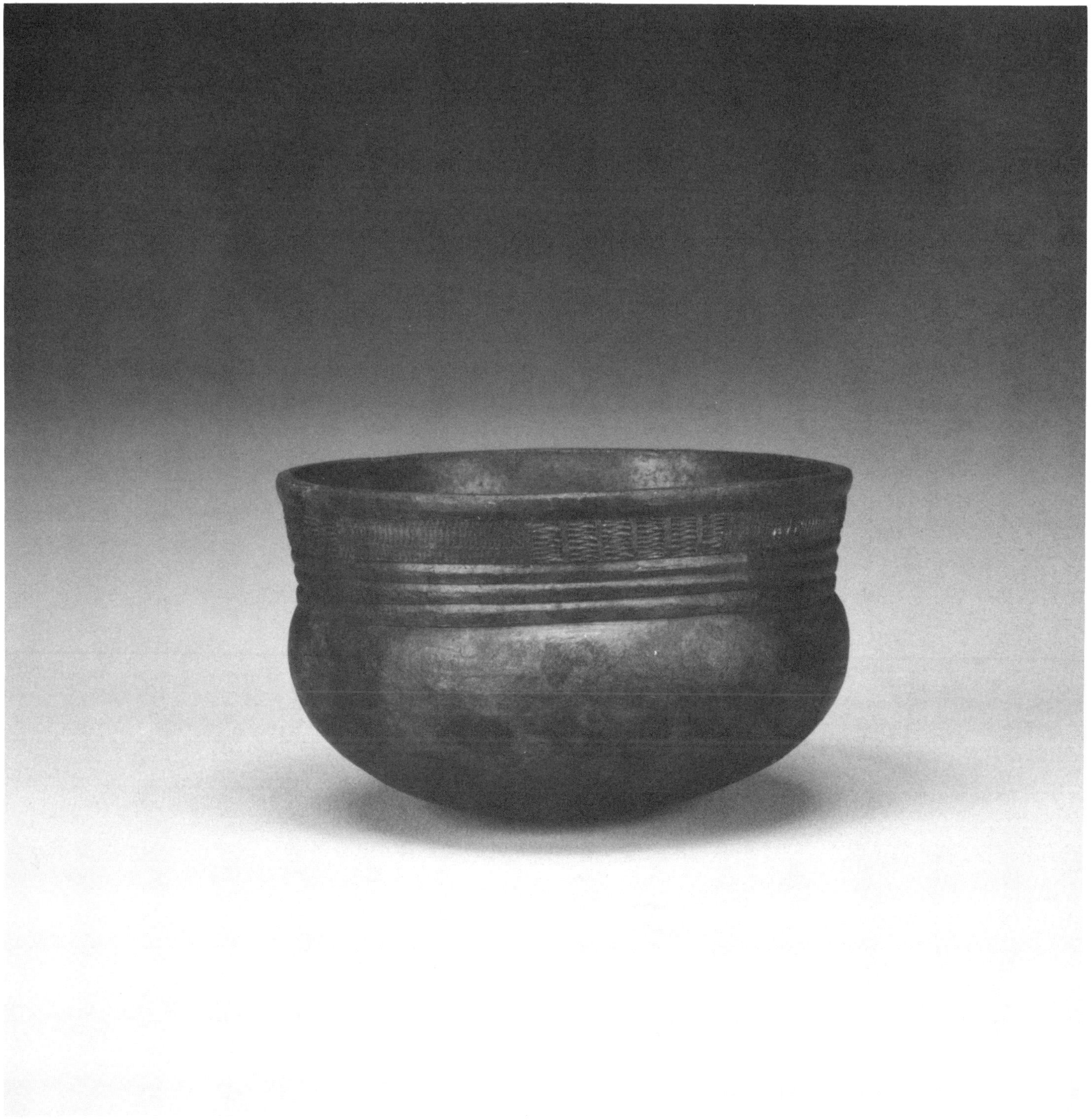

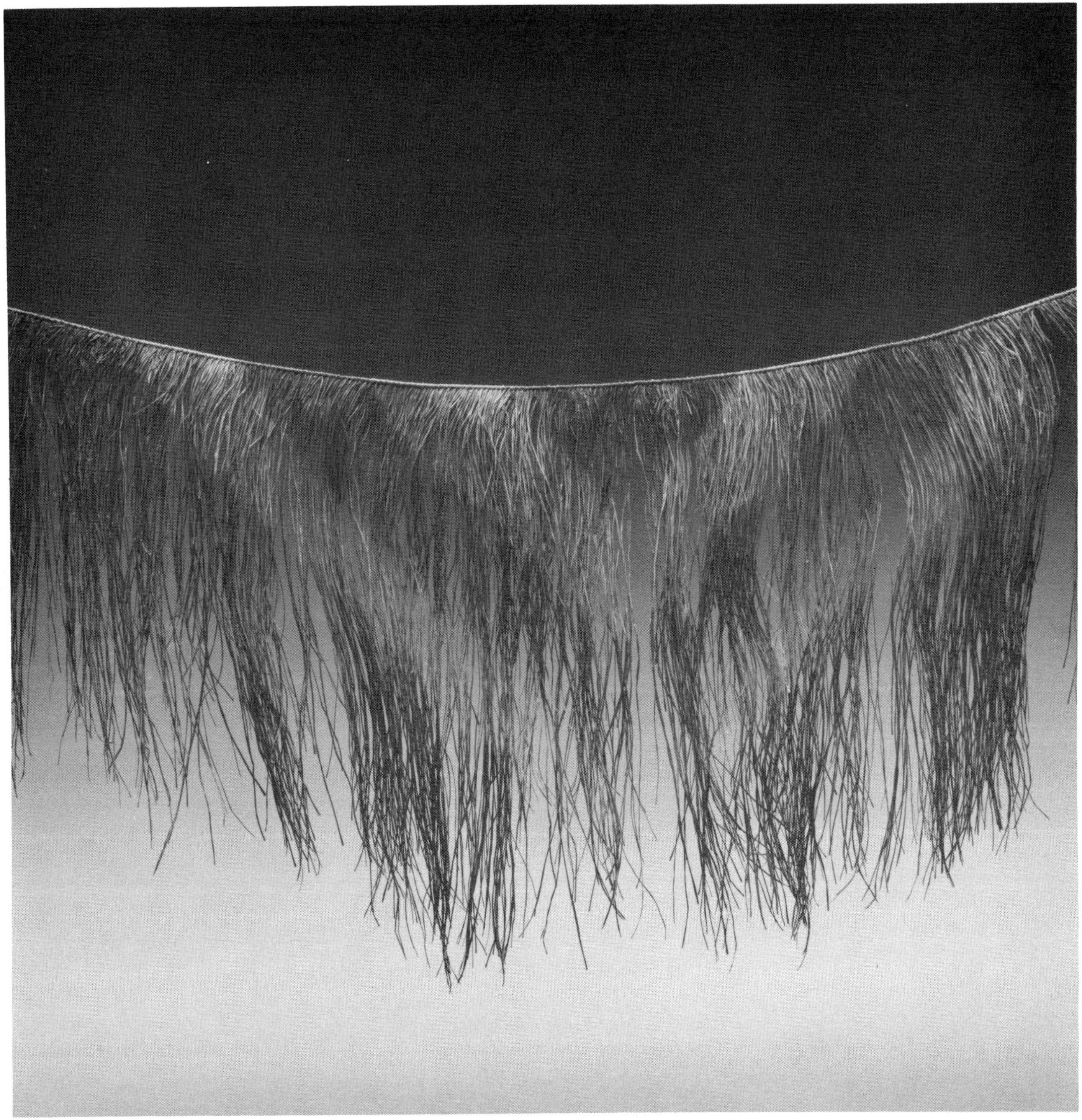

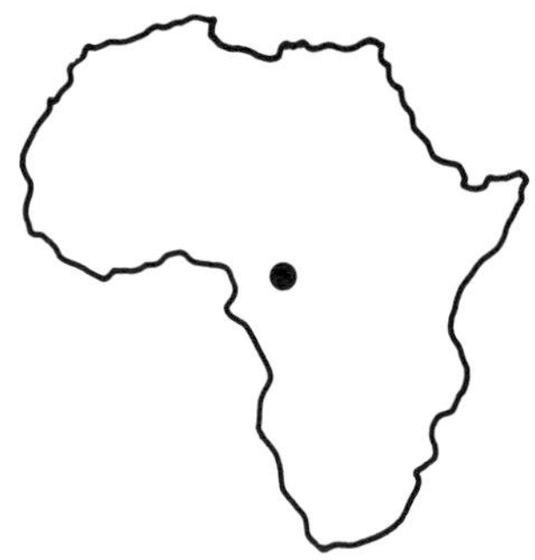

Skirt (E2,317)

Ngala, Zaire

Raffia, dye

L. 81 cm.

A woman's skirt from the Ngala of the upper Congo River. The subtle design was produced by tie-dying the raffia strands. *Gift of Mr. William C. Endicott, 1892. Collected by E.J. Glave, ca. 1883-1889.*

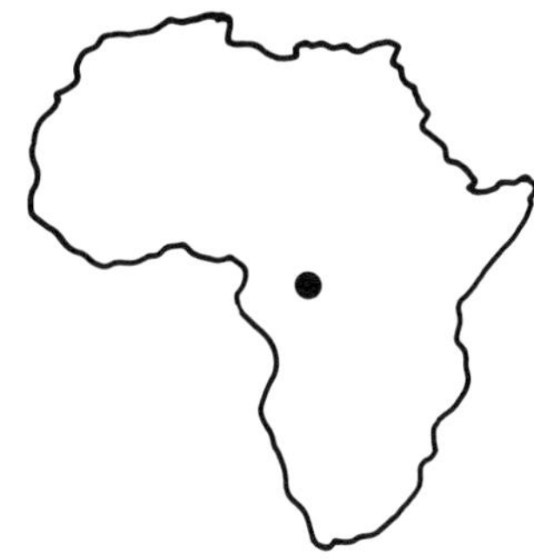

Sword (E2,335)

Ngala, Zaire

Iron, wood, leather, brass

L. 59 cm.

A specialized type of sword used for executions and sacrifices. *Gift of Mr. William C. Endicott, 1892. Collected by E.J. Glave, ca. 1883-1889.*

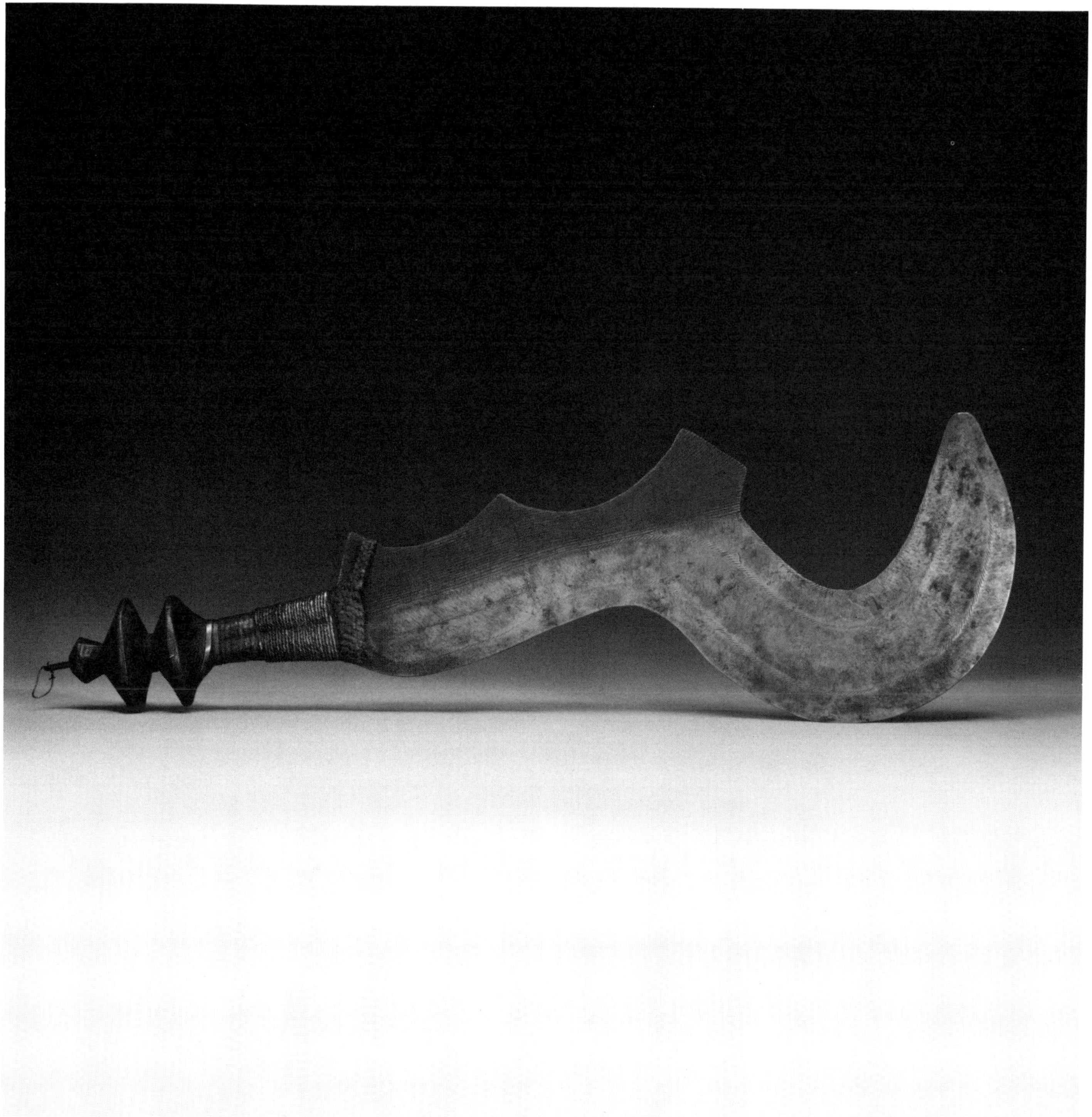

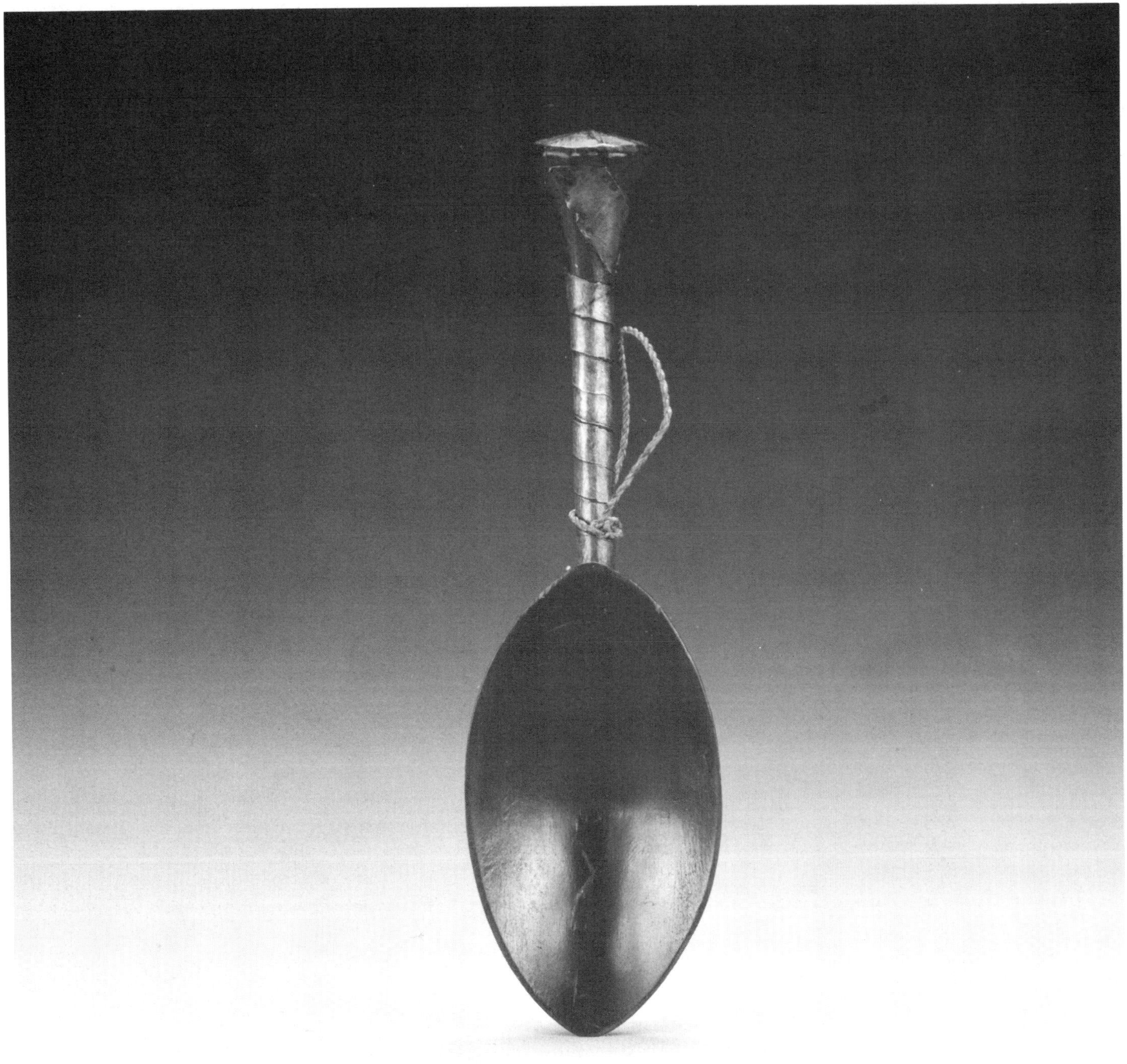

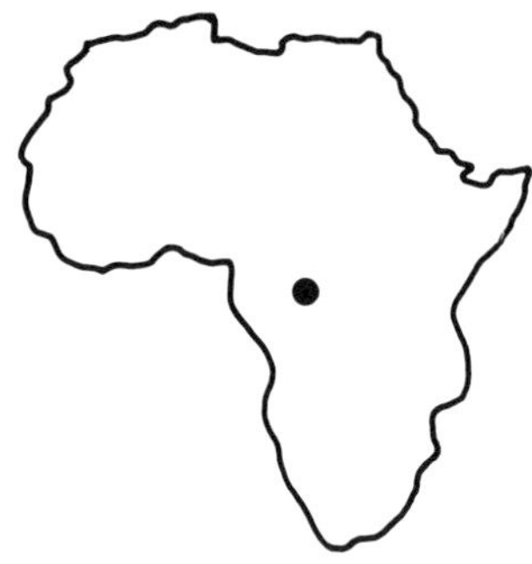

Spoon (E2,329)

Mongo, Zaire

Wood, brass, vegetable fiber

L. 16 cm.

This beautifully designed and polished spoon was made by the Mongo of the Maringa River area. *Gift of Mr. William C. Endicott, 1892. Collected by E.J. Glave, 1883-1889.*

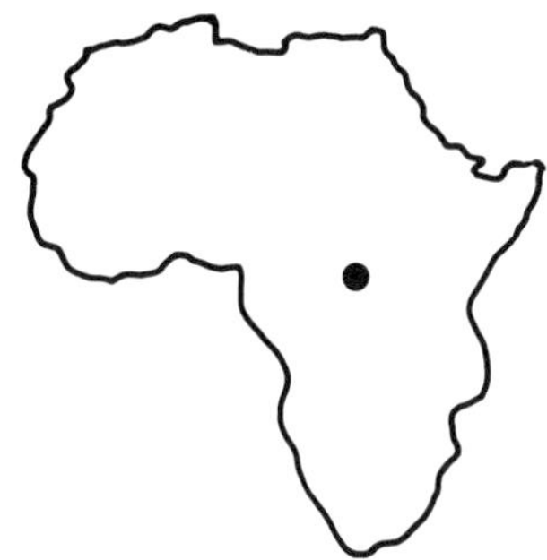

Arrows (E13,033)

Mbuti, Zaire

Bamboo, leather, iron,
vegetable fiber

L. 62-66 cm. *Detail*

The Mbuti Pygmies live in the
Ituri forest of northern Zaire, in-
termingling with the Negroid
tribes in the area. Racially distinct
from the Negroid peoples which
occupy most of sub-Saharan
Africa, the Pygmies are nomadic
hunters and gatherers who do not
traditionally plant crops or raise
livestock. Mbuti hunting is
generally done with nets and
snares; these decorated arrows
may be from the Efe, a sub-group
of the Mbuti. *Gift of William G.
Sewall, 1910. Collected ca.
1908-1909.*

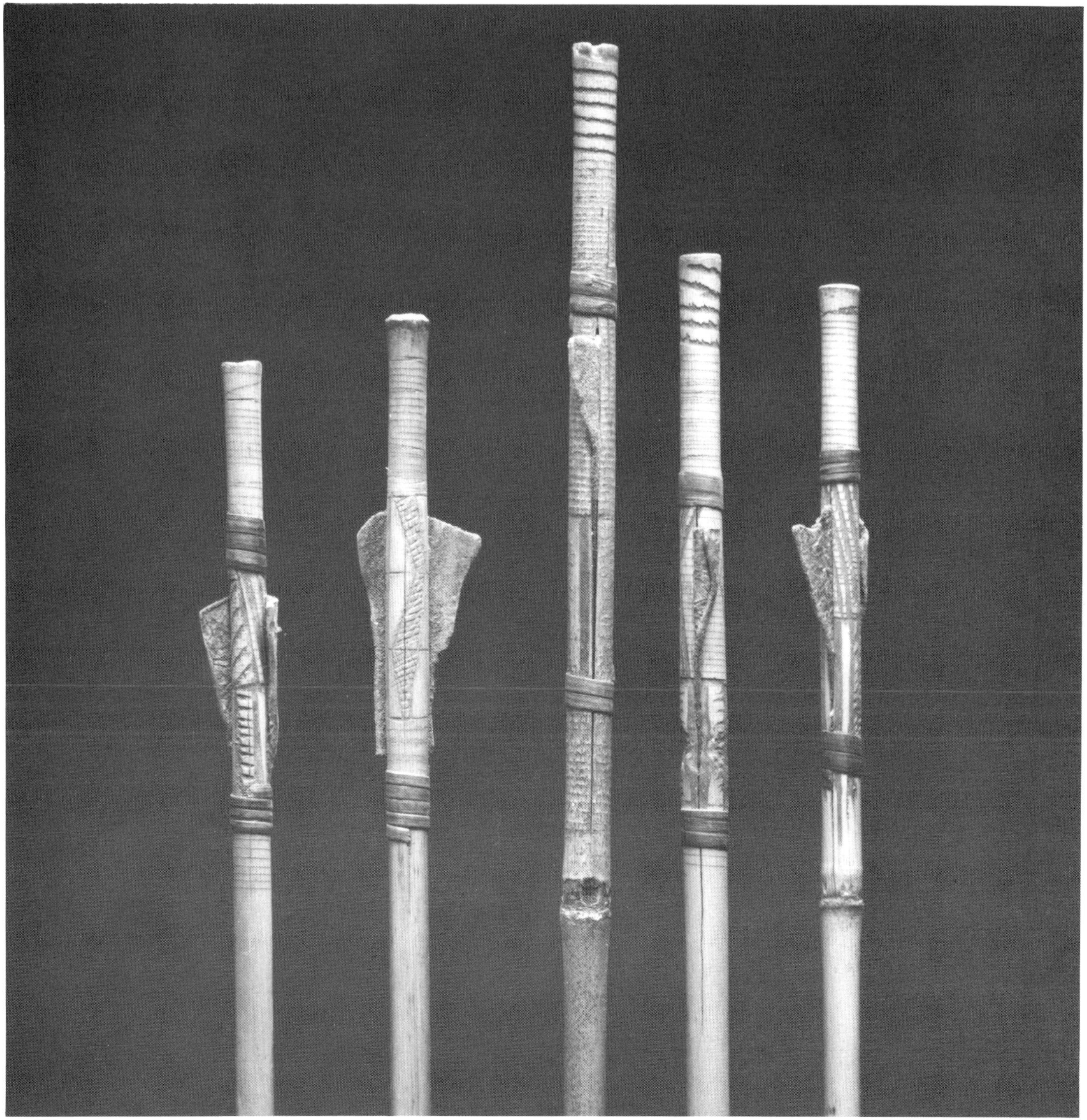

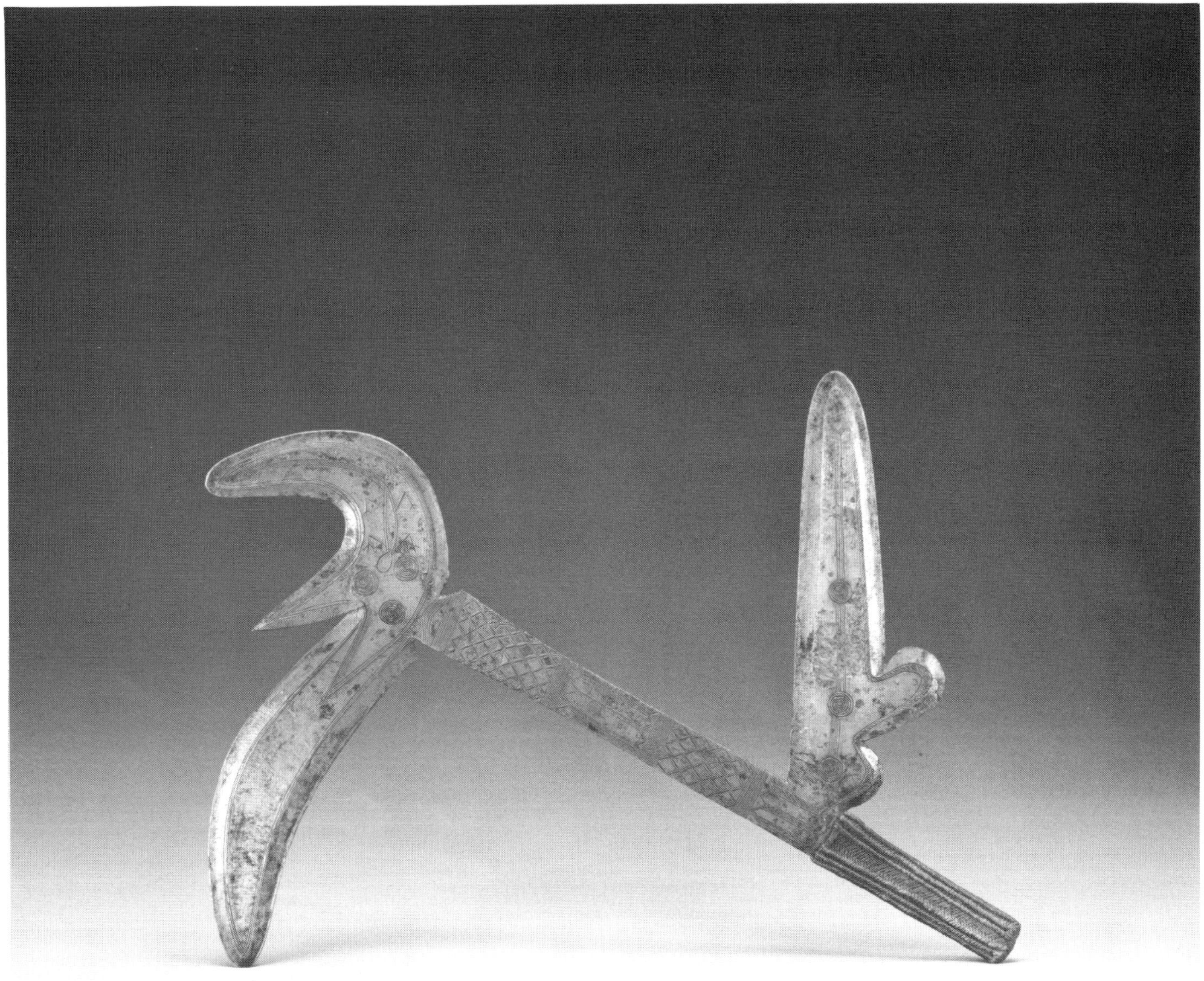

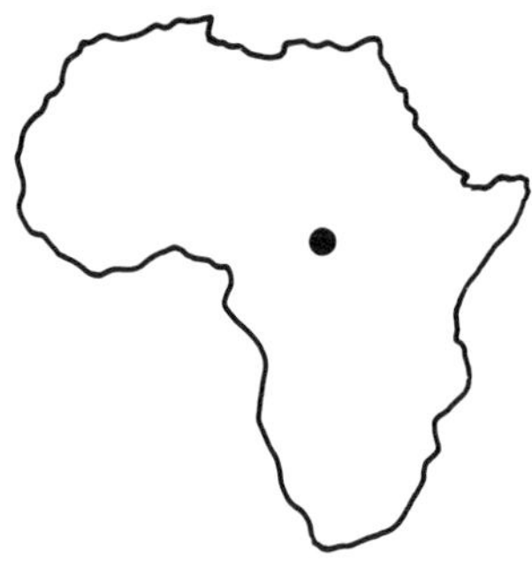

Throwing Knife (E14,363)

Azande, Zaire

Iron, cordage

L. 46 cm.

Iron - smelting technology has existed in sub-Saharan Africa since about 500 B.C. In addition to the development of tools for agriculture and woodworking, a number of edged weapon types have evolved. One of the most lethal is the throwing knife, whose multi-edged design insured penetration regardless of how the weapon struck an opponent. *Gift of Dr. Charles G. Weld, 1910.*

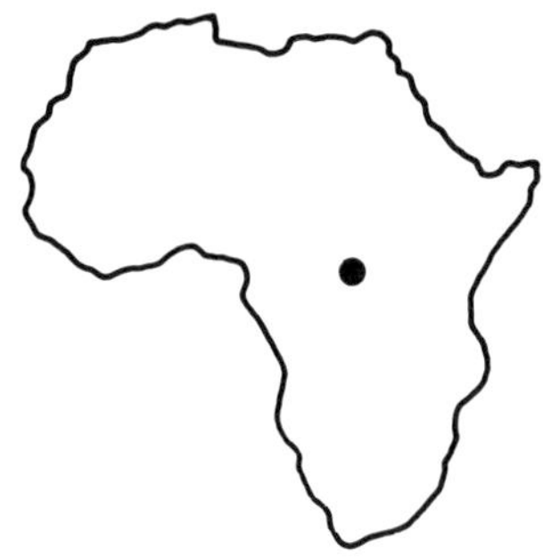

Figure (E27,332)

Mangbetu, Zaire

Ivory

L. 51 cm. *Detail*

Women of the Mangbetu of northern Zaire wear an elaborate hairstyle, depicted in this figure carved on the end of an elephant tusk. *Gift of Mrs. Augustus P. Loring, 1947.*

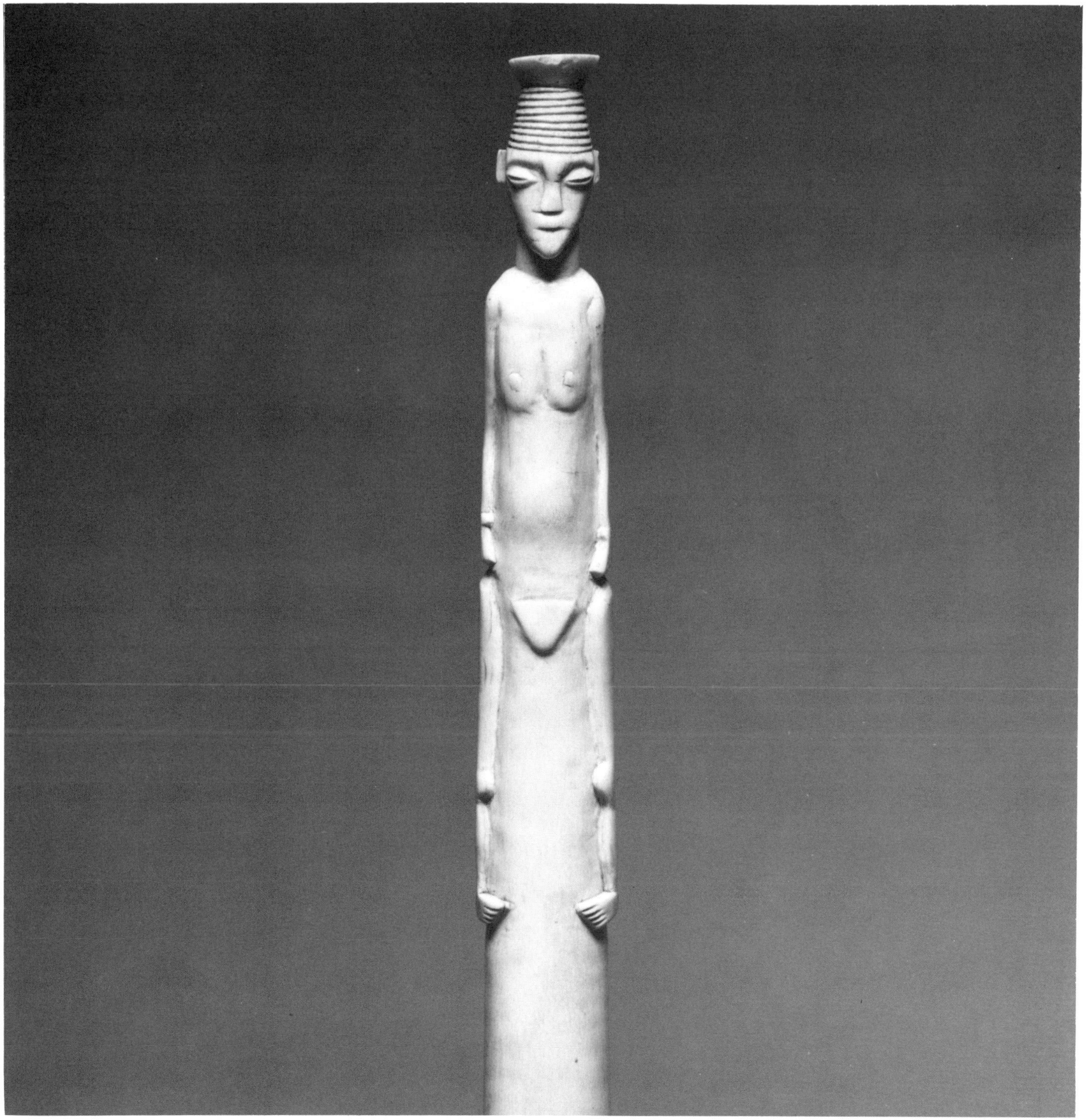

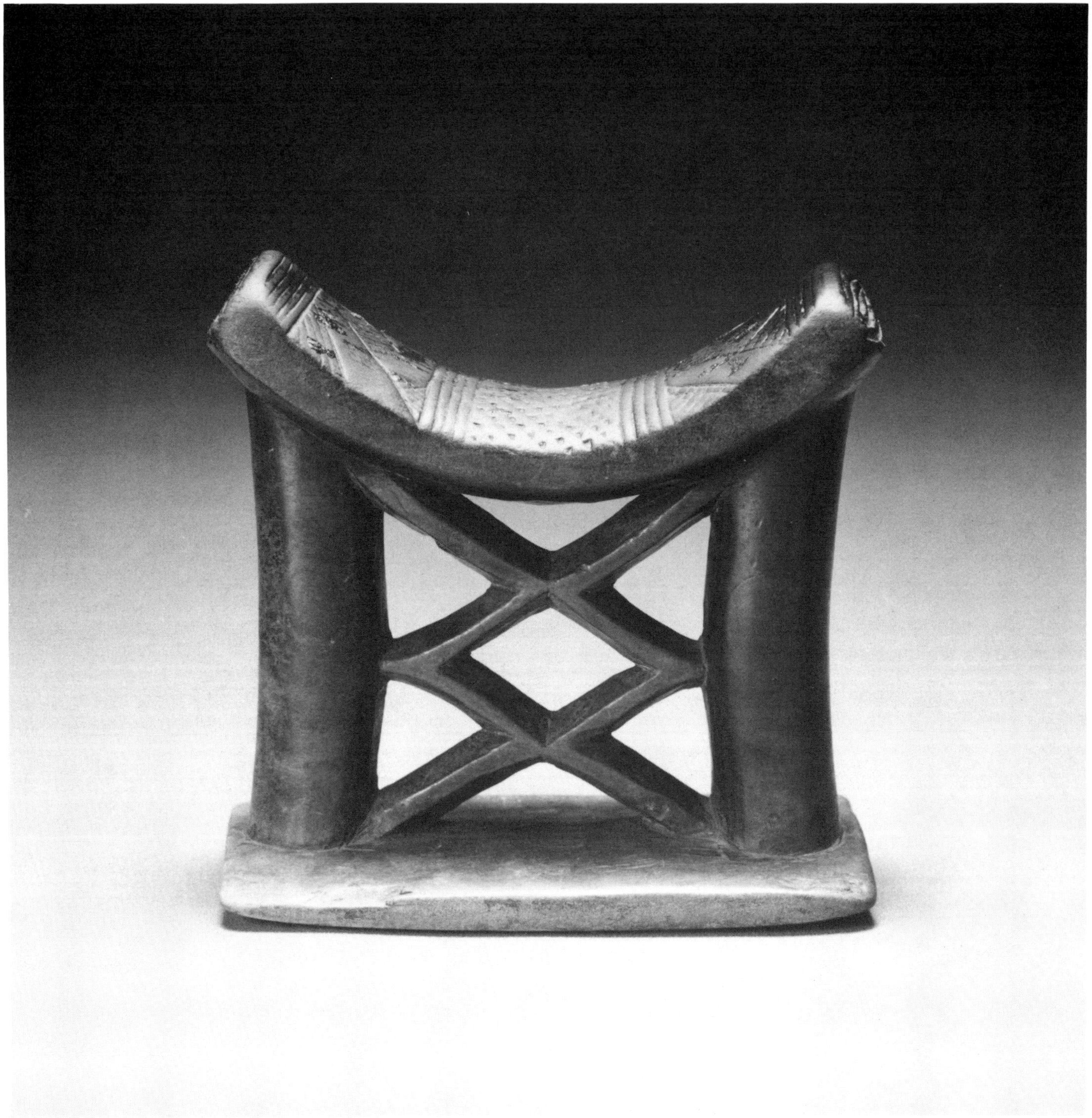

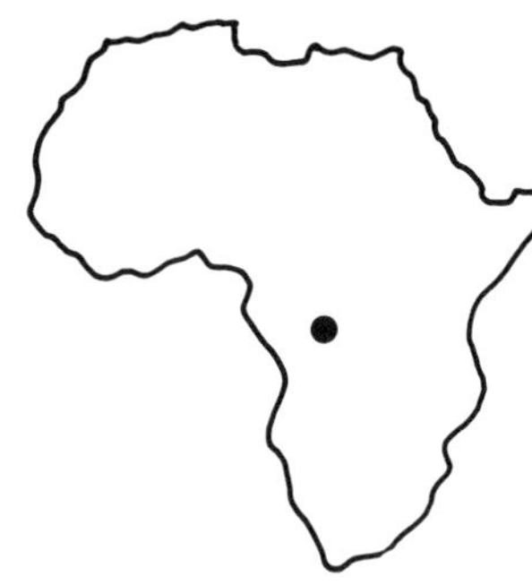

Headrest (E5,918)

Probably Kuba, Zaire

Wood

H. 15 cm.

The Kuba are a group of about eighteen tribes related by culture and language. Collectively, they possess a rich artistic tradition including masks, figures, and an assortment of highly decorated functional objects and textiles. This well-worn headrest has interlocking geometric patterns typical of Kuba surface decoration. *Gift of Mrs. Charles G. Loring, 1904.*

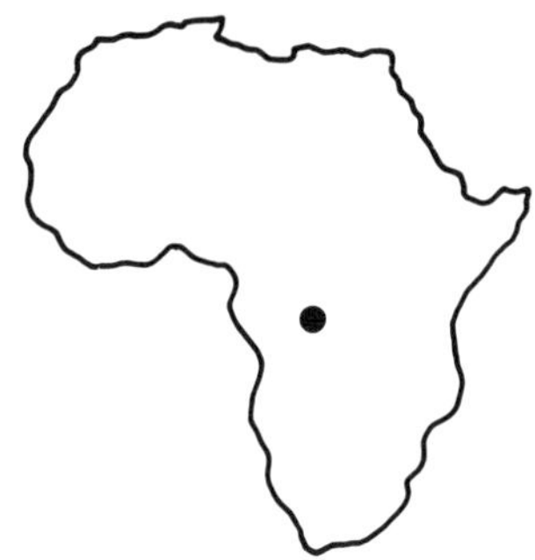

Wine Cup (E4,112)

Kuba, Zaire

Wood

H. 15 cm.

Wine Cup (E27,644)

Kuba, Zaire

Wood

H. 12 cm.

Initiated Kuba men drink a mildly intoxicating palm wine from cups such as these. *E4,112, Gift of Mr. Augustus Hemenway, 1897; E27,644, Gift of Rev. Thomas Adams, 1948. Collected ca. 1891-1897.*

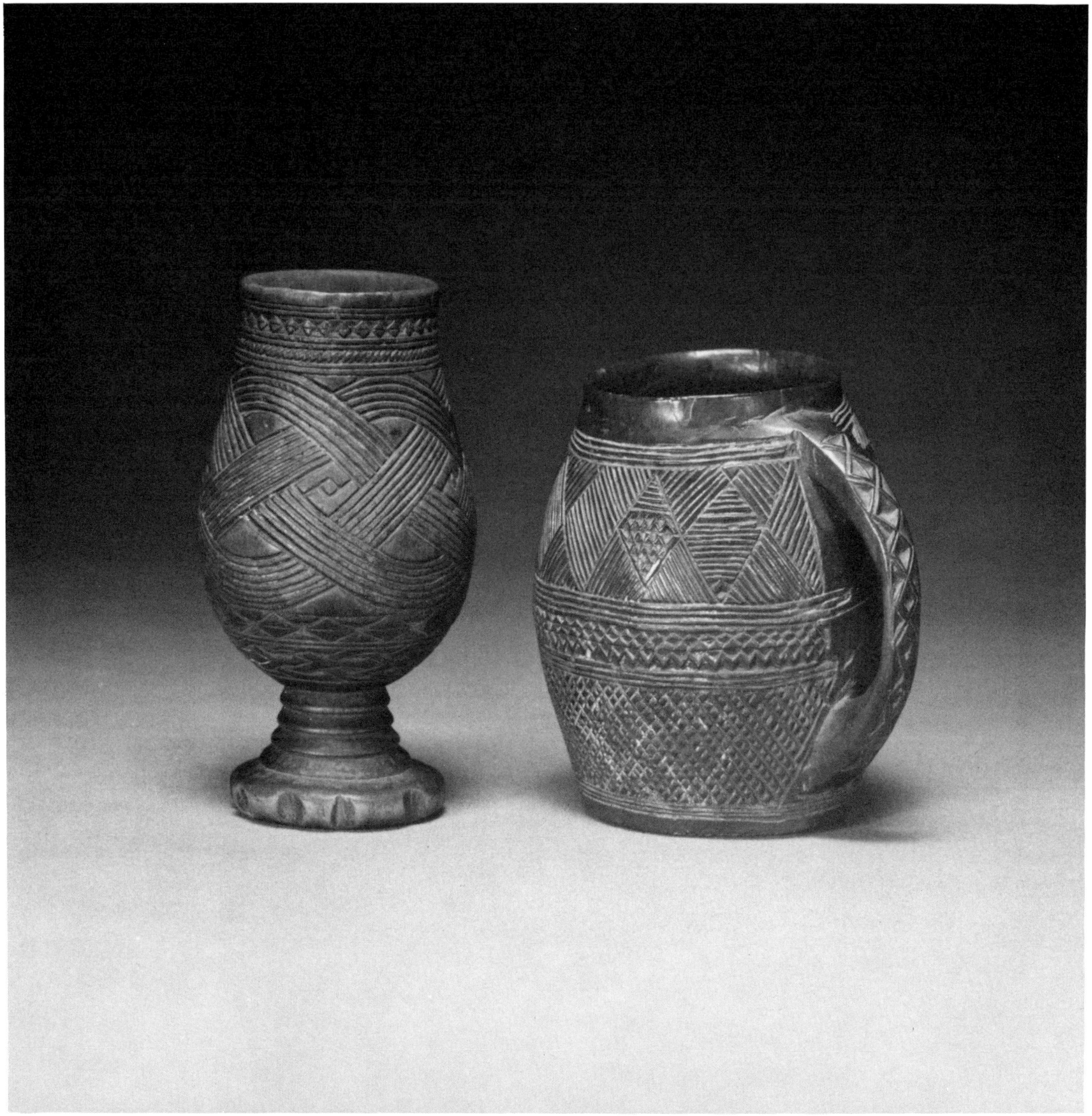

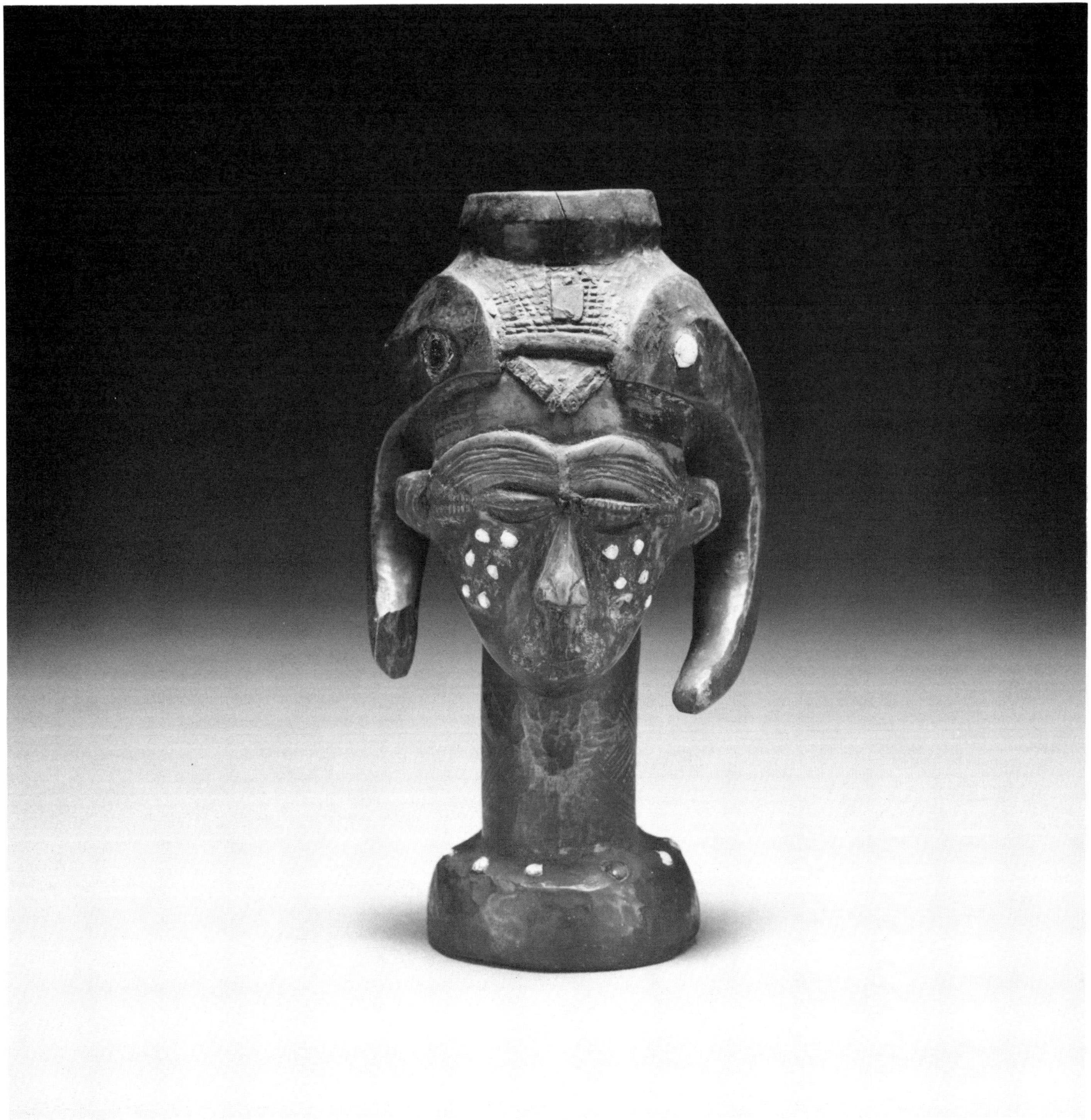

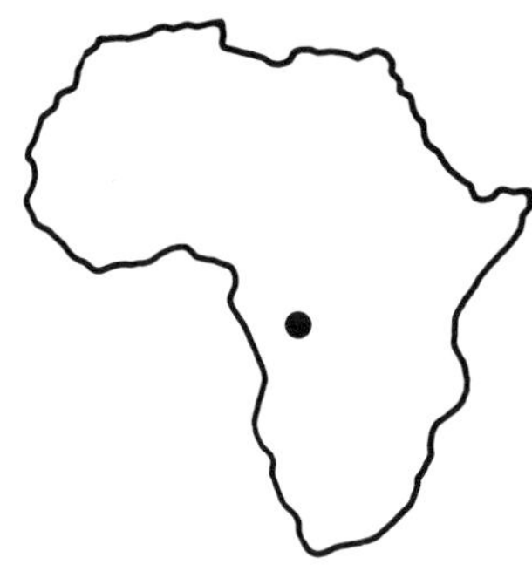

Wine Cup (E5,917)

Kuba, Zaire

Wood, shell

H. 24 cm.

This very old and beautifully patinated Kuba palm wine cup is of a type restricted to royal use. *Gift of Mrs. Charles G. Loring, 1904.*

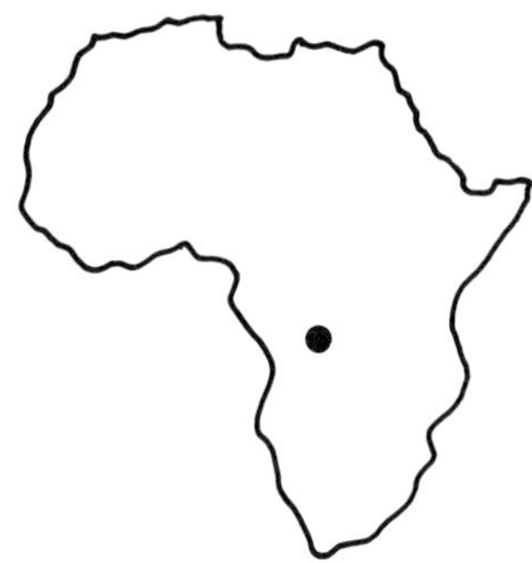

Pipe (E2,331)

Kuba, Zaire

Wood, bone

L. 59 cm. *Detail*

This fine old pipe, in typical Kuba style, has a bowl in the form of a human head. *Gift of Mr. William C. Endicott, 1892. Collected by E.J. Glave, ca. 1883-1889.*

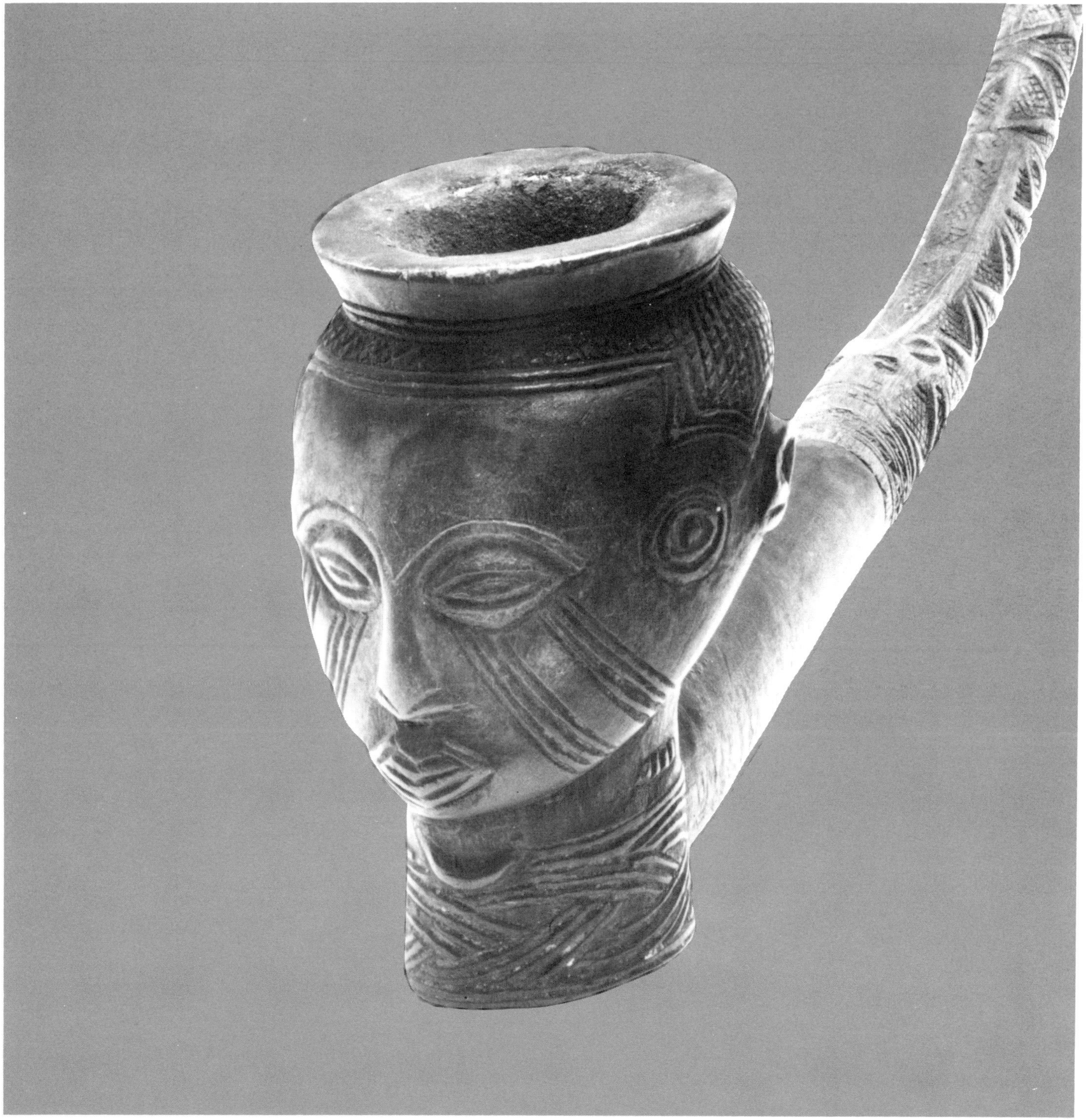

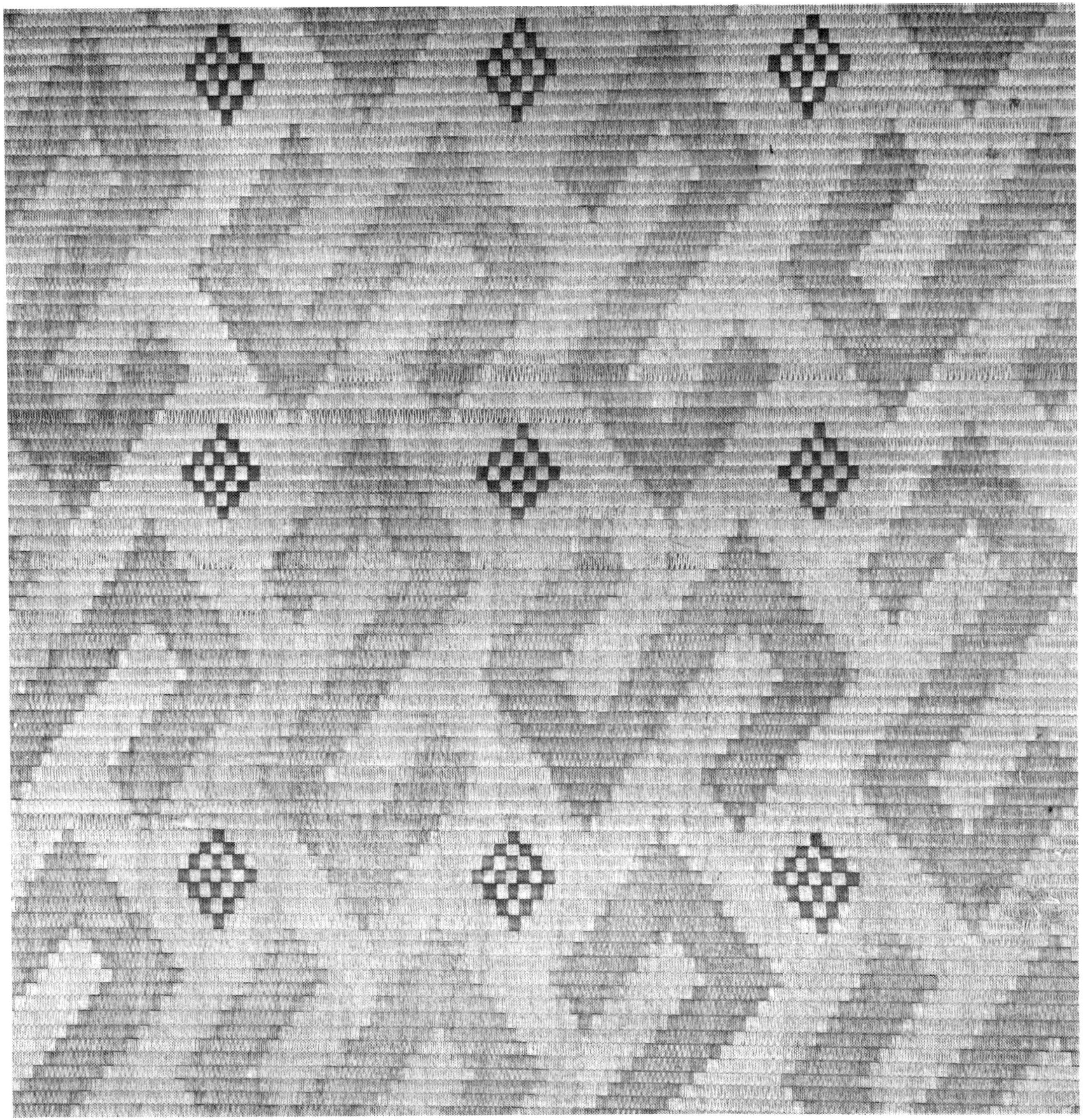

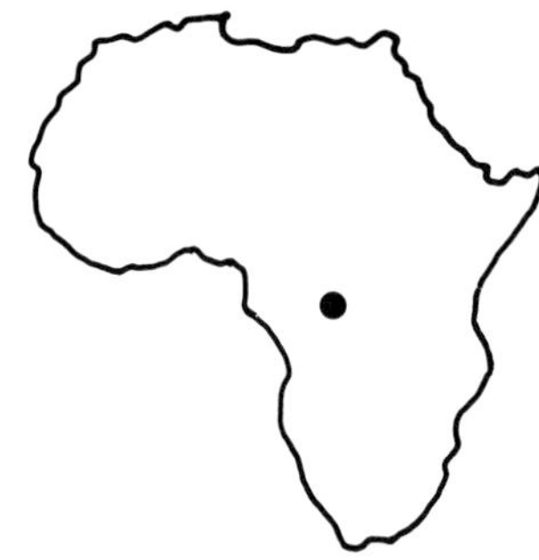

Mat (E27,652)

Probably Kuba, Zaire

Split cane, vegetable fiber, dye

L. 295 cm. *Detail*

A sleeping mat for an elite Kuba household. *Gift of Rev. Thomas Adams, 1948. Collected ca. 1891-1897.*

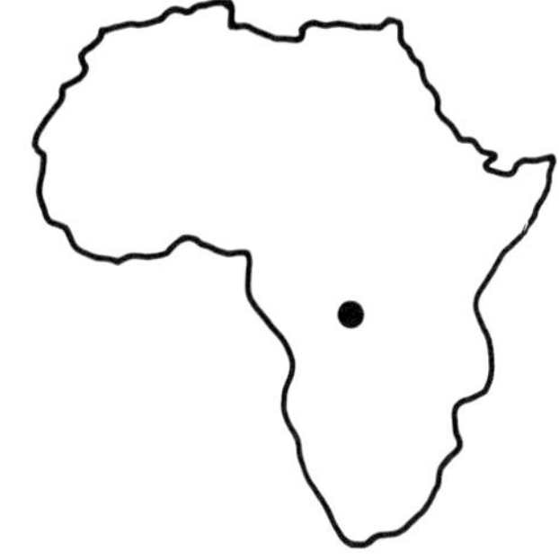

Textile (E16,911)

Kuba, Zaire

Raffia, dye

L. 56 cm. *Detail*

Textile (E16,912)

Kuba, Zaire

Raffia

L. 53 cm. *Detail*

Sometimes referred to as "Kassai velvet", these decorated raffia textiles have a plush pile surface achieved by introducing tiny bundles of fiber into the stitching of a plain-weave cloth and snipping the ends to a uniform length. Kuba women decorate the cloth, which is woven by men. Elaborate textiles were reserved for royal use. *E16,911 & E16,912, gift of Miss Caroline M. Grover, 1917*

65

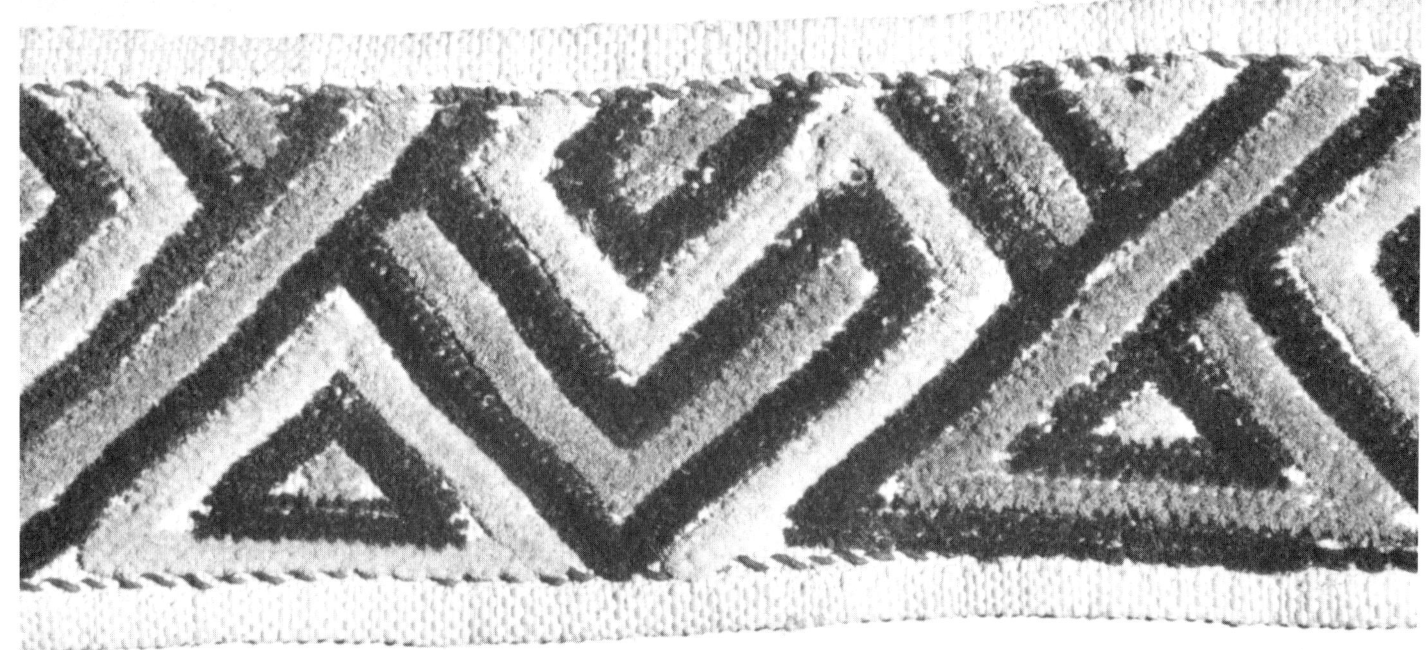

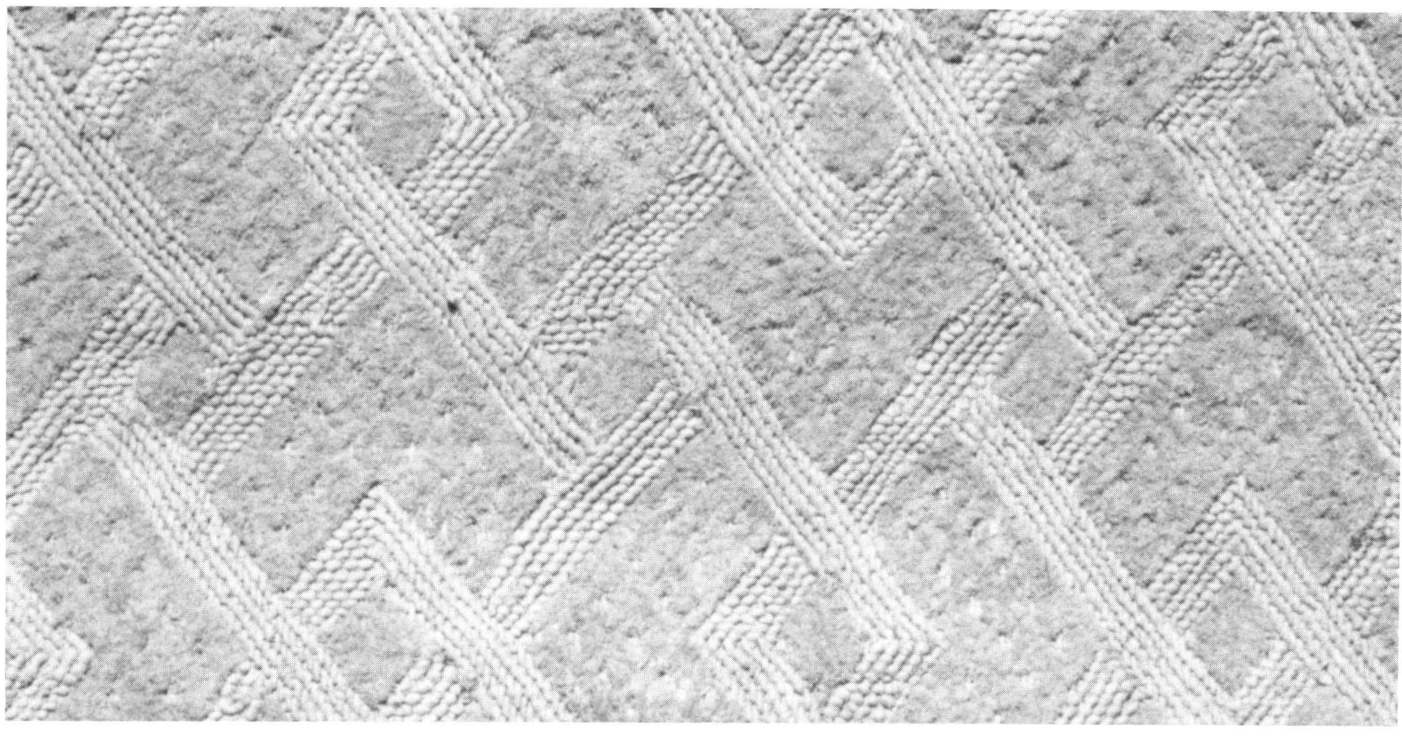

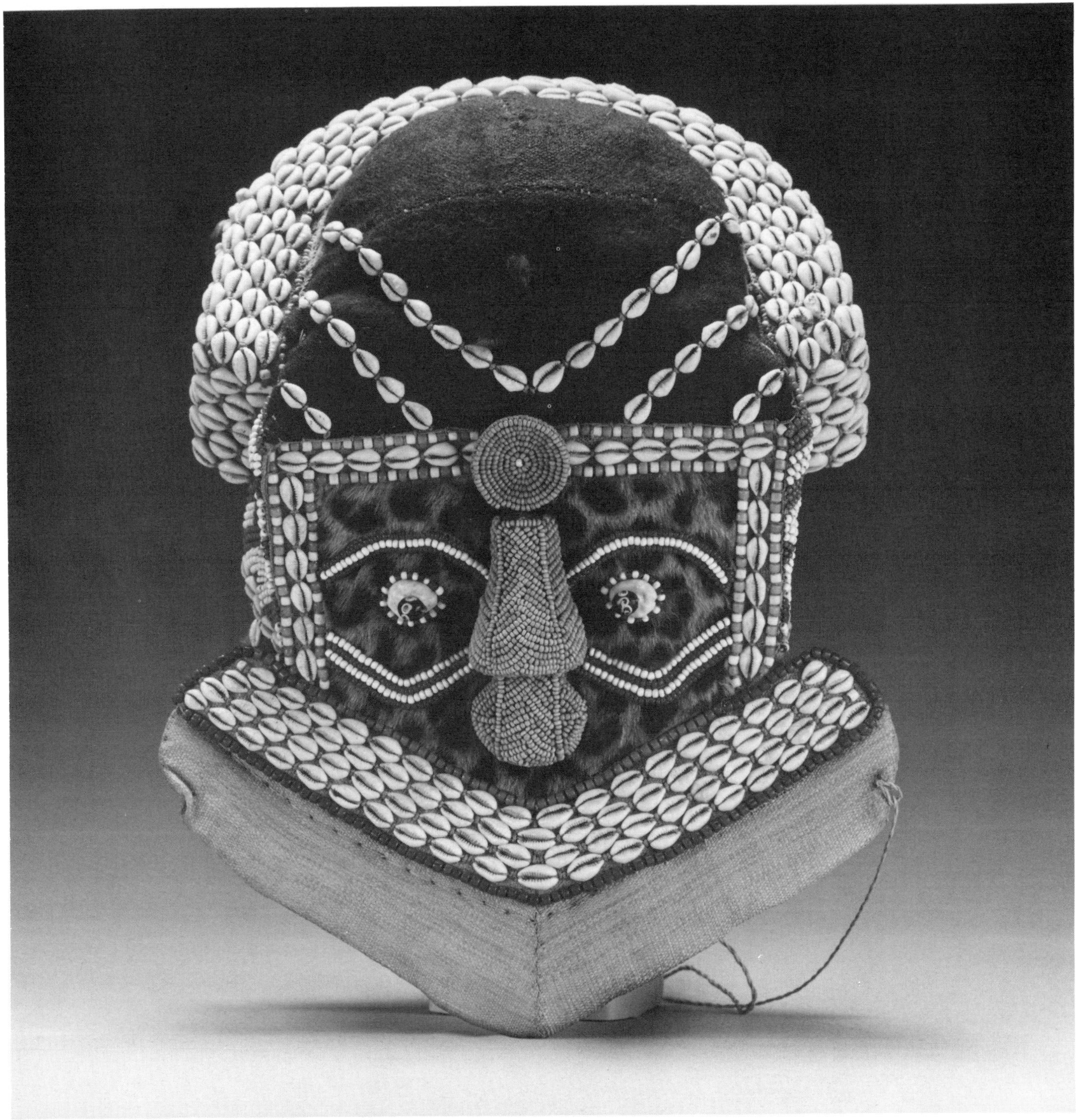

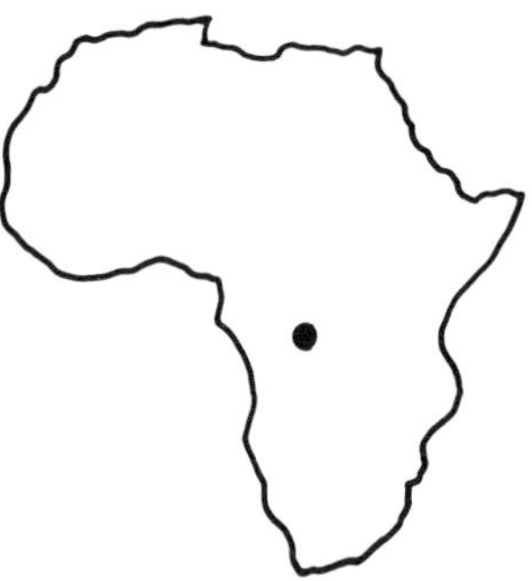

Mask (E14,376)

Kuba, Zaire

Cloth, woven raffia, leopard fur, glass beads, cowries

H. 48 cm.

In addition to a rich tradition of wood carving and textile manufacture, the Kuba produce a composite mask called *mashamboy*, of which this is a particularly fine example. The mask represents the primordial ancestor *Woot*, and is used in initiation ceremonies. *Gift of Dr. Charles G. Weld, 1910.*

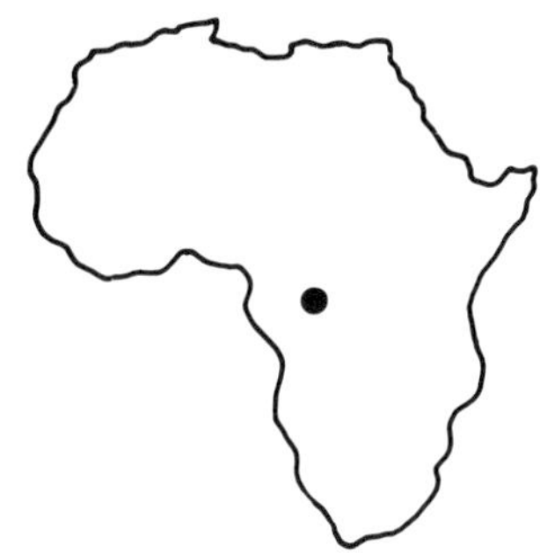

Shield (E2,313)

Group uncertain, Zaire

Wood, vegetable fiber, raffia

H. 143 cm.

Originating in an undetermined tribe of the upper Congo River, this shield is a masterpiece of symmetry and basketwork. Since the construction is not substantial enough to have been an effective barrier to spears or arrows, the shield was probably used as a parrier. *Gift of Mr. William C. Endicott, 1892. Collected by E.J. Glave, ca. 1883-1889.*

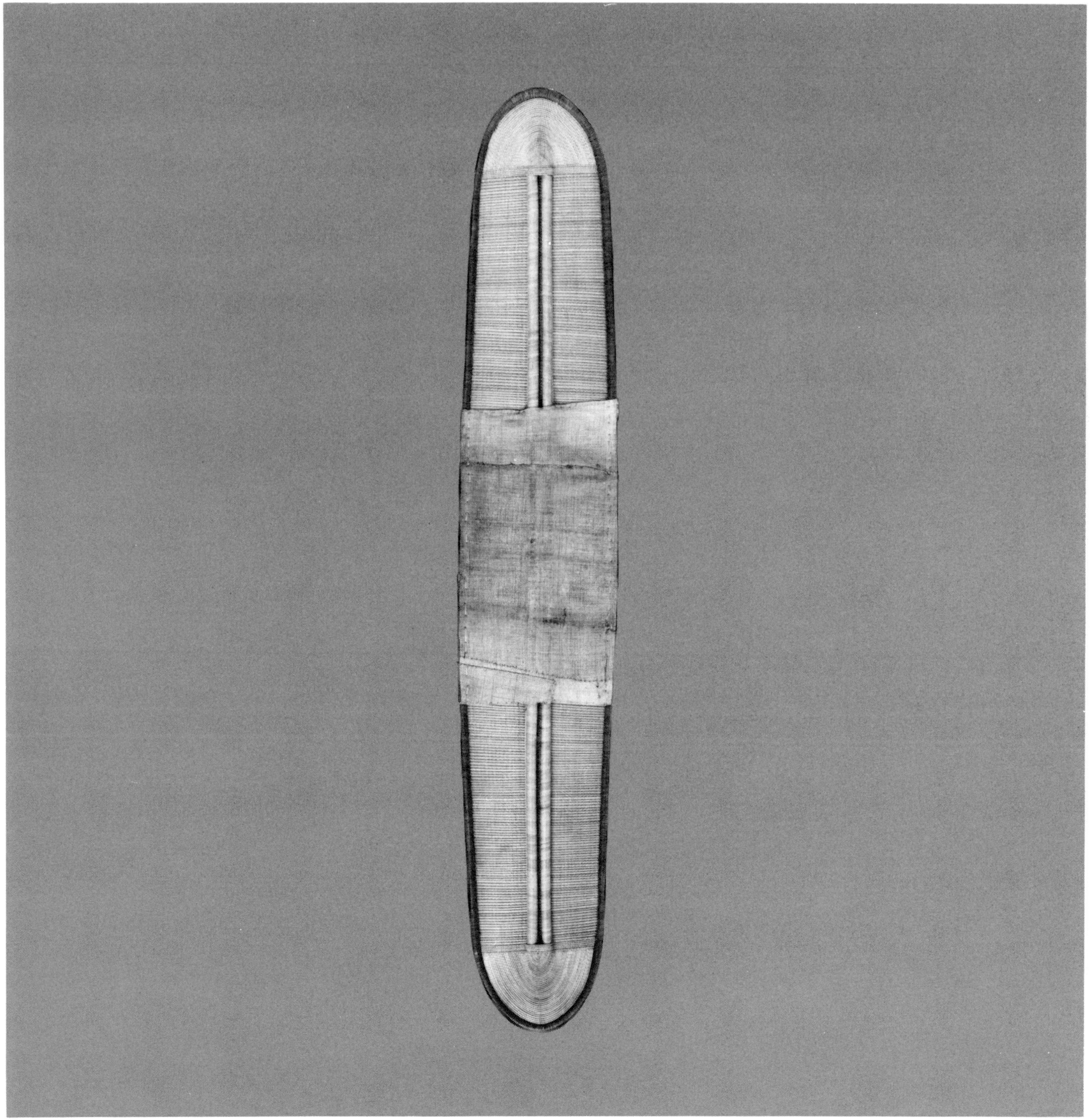

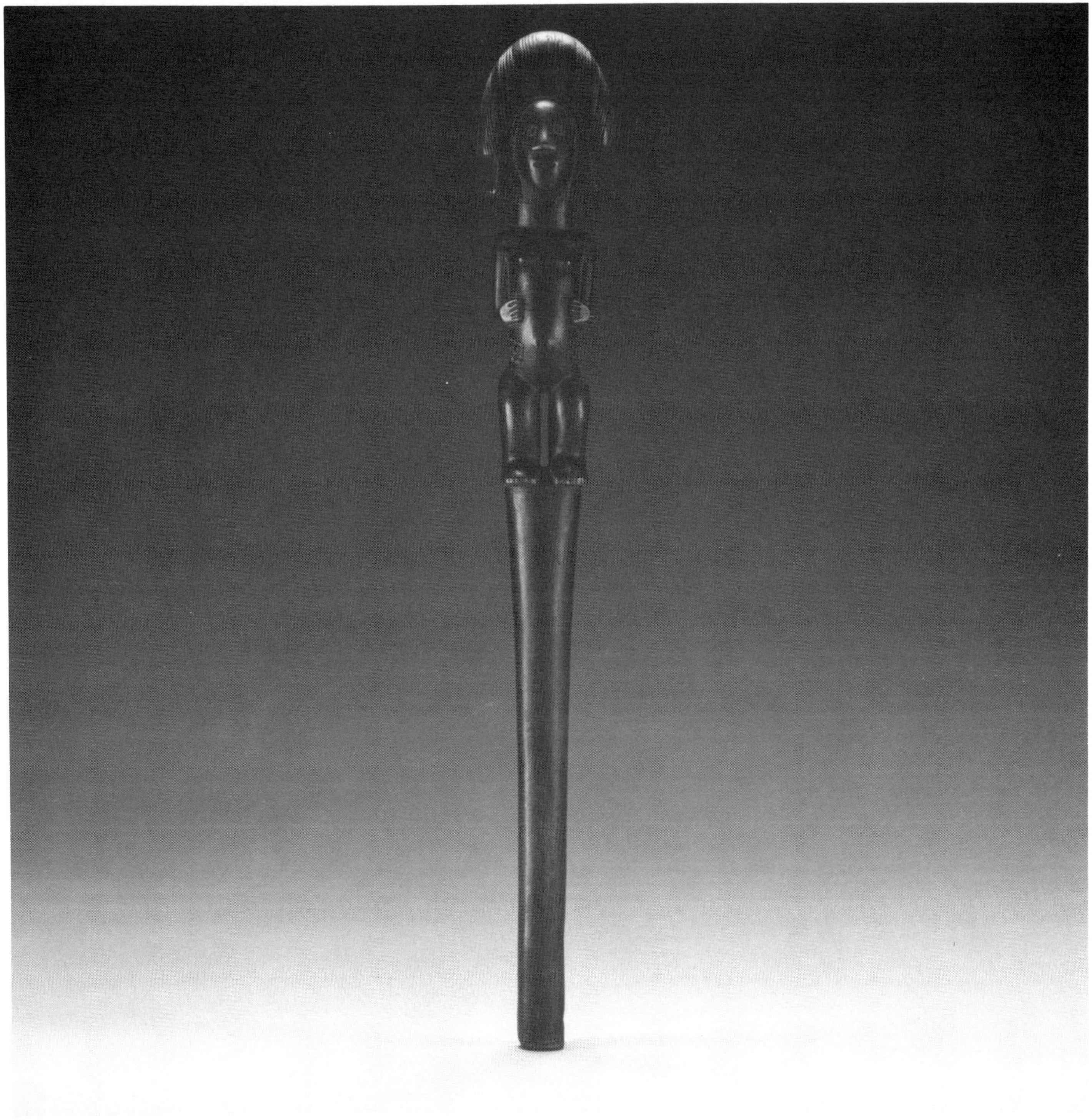

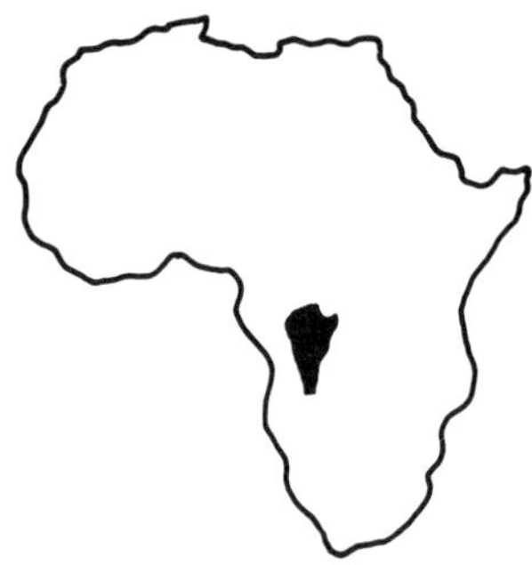

Staff (E6,737)

Probably Chokwe, Angola-
Zaire-Zambia

Wood

H. 43 cm.

The Chokwe originally existed as a vassal state of the Lunda empire until the demise of the latter in the late 19th century. There followed a period of Chokwe expansionism; their territory assuming its present boundaries in northeastern Angola, southern Zaire and portions of Zambia. Chokwe artists flourished under the patronage of the ruling aristocracy producing a wide variety of royal accessories, sculpture, masks, and elaborately decorated functional objects. This staff is probably a symbol of office. *Gift of Mrs. A.E. Govea, 1894.*

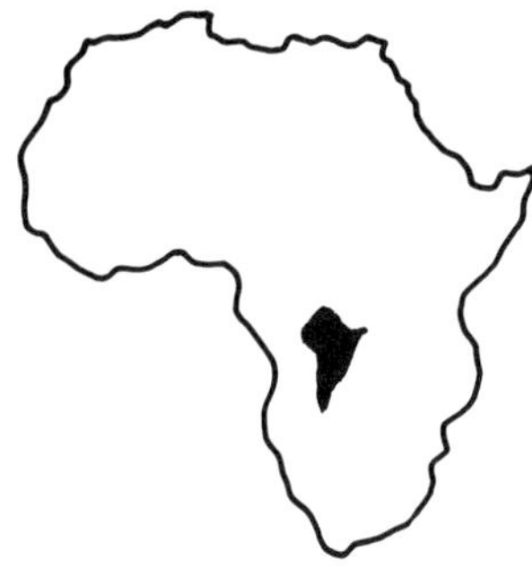

Chair (E29,207)

Chokwe, Angola-Zaire-
Zambia

Wood, animal skin

H. 75 cm.

The form of this chair is derived
from European prototypes
brought to Angola during the
16th century by Portuguese of-
ficials. This is a comparatively
austere example compared with
others of Chokwe manufacture,
which are often elaborately carved
with figures. *Gift of Mr. Austin L.
Moore, 1951.*

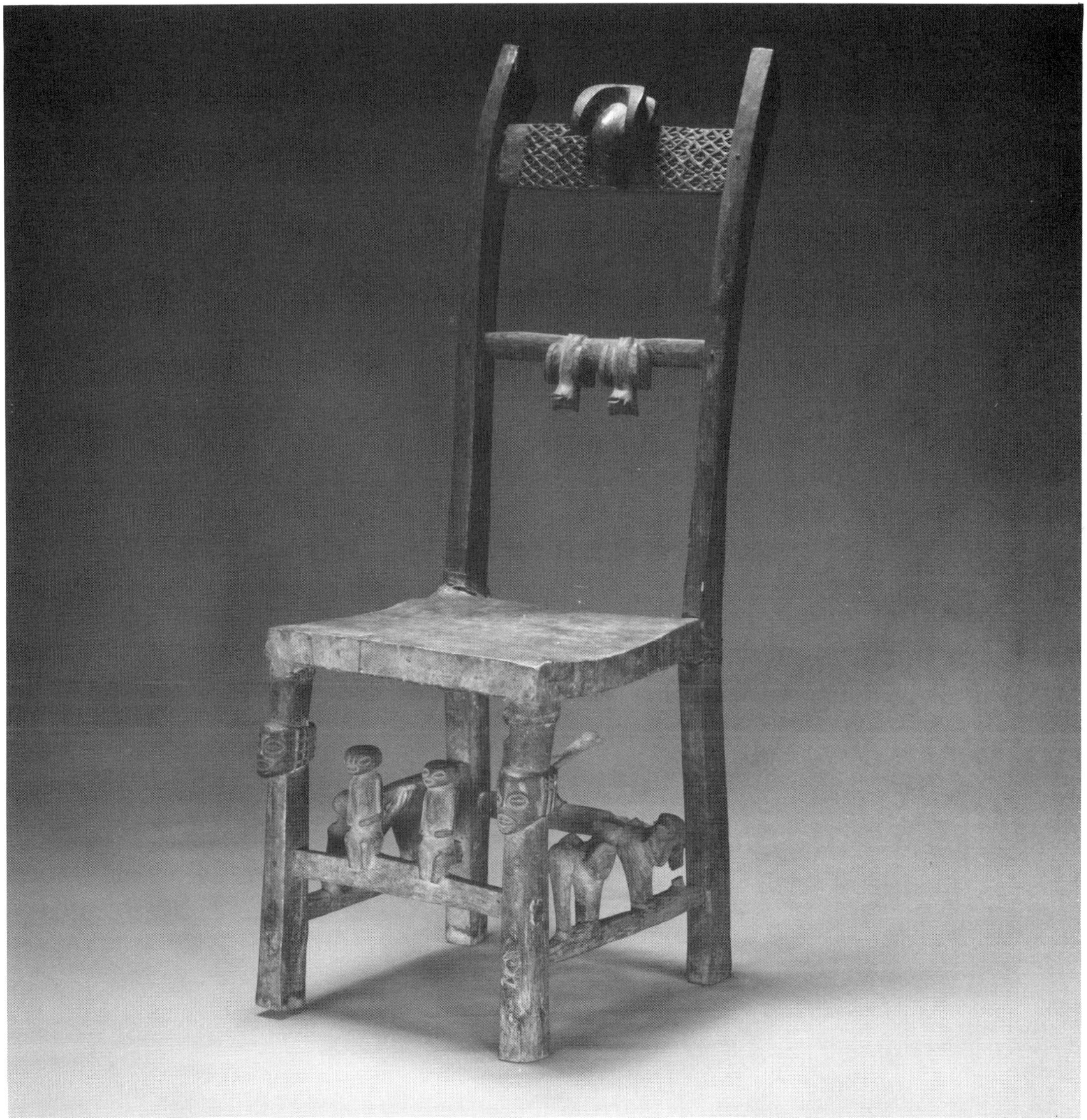

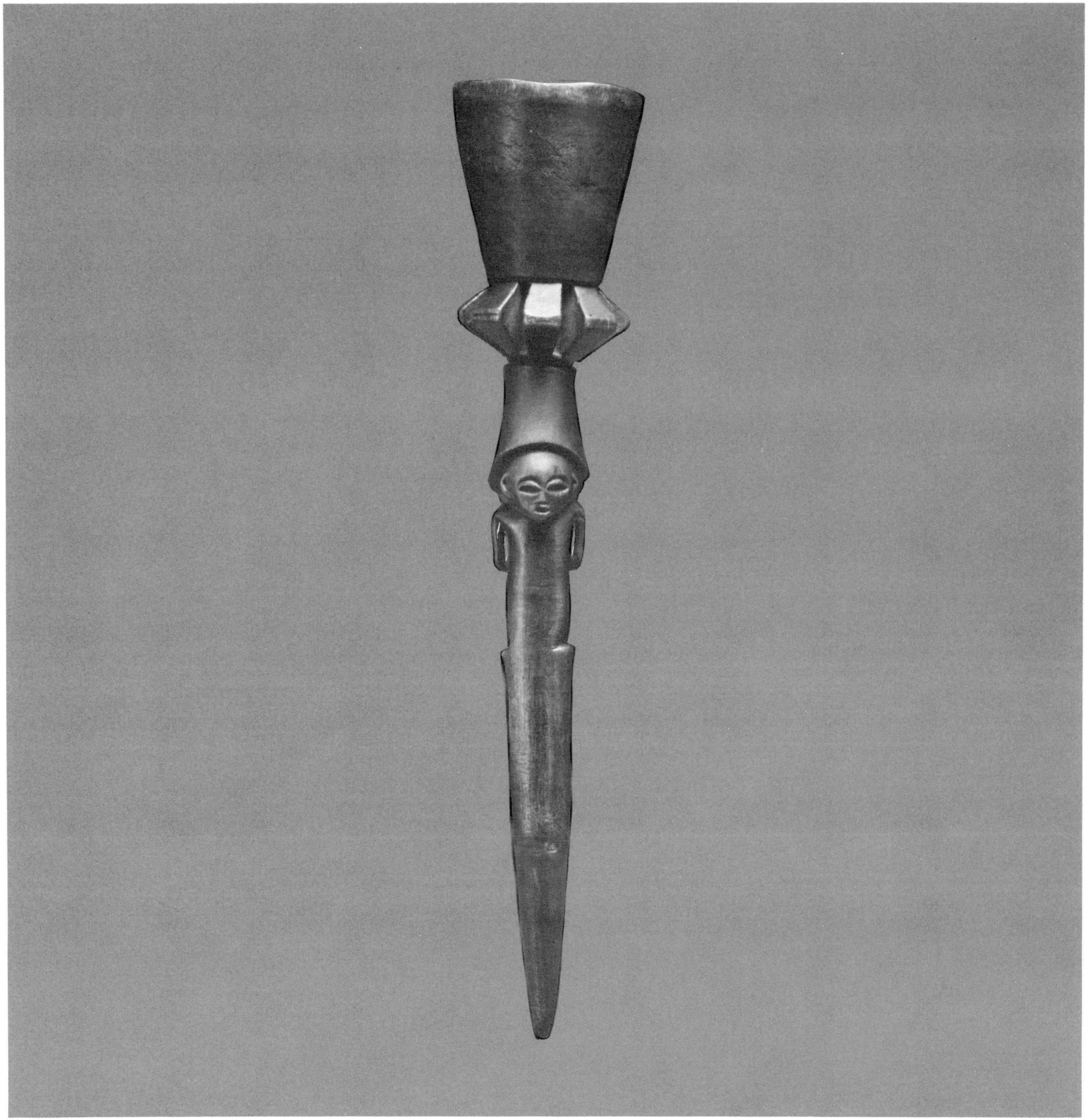

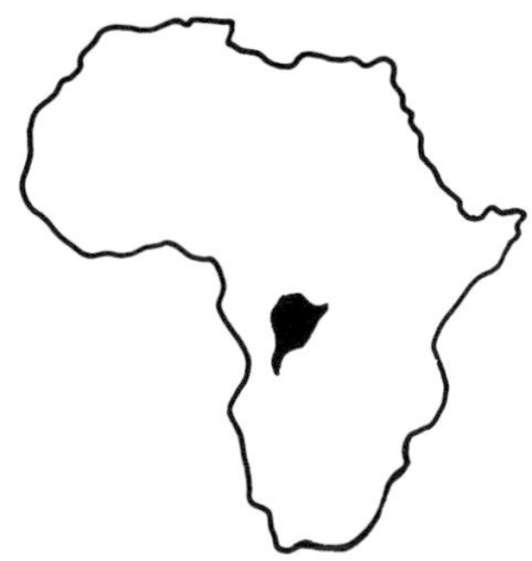

Mortar (E36,741)

Probably Chokwe, Angola-
Zaire-Zambia

Wood

H. 50 cm.

Small mortars such as this were used for grinding leaf tobacco into snuff. *Gift of Mr. Stephen Wheatland, 1959.*

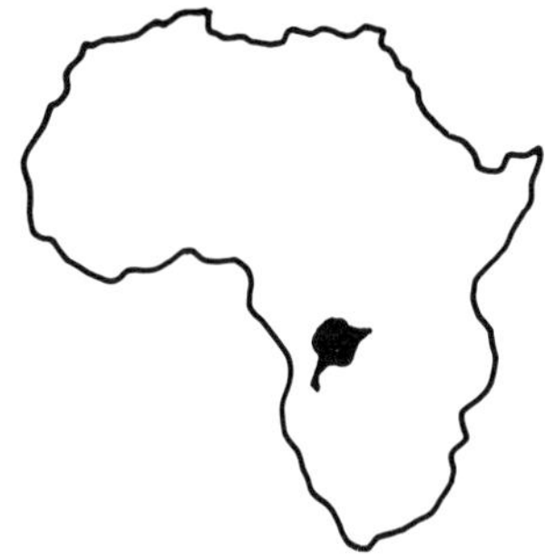

Comb (E34,143)

Chokwe, Angola-Zaire-
Zambia

Wood

L. 15 cm.

A delicately carved ornamental
comb surmounted with a female
figure. *Gift of Mr. Oscar Meyer,
1957.*

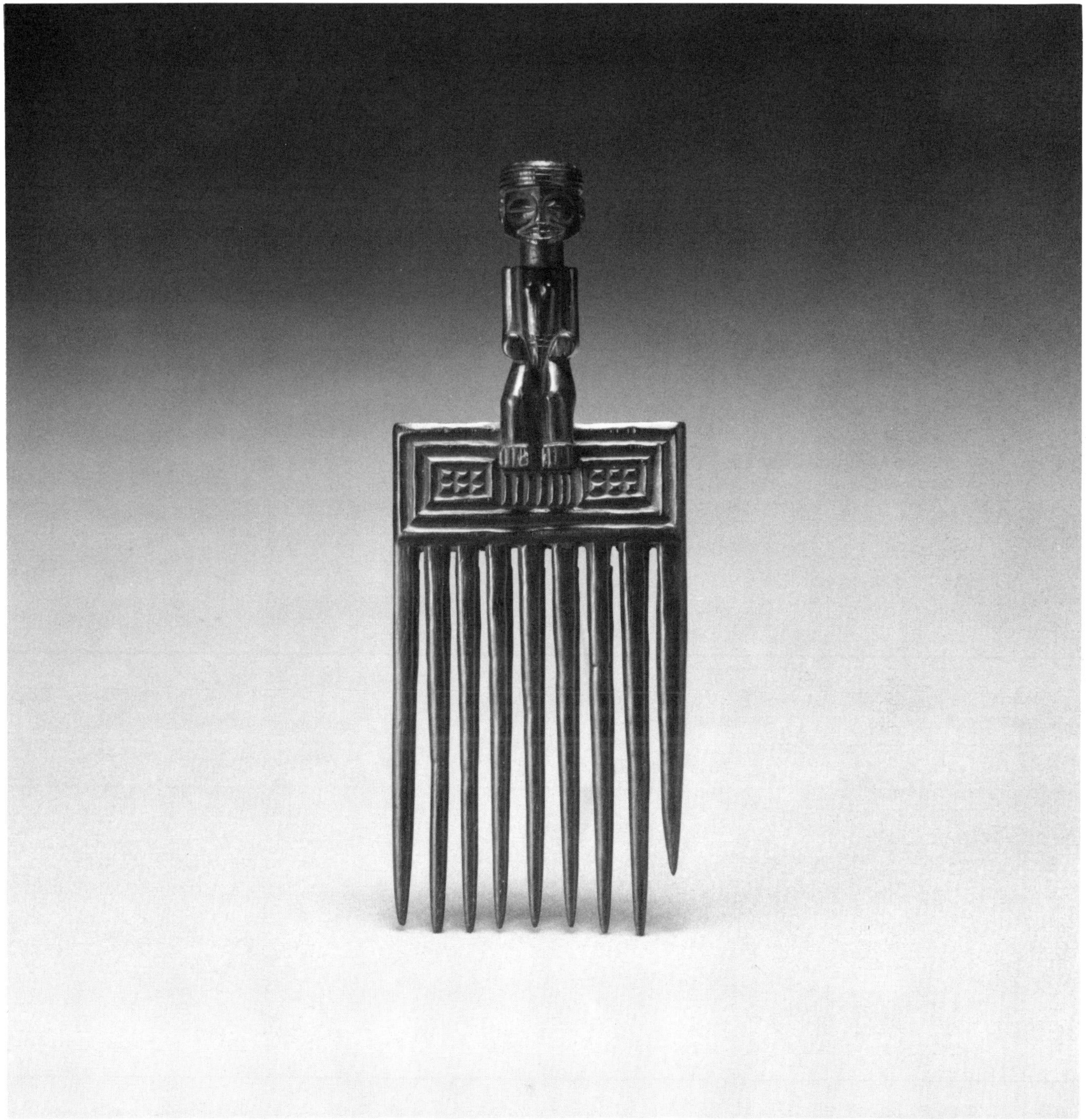

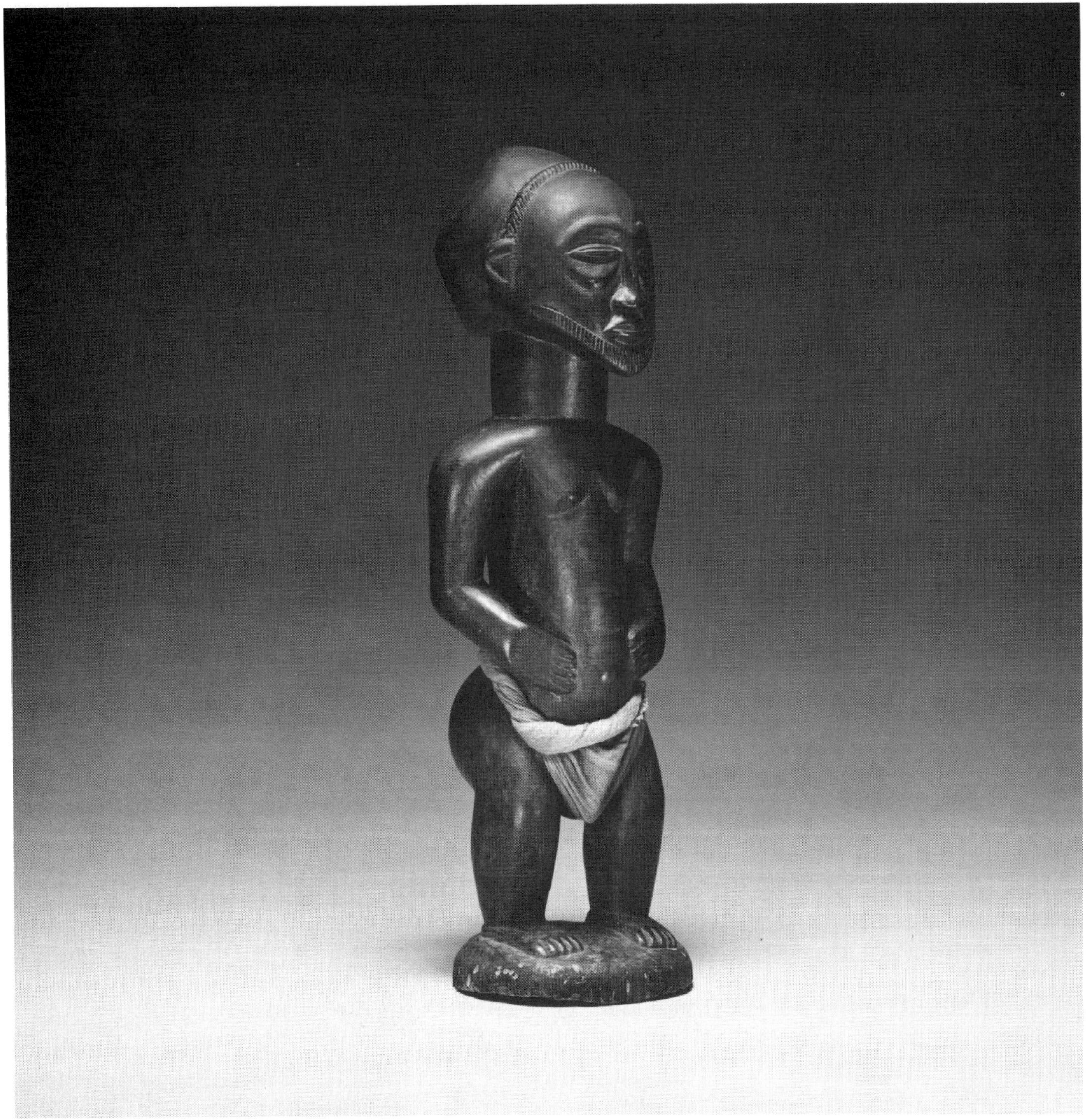

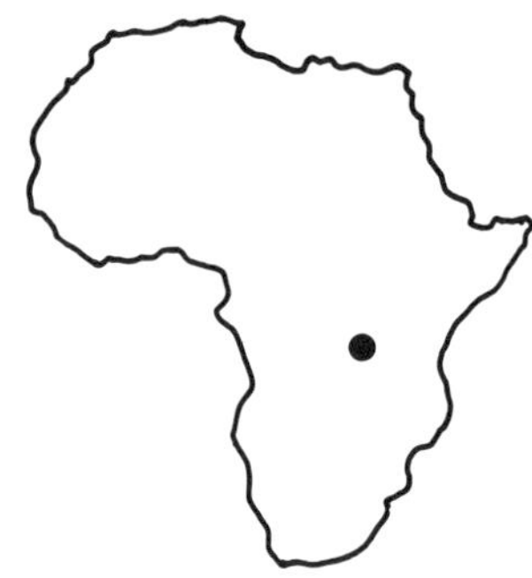

Figure (E72,092)

Buye, Zaire

Wood, cloth

H. 52 cm.

The art of the Buye, better known as the Luba-Hemba, is characterized by extensive use of spheres and circles. This tendency is evident in the rounded body contours of this male ancestor figure. *Anonymous gift, 1981.*

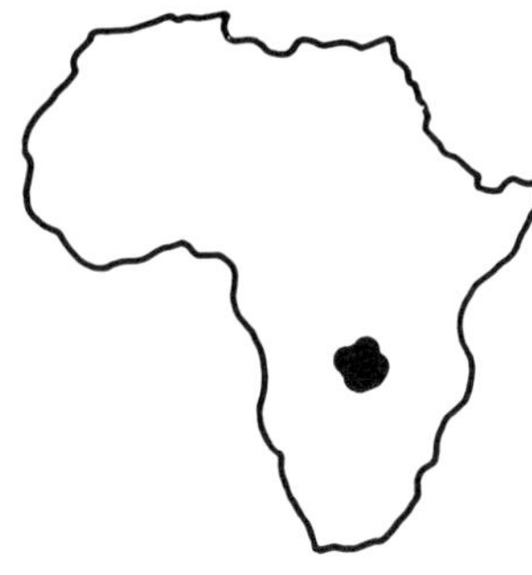

Sword and Scabbard
(E21,994)

Luba, Zaire

Iron, wood, leather

L. (sword) 50 cm.

A Luba sword with an unusually ornate scabbard. *Gift of the heirs of George C. Stone, 1936.*

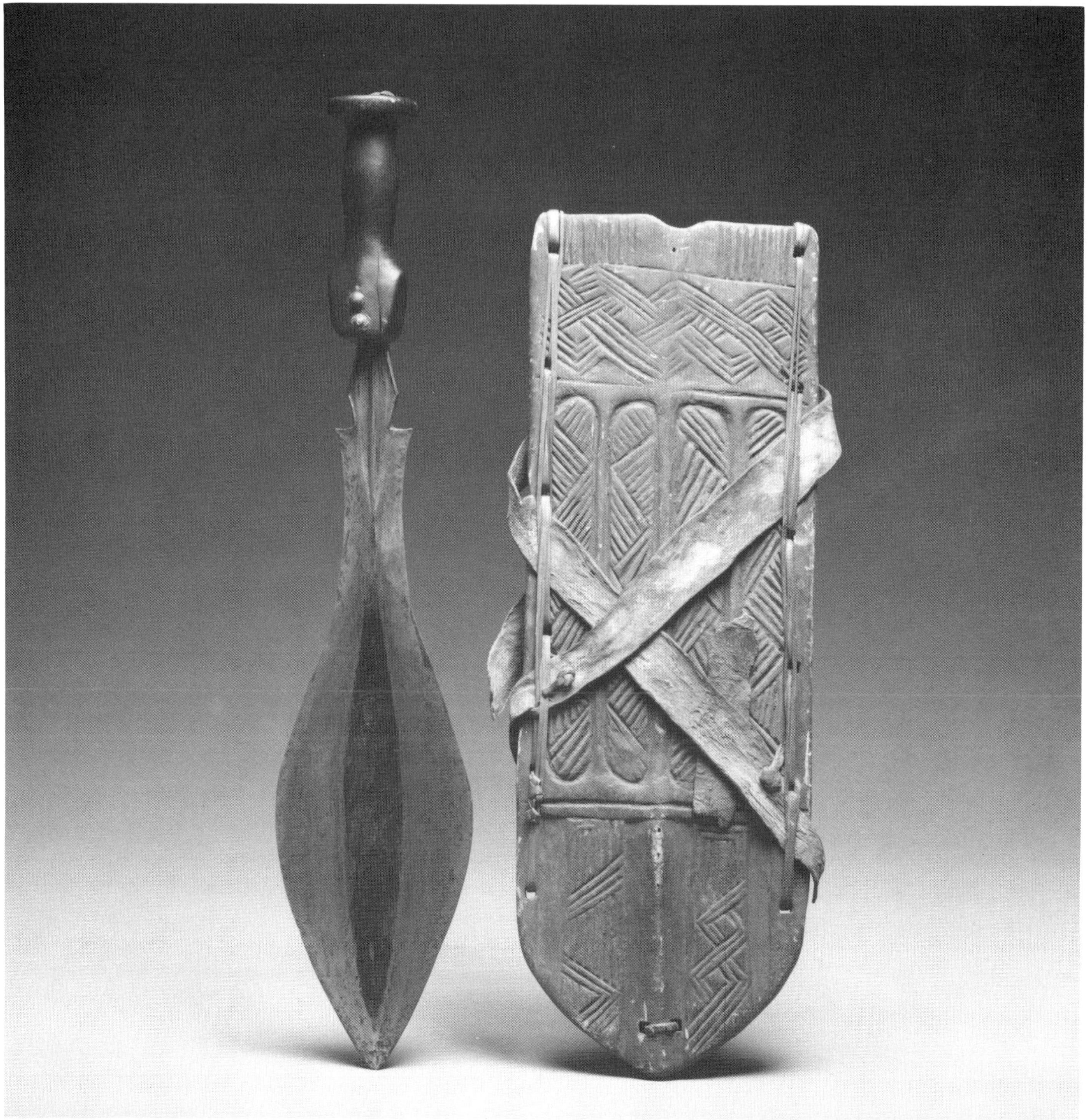

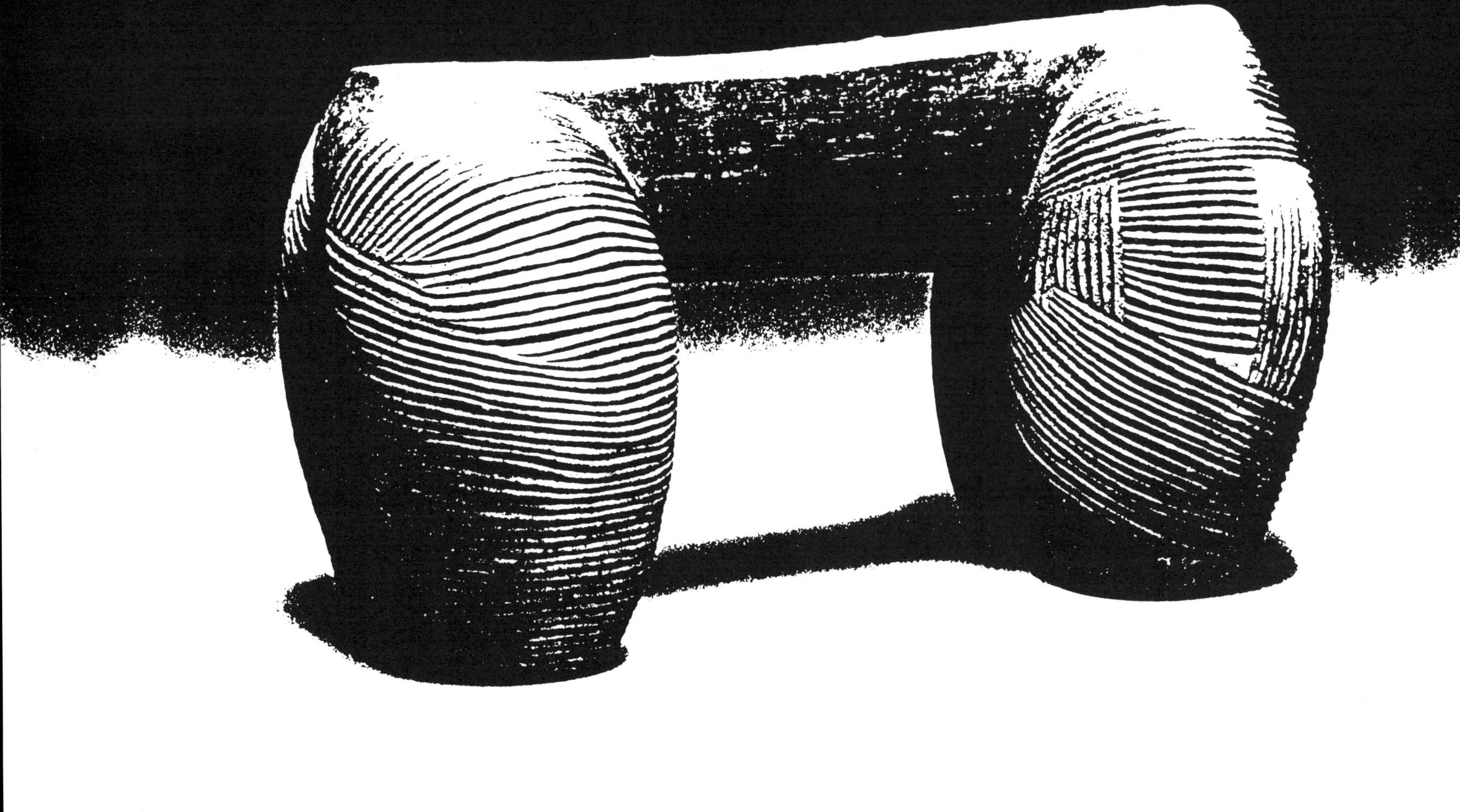

The Lakes Region and Southern Africa

East and South of the Congo basin, a vast interior plateau rises from the coastal lowlands to an altitude of 3,000 - 6,000 feet. The eastern region is marked by mountains and rift valleys which form catchments for a chain of large lakes, including Lakes Victoria, Tanganyika, and Malawi. Except for a strip of rain forest along the Indian Ocean coast and desert and semi-desert in the southwest, the region is covered with savanna and temperate grasslands that support large herds of grazing animals.

Bantu peoples predominate in this region, having displaced the indigenous Bushmen during the centuries before European contact. Agriculture is universal among the Bantu and most groups also raise cattle for milk and meat. Bushmen survive in the marginal environments in and near the Kalahari Desert, where they pursue their traditional livelihood of hunting and gathering.

Islamic dominance in virtually all of northern Africa, except Ethiopia, extended down the east African coast to encompass indigenous peoples, collectively called Swahili (coast people, in Arabic). The strictures of Islam, along with the ancient coastal intermixture of peoples and cultures, may account in part for the rarity of figural sculpture and the extensive geometric decoration applied to utilitarian objects. In addition, herding peoples of interior grasslands and veld, often lacking permanent abodes, confined their belongings and artistic talents to portable functional objects. The stone ruins of Great Zimbabwe and other Monomotapa sites are evidence of a centuries-old native trading network that once stretched far inland. The Sotho, Shona, Zulu and other southern tribes have been subjected to the prolonged influence of European traders, missionaries, and colonists.

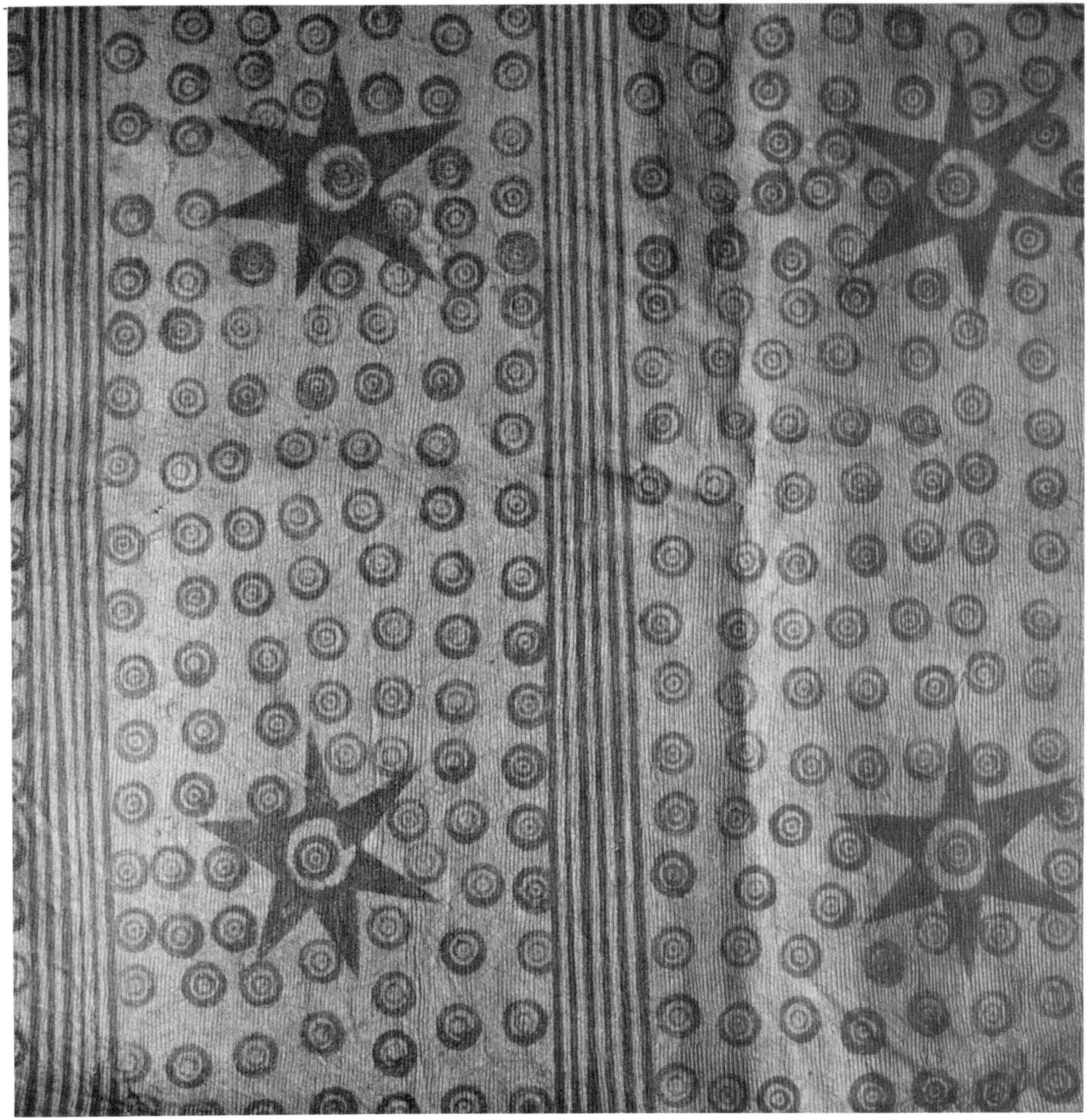

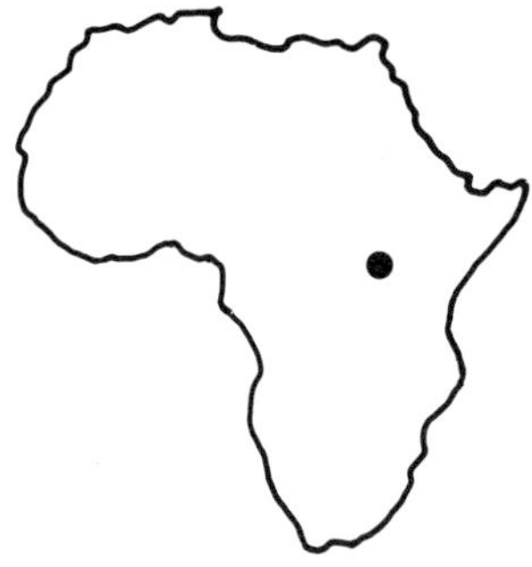

Bark Cloth (E23,804)

Probably Ganda, Uganda

Vegetable fiber, dye

L. 280 cm. *Detail*

Bark cloth is usually derived from the inner bark of the fig, *Ficus natalensis*, which is stripped from the tree, softened by soaking or steaming, and beaten on a log anvil using a specialized beater. The Ganda are noted for the production of a high-quality bark cloth, sometimes stenciled as in this example, which is used for clothing and mats. *Gift of the estate of Miss Mary Brooks, 1941.*

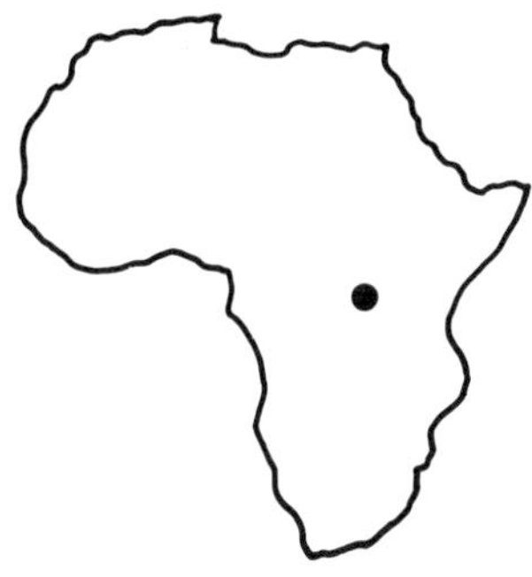

Drum (E13,024)

Ganda, Uganda

Wood, animal skin

H. 47 cm.

A typical Ganda drum; the twisted hide lacings both tune the drum and provide an interesting decorative effect. *Gift of Mr. William G. Sewall, 1910. Collected ca. 1908-1909.*

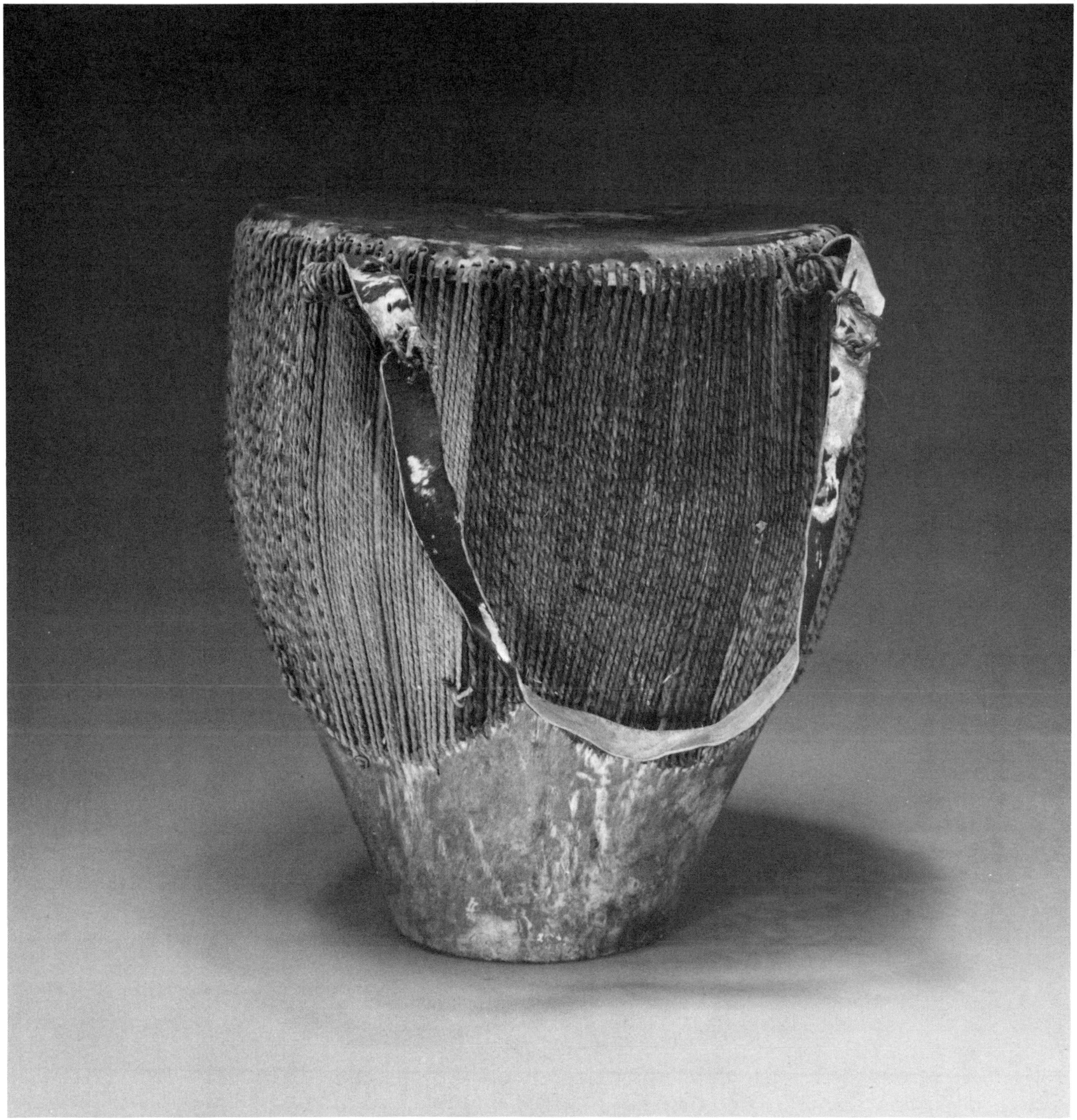

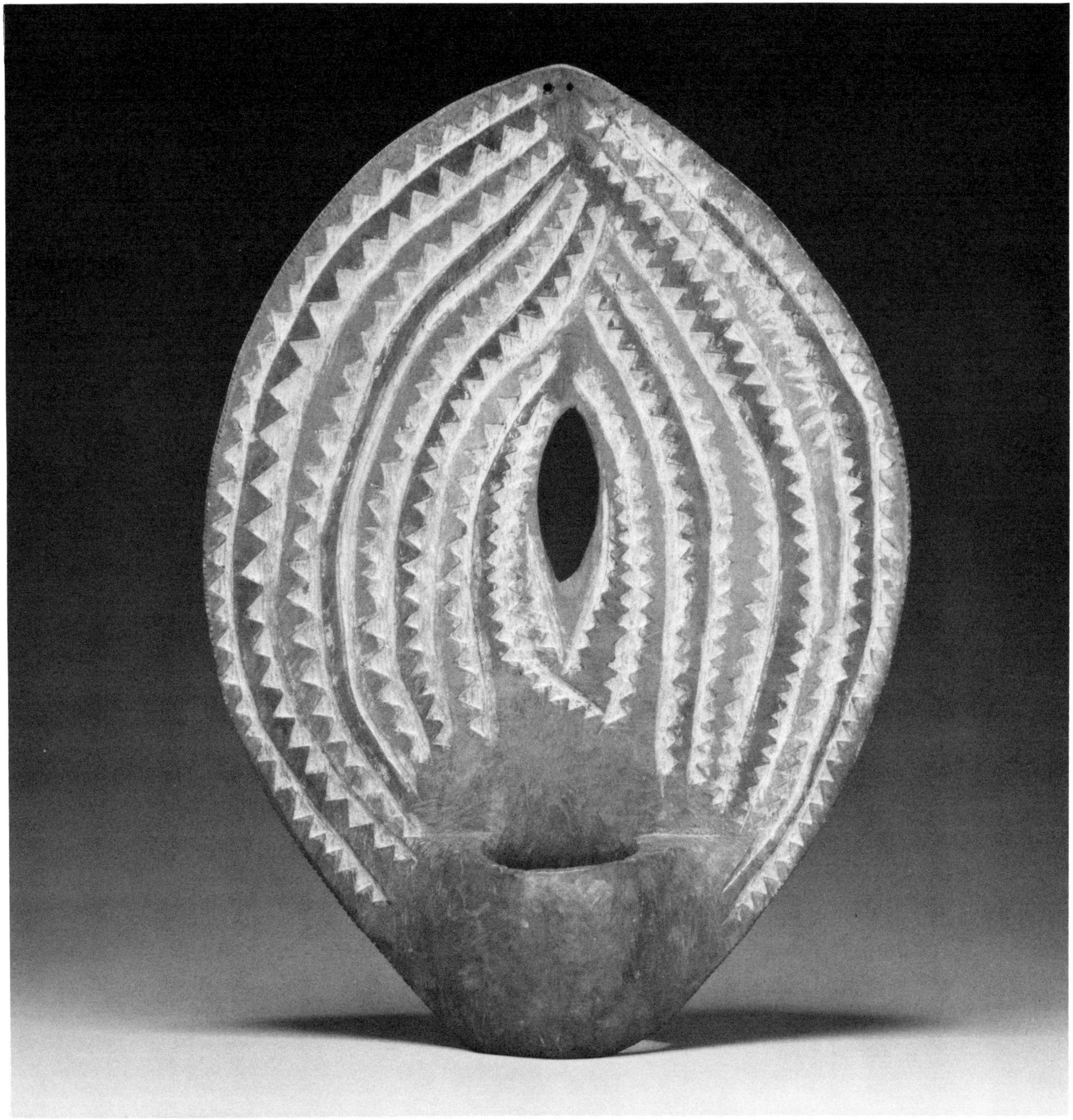

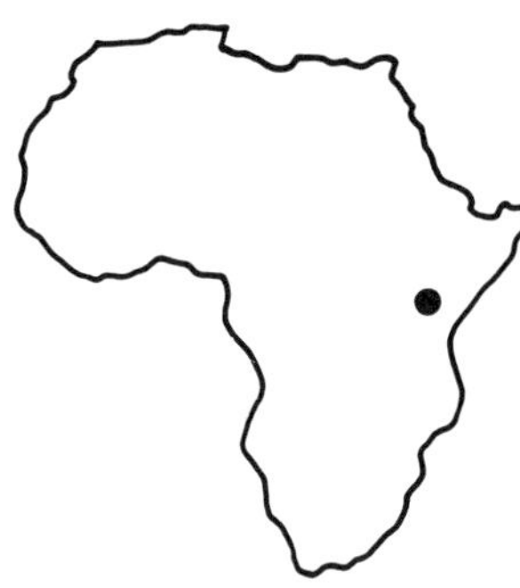

Dance Shield (E38,098)

Kikuyu, Kenya

Wood, pigment

H. 56 cm.

Shields such as this are used in ceremonies surrounding the achievement, by circumcision, of the first of three initiation levels by Kikuyu males. The designs on the front of the shield denote the initiate's age-grade and clan. *Donor unknown, prior to 1962.*

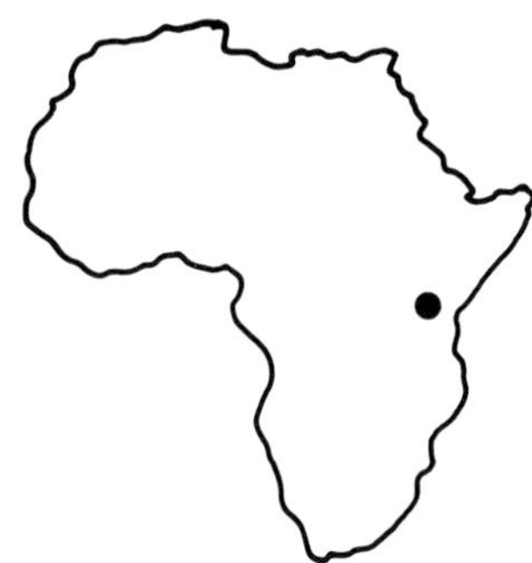

Container (E29,193)

Kamba, Kenya

Gourd

D. 15 cm.

The Kamba live south of the Kikuyu, with whom they are linguistically related. Their lifestyle, however, which includes a heavy reliance upon cattle for food, is more closely akin to the Masai, their neighbors to the west. In the nineteenth century, Kamba frequently accompanied Swahili traders to and from the coast. The western sailing vessel depicted on this gourd container may have been inspired on such a trip. *Gift of Albert Fowler, 1951.*

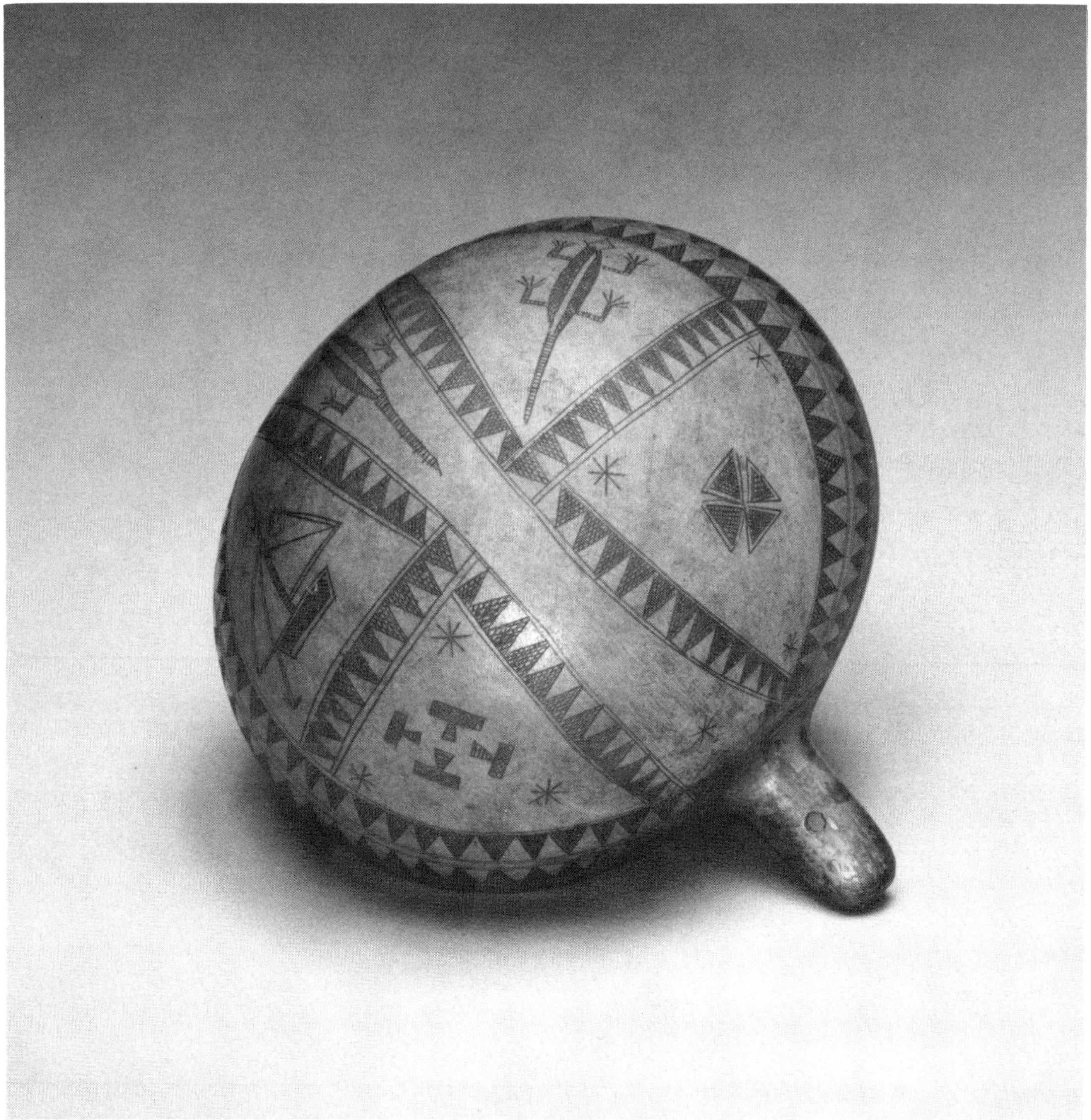

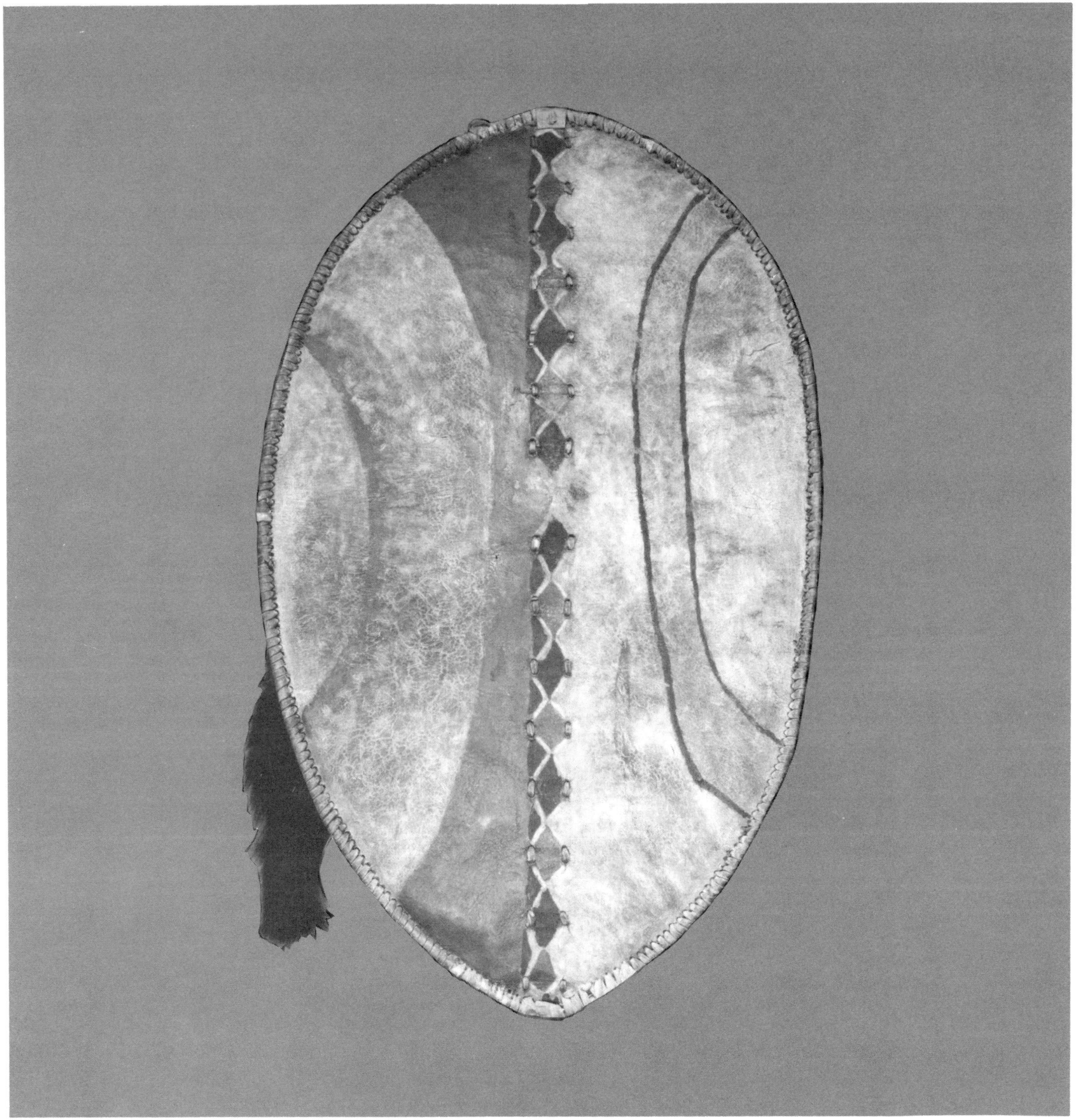

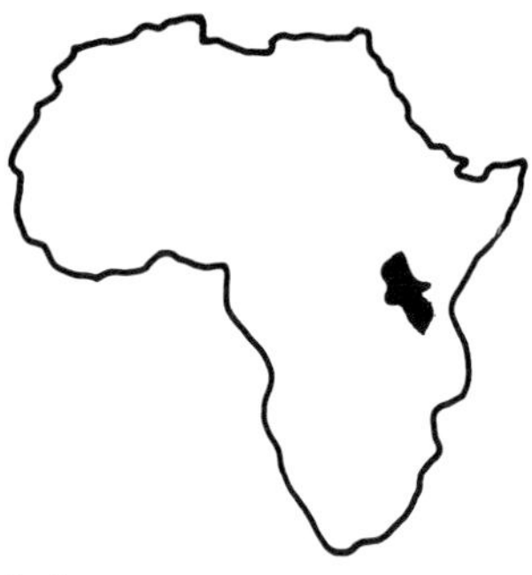

Shield (E13,017)

Masai, Kenya-Tanzania

Hide, wood, pigment

H. 104 cm.

The Masai of Kenya and Tanzania are nomadic pastoralists, deriving meat, milk and blood, the latter consumed fresh, from their cattle. The complex, painted designs on Masai warrior's shields represent the age-grade, and village of its owner. *Gift of Mr. William G. Sewall, 1910. Collected ca. 1908-1909.*

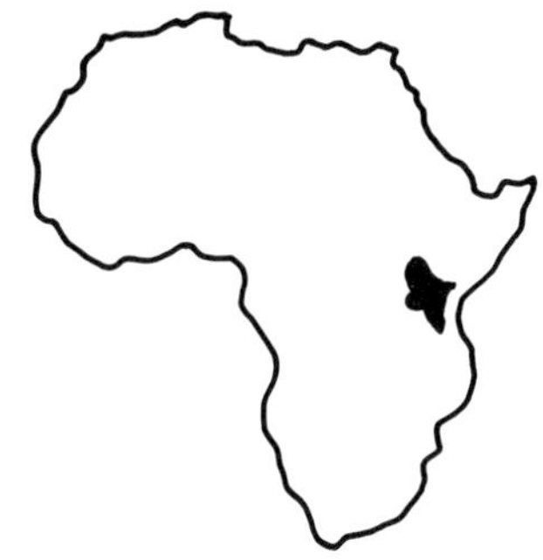

Collar (E18,978)

Masai, Kenya-Tanzania

Leather, glass beads, pigment

D. 24 cm.

A woman's collar of beaded
leather. *Museum purchase, 1923.*

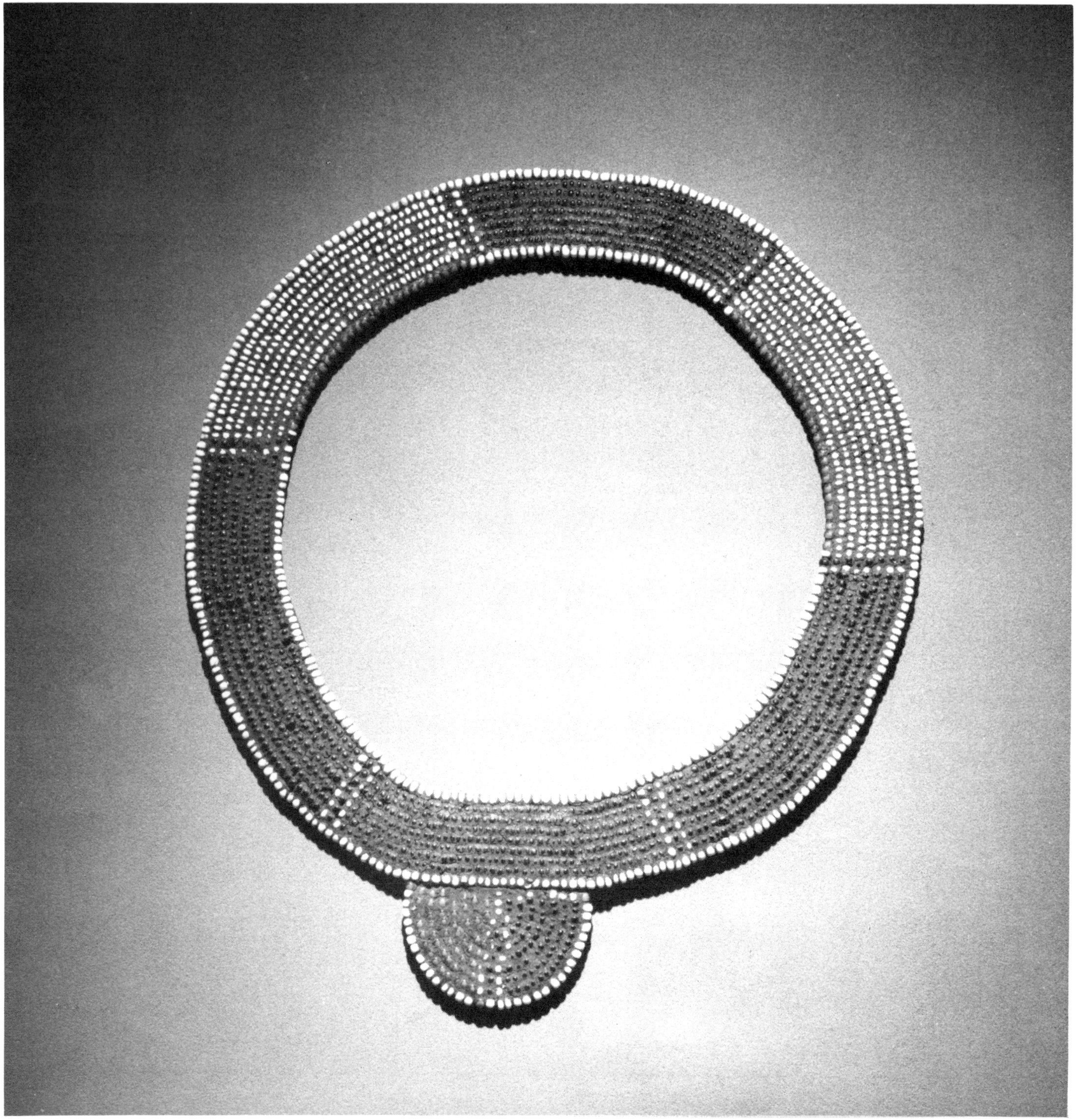

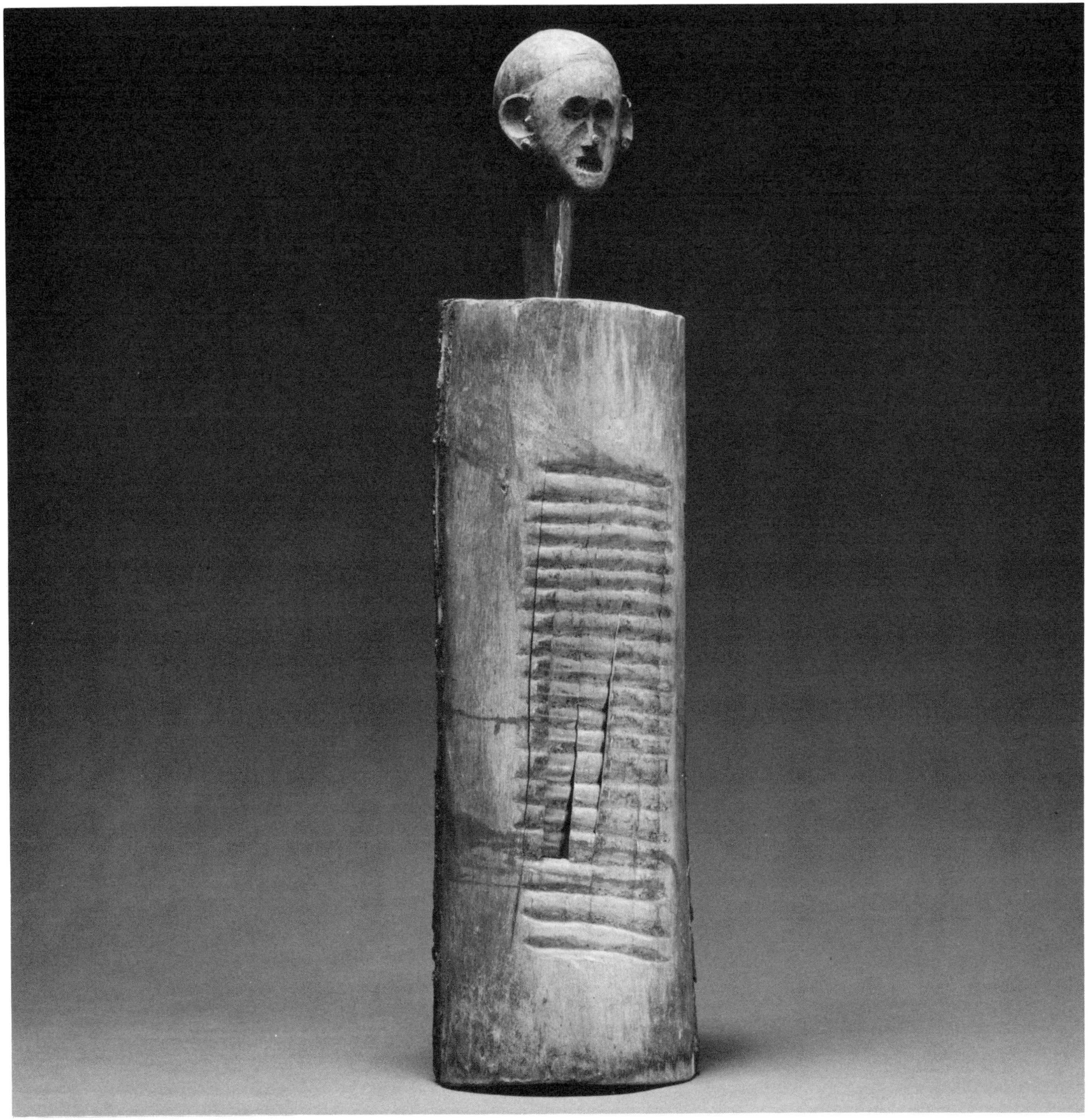

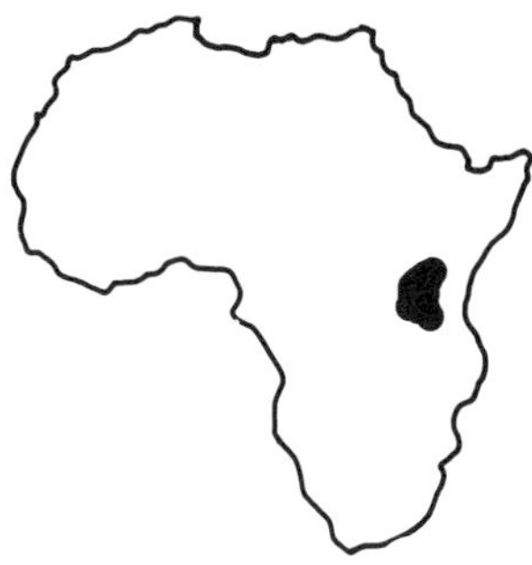

Idiophone (E6,749)

Possibly Sukuma or
Nyamwezi, Tanzania

Wood, metal, resin

H. 81 cm.

Little is known of this piece other
than it was collected at Zanzibar.
The original catalog entry says
that it came from the coastal interior of East Africa, and it is here
tentatively attributed to the
Sukuma or Nyamwezi of Tanzania on the basis of illustrations
of their carving. The instrument
was apparently played by pulling
a stick across the exterior cor-
rugations to produce a rasping
sound. *Gift of E. Emmerton,
1846.*

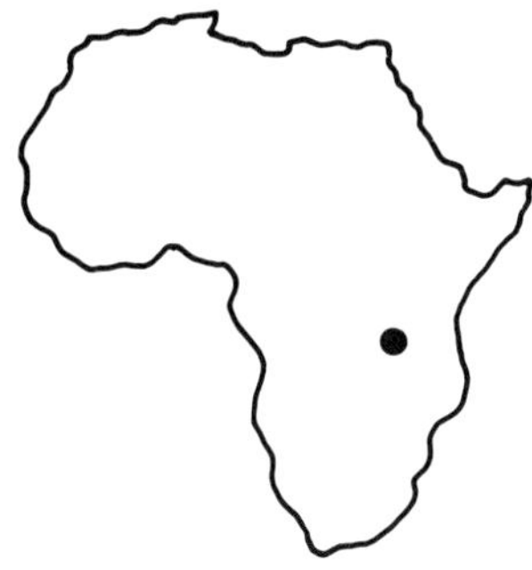

Headrest (E18,488)

Group uncertain,
Tanzania

Wood

H. 21 cm.

Reported to have been collected
on the eastern shore of Lake
Tanganyika. *Gift of Mrs. William
G. Farlow, 1922.*

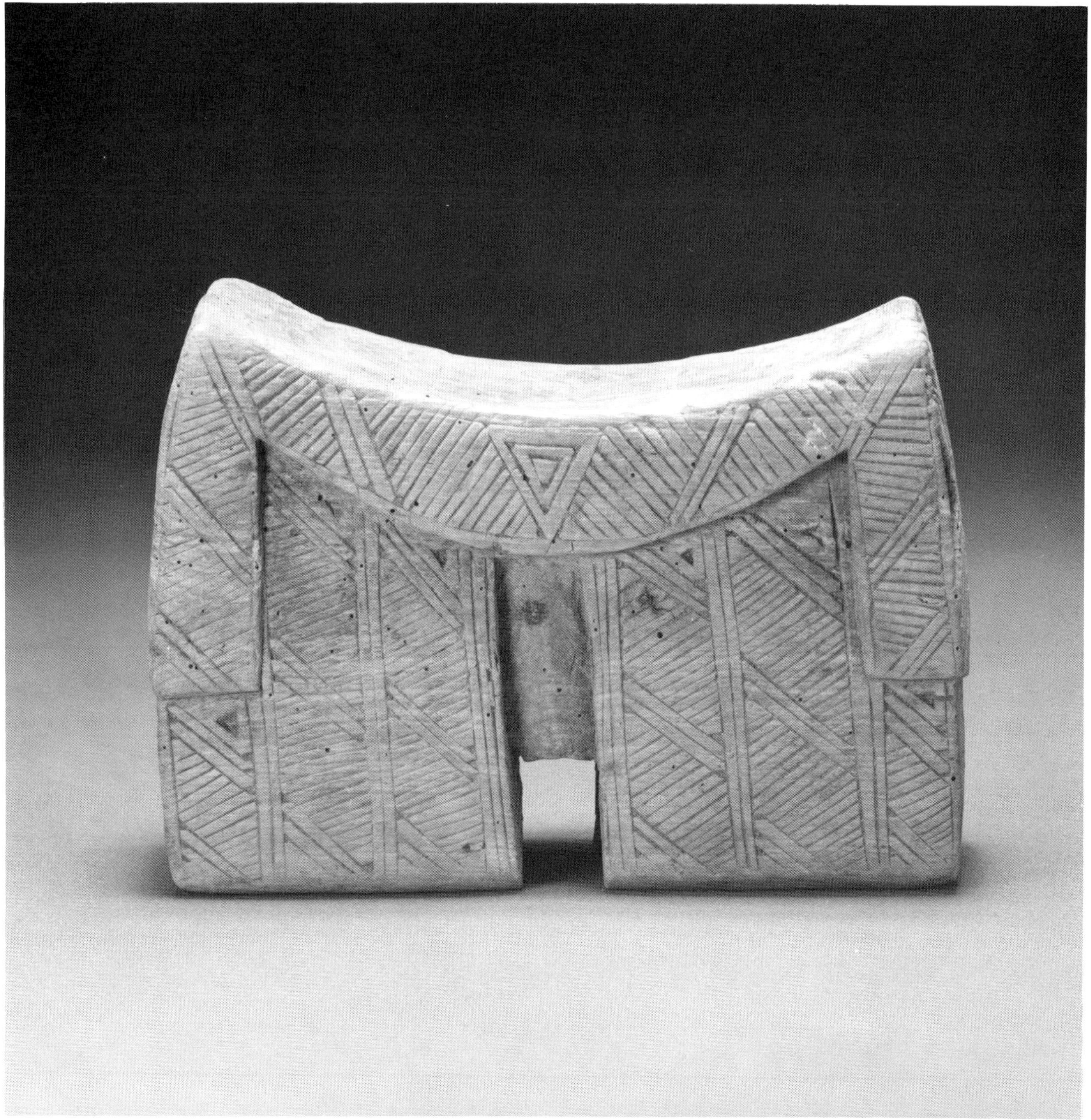

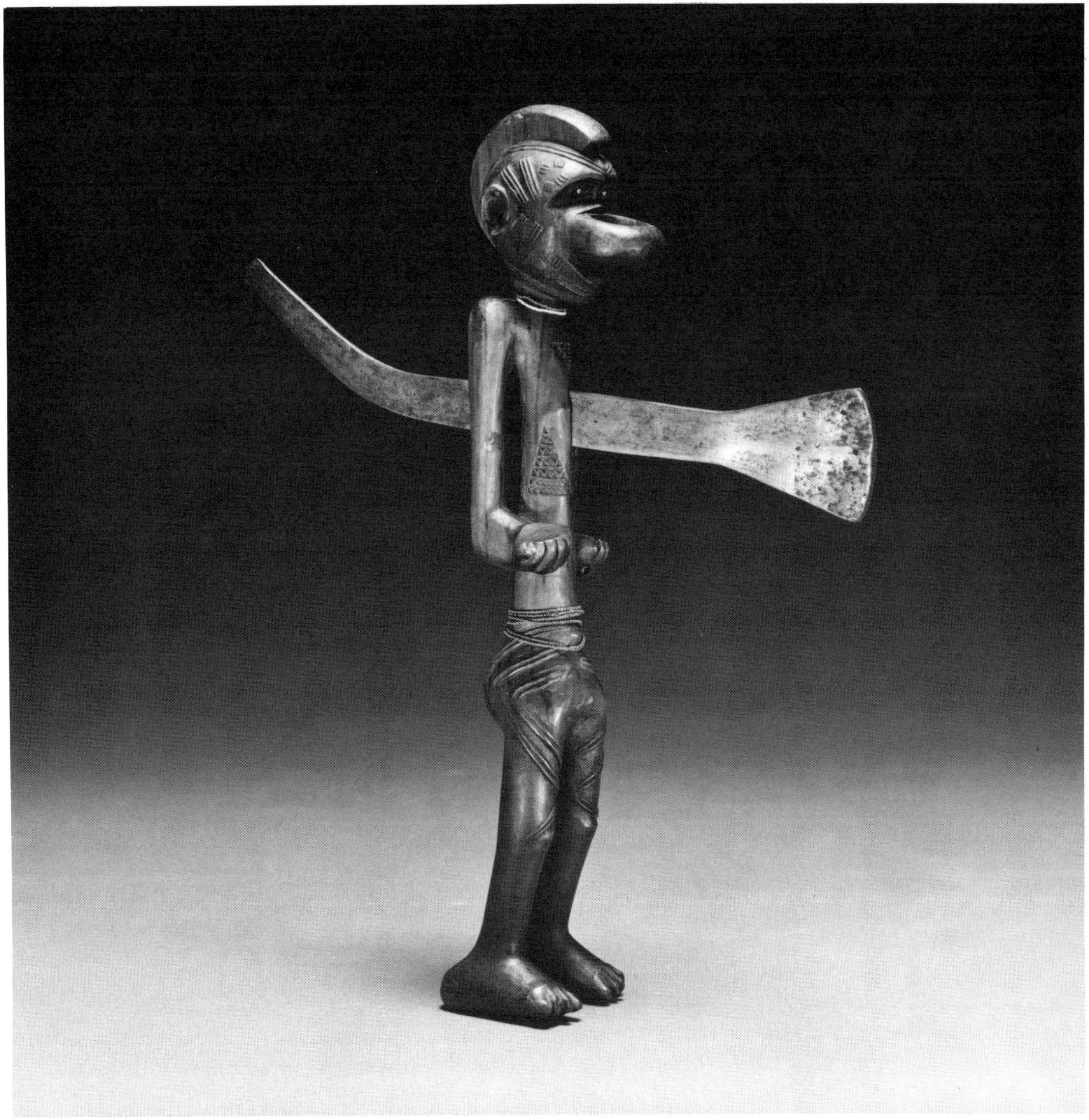

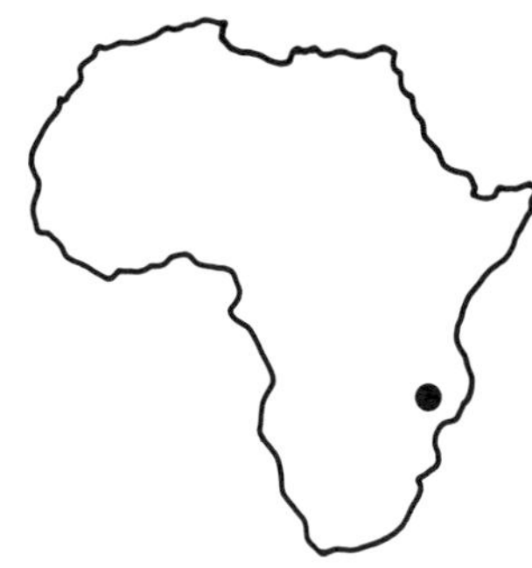

Axe (E6,765)

Nyanja, Malawi

Wood, iron, glass beads

H. 46 cm.

One of the largest cultural regions in Africa is that of the Central Bantu; it comprises an irregular band from the mouth of the Congo River eastward to the Indian Ocean. While the western portion of this province includes a number of societies with well-studied artistic traditions including the Kongo, Yaka, Kuba and Chokwe, the peoples and art of the eastern portion of the province are less well known. This extraordinary carving is from the Nyanja, one of the easternmost of the central Bantu peoples, who live in the area south of Lake Nyasa. It is unlikely that the axe was functional; rather, it was probably an emblem of prestige or authority. The figure depicts a female, since the upper lip is distended by a now-missing plug or labret of ivory. *Ex Essex Institute collection, 1867. Collected by Edward Ropes ca. 1855-1860.*

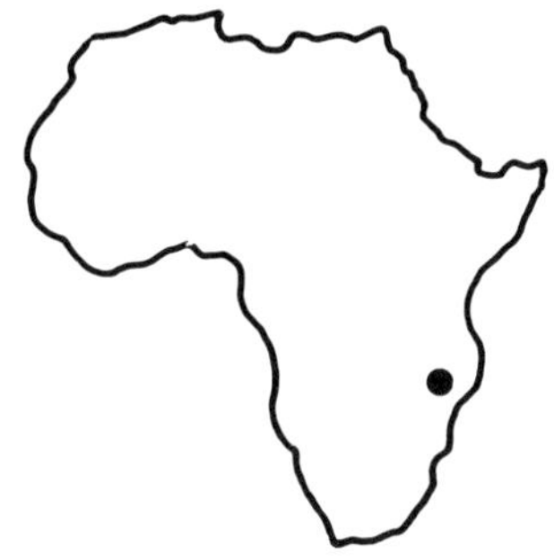

Basket (E6,777)

Nyanja, Malawi

Bark, vegetable fiber, pigment

H. 12 cm.

The pleasing geometric design of this Nyanja basket is achieved by incising the bark sides and filling the grooves with red and white pigment. *Gift of Mrs. E.A. Emmerton, 1895.*

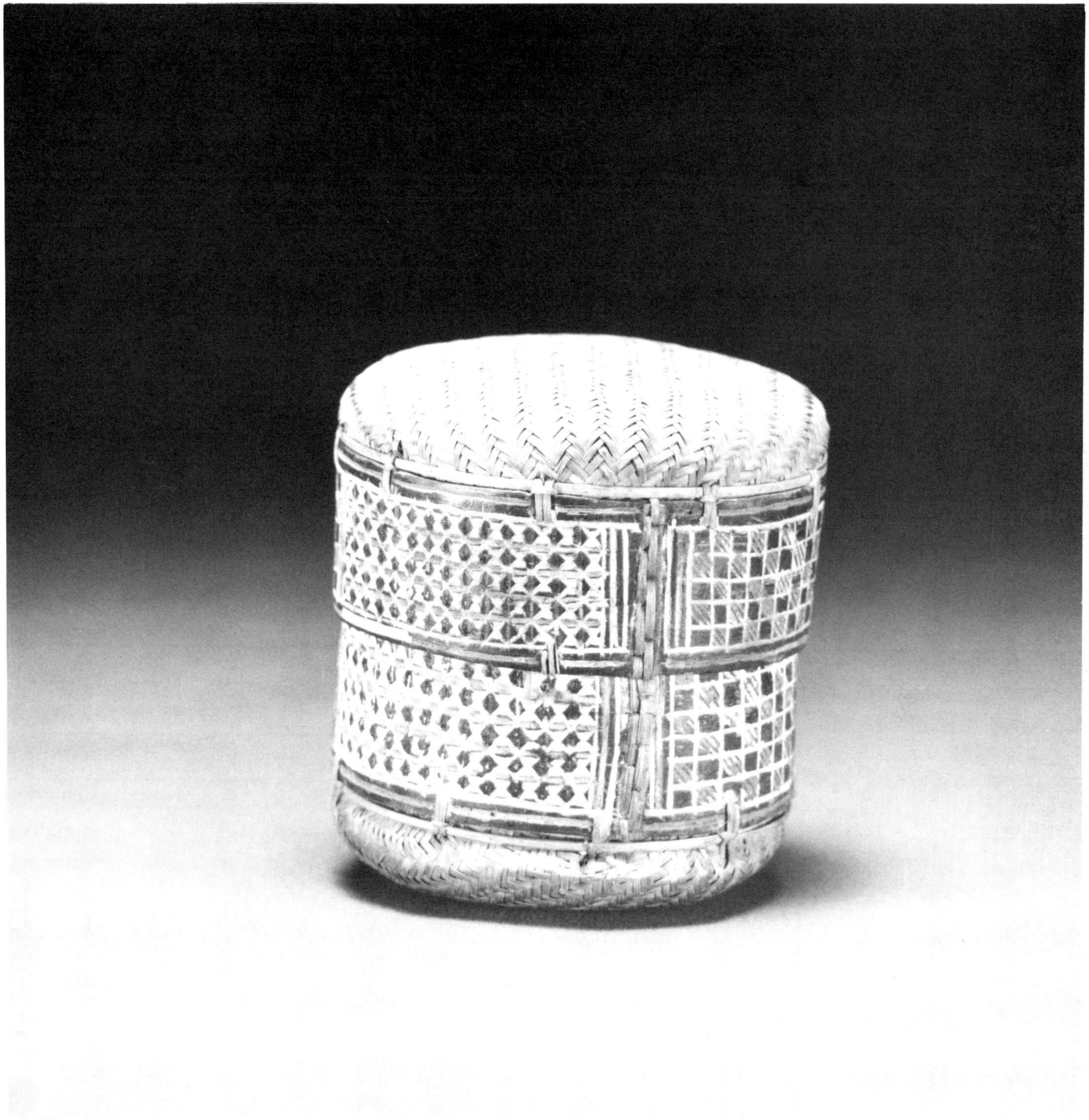

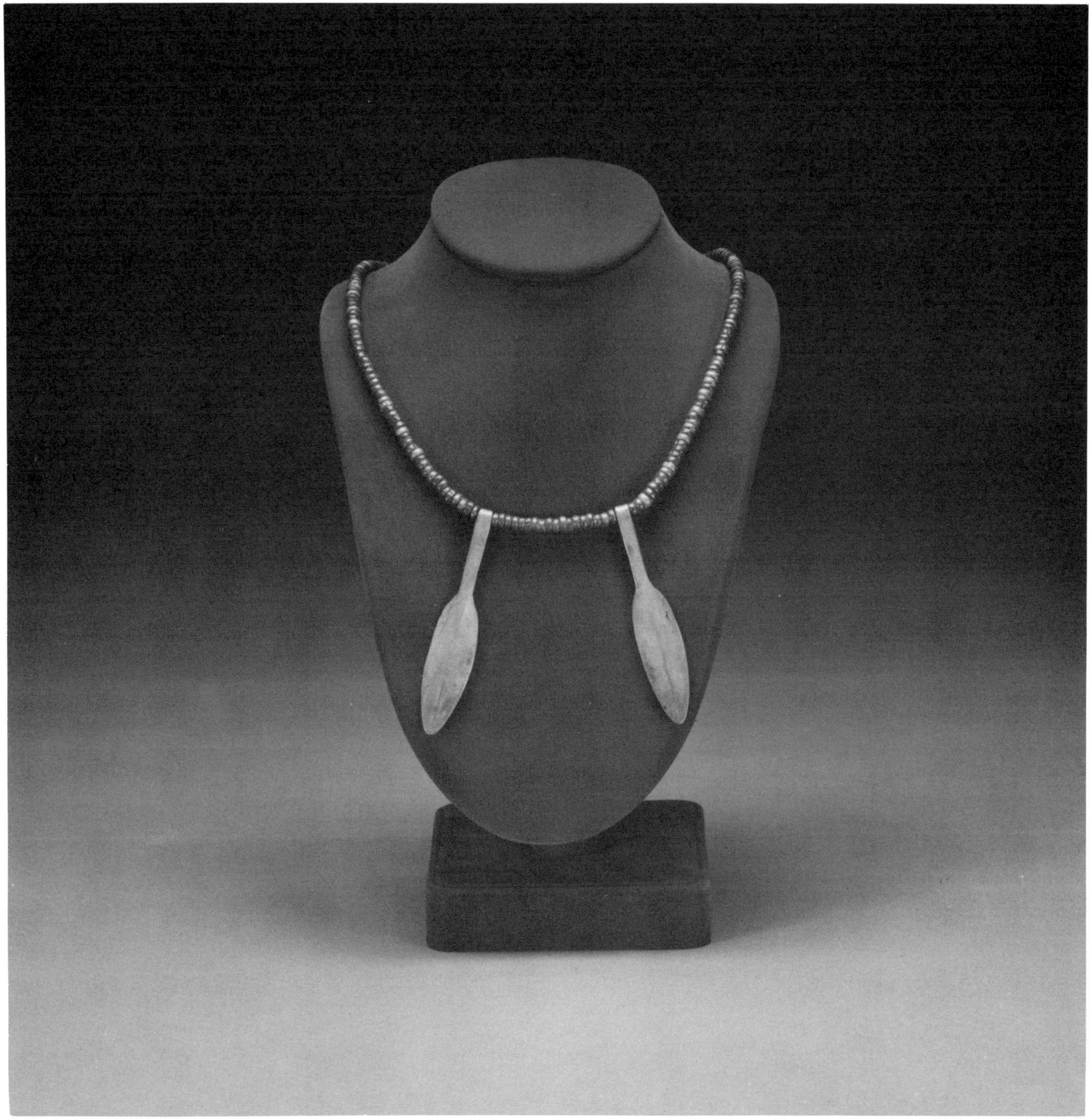

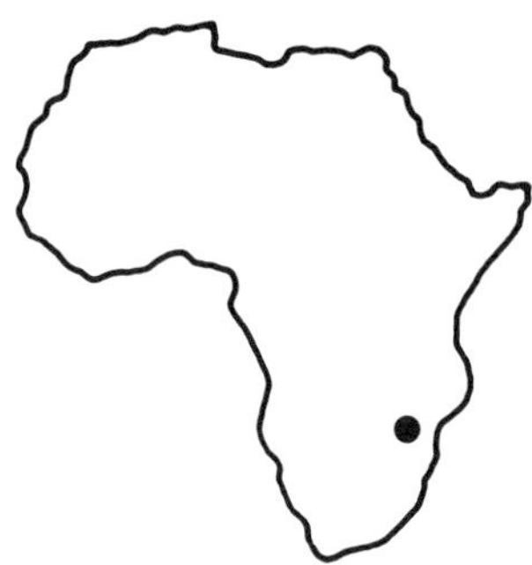

Necklace (E18,252)

Shona (Karanga), Zimbabwe

Brass, cordage

D. (excluding pendants) 20 cm.

The Karanga are one of six groups which are collectively referred to as the Shona. *Gift of Amy and Clara Curtis, 1921.*

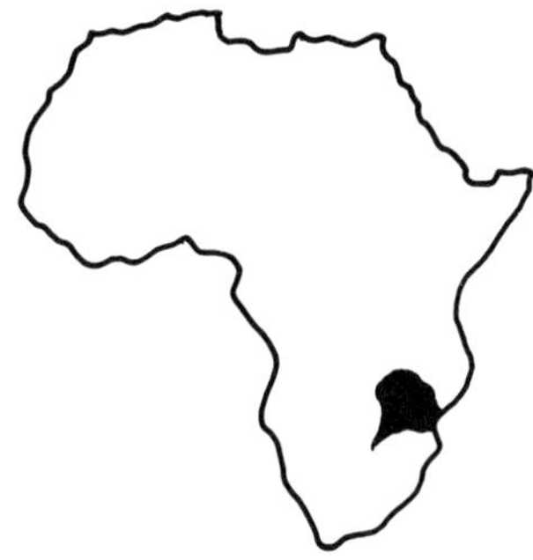

Headrest (E17,692)

Shona, Zimbabwe-
Mozambique

Wood, wire repairs

H. 17 cm.

South of the Congo River basin
and lakes region, figurative
sculpture is rare; most creative ef-
fort is directed toward the
embellishment of functional objects. Although this well-worn
Shona headrest is of a common
form, the carving displays an ex-
ceptional vitality. *Museum purchase, 1919.*

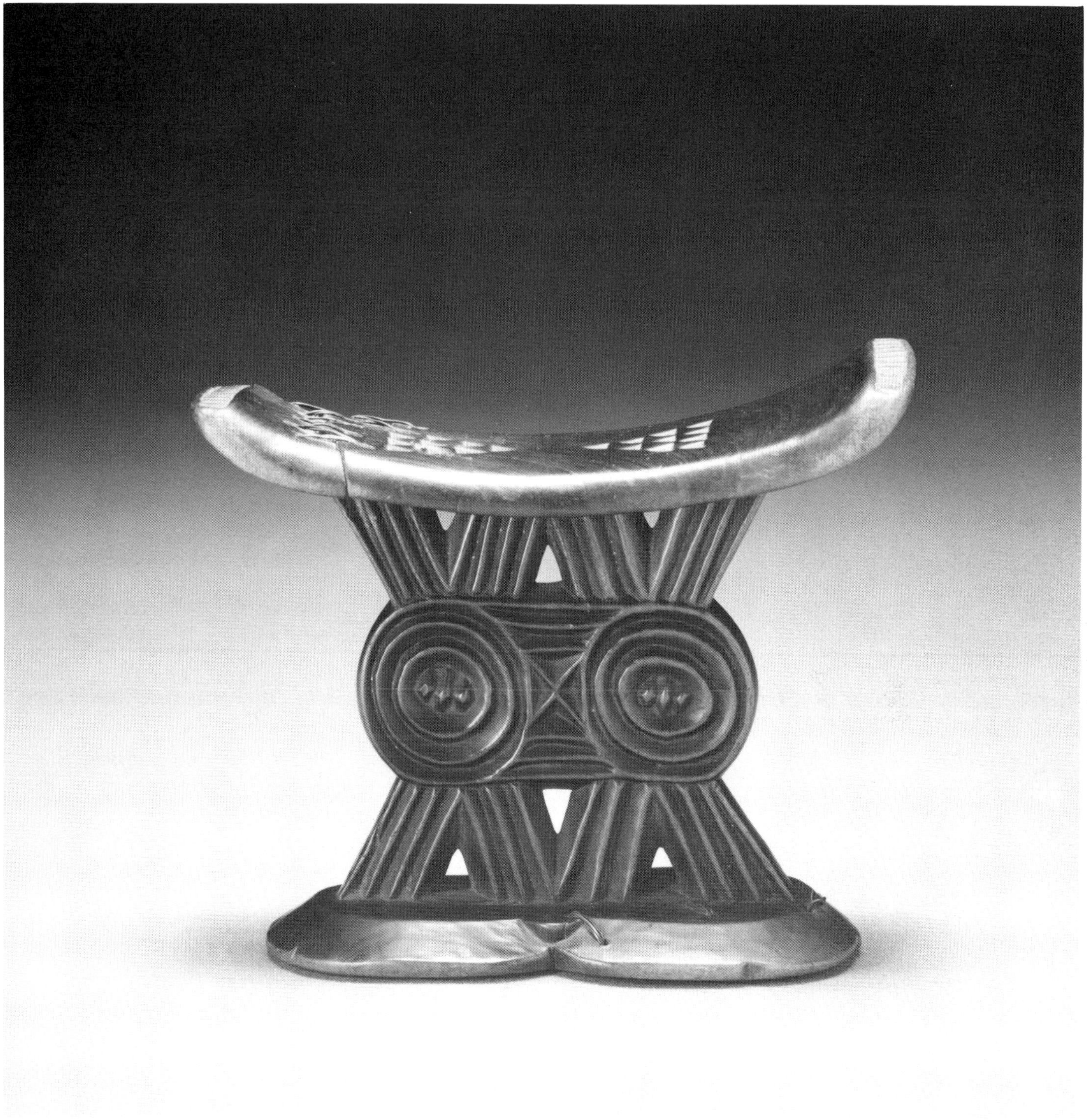

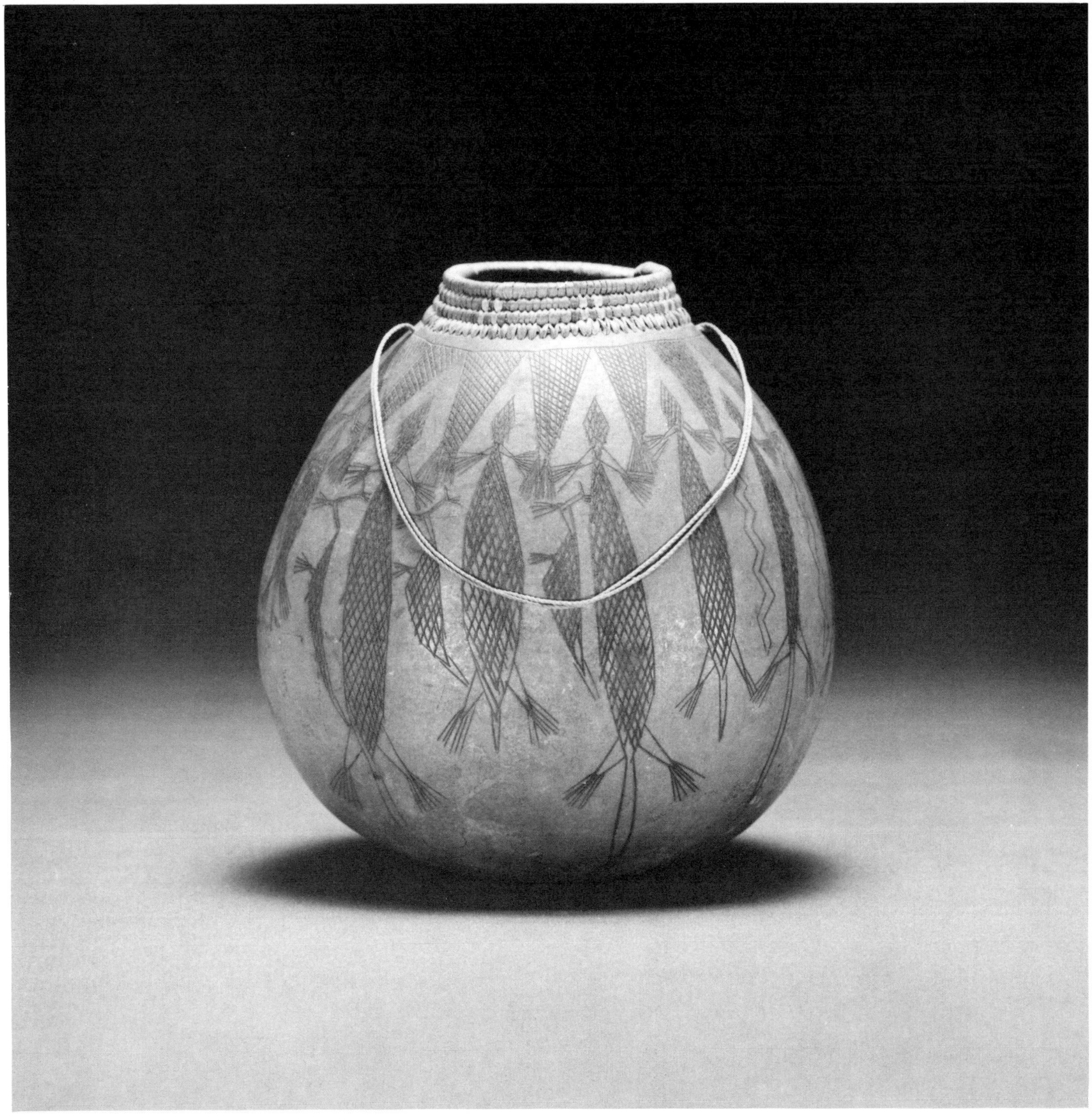

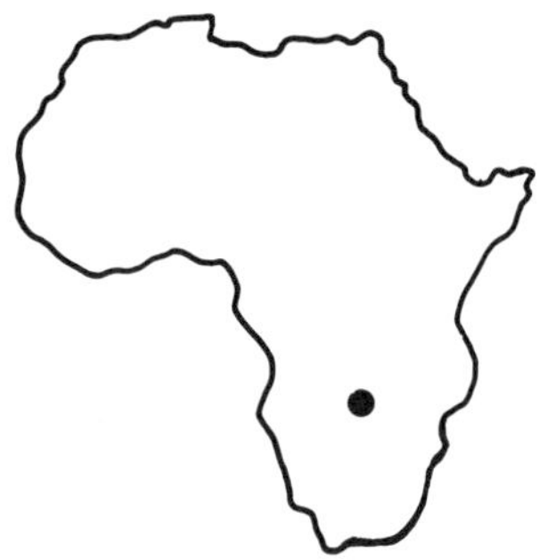

Container (E7,941)

Lozi, Zambia

Gourd, vegetable fiber

H. 22 cm.

The Lozi live in the vicinity of the Zambezi River in western Zambia. The lizard-like motifs on this gourd container may represent crocodiles. *Gift of the estate of Dr. Helen A. Michael, 1905.*

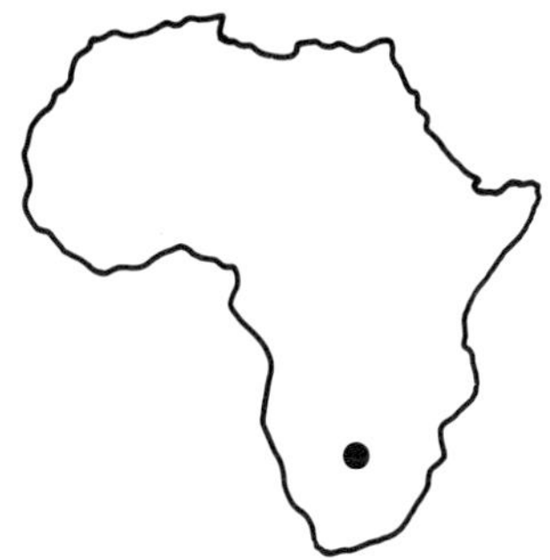

Water Container (E50,689)

Probably Ohekwe,
Botswana

Ostrich egg, pigment

L. 16 cm.

The Bushmen of southwestern
Africa are the descendents of
prehistoric hunting peoples who
originally occupied much of east
Africa as well. Contemporary
Bushmen live in and around the
Kalahari Desert, where rainfall
averages less than 20 inches per
year. In this arid environment
water is a vital commodity, and
stores of it are traditionally kept in
ostrich eggs. Sealed with a plug,
several could be carried in net
bags or cached for future use. The
containers were frequently
engraved with geometric or
representational designs and rub-
bed with black pigment for con-
trast. *Gift of Dr. John B. Sears,
1974. Collected 1963.*

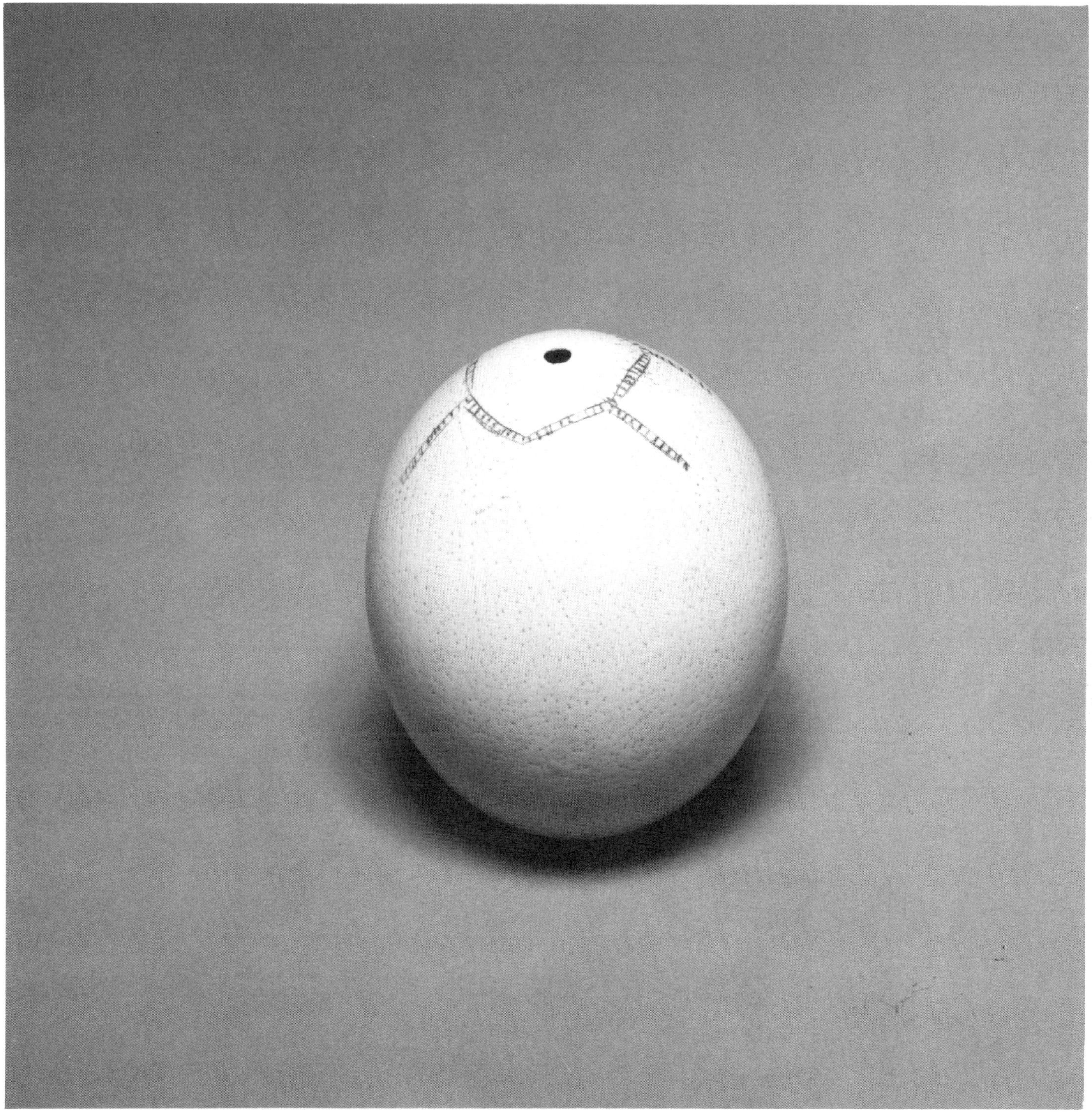

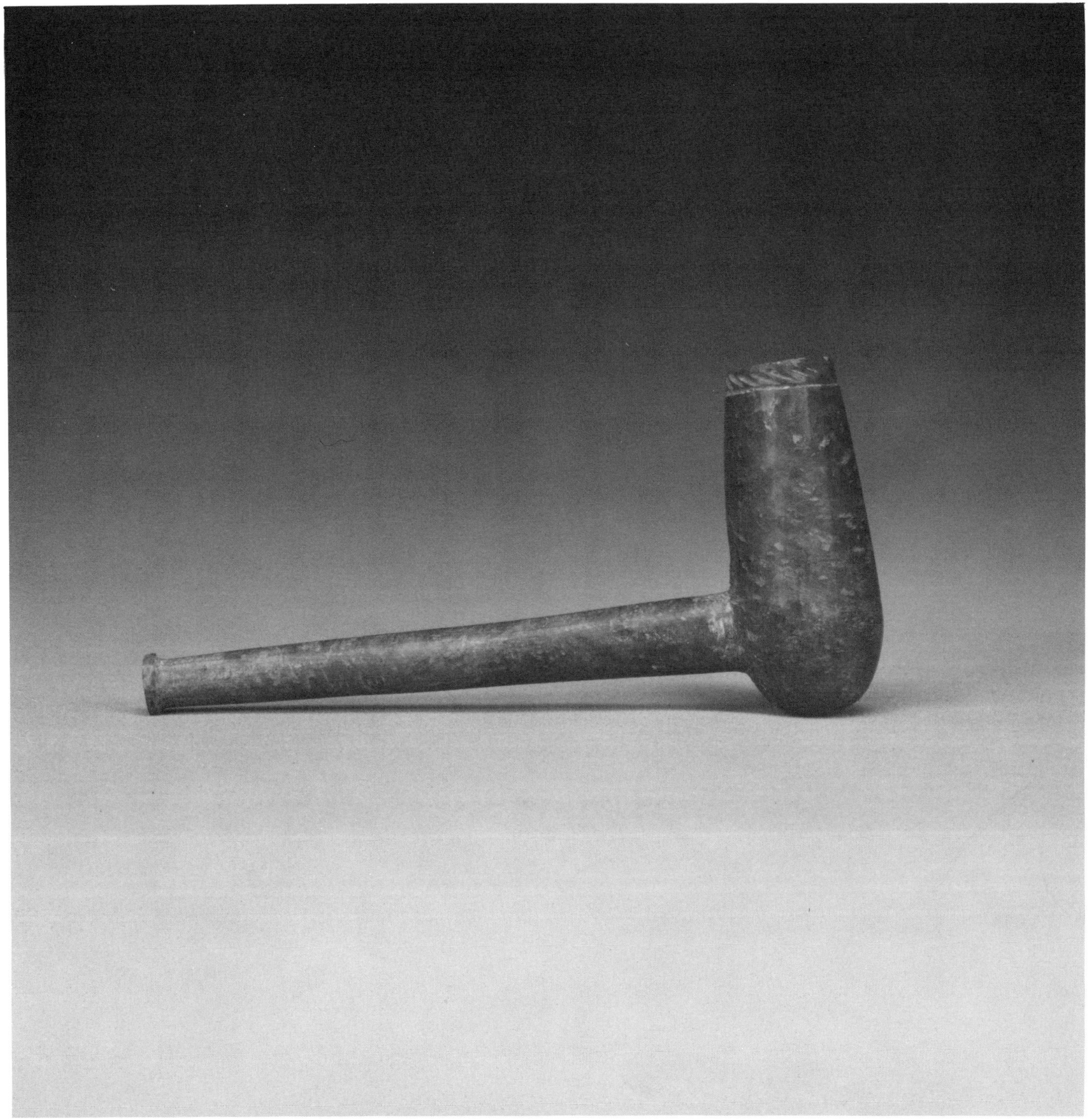

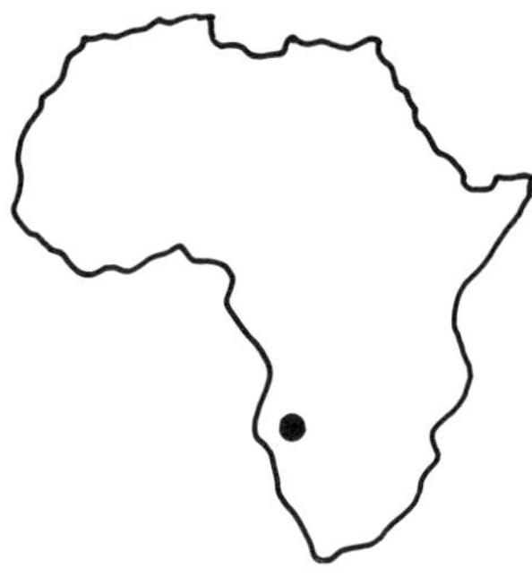

Pipe (E8,655)

Bergdama, Namibia

Steatite

L. 12 cm.

The Bergdama are one of the westernmost of the Bushmen groups, inhabiting the area immediately to the east of the Namib Desert. Bushmen pipes are typically in the form of a flared cylinder; this one is modelled after the European form and is carved from a single piece of stone. *Gift of Alfred S. Peabody, 1880.*

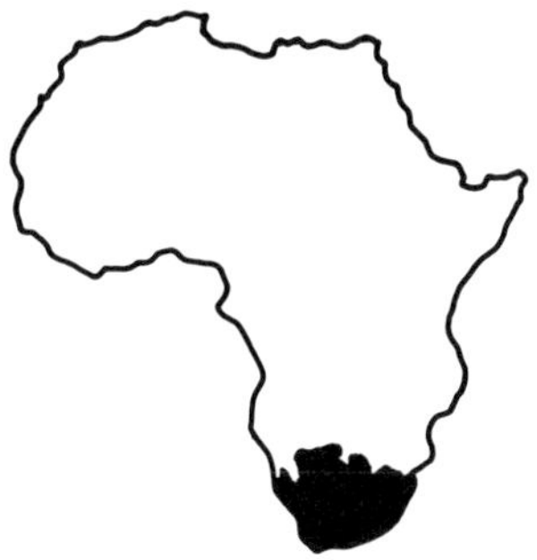

Chest Ornament (E39,470)

Group uncertain, Namibia-Botswana-South Africa

Ostrich egg shell, mollusc shell, glass beads

D. (of loop) 24 cm.

The Bushmen make large quantities of beads from ostrich egg shell, drilling the holes with stone-tipped drills. Strung together in strands, they are used for necklaces, belts, and other types of personal adornment. The beads are widely traded in the area. *Gift of Mr. Augustus P. Loring from the estate of Mrs. James Duncan Phillips, 1963.*

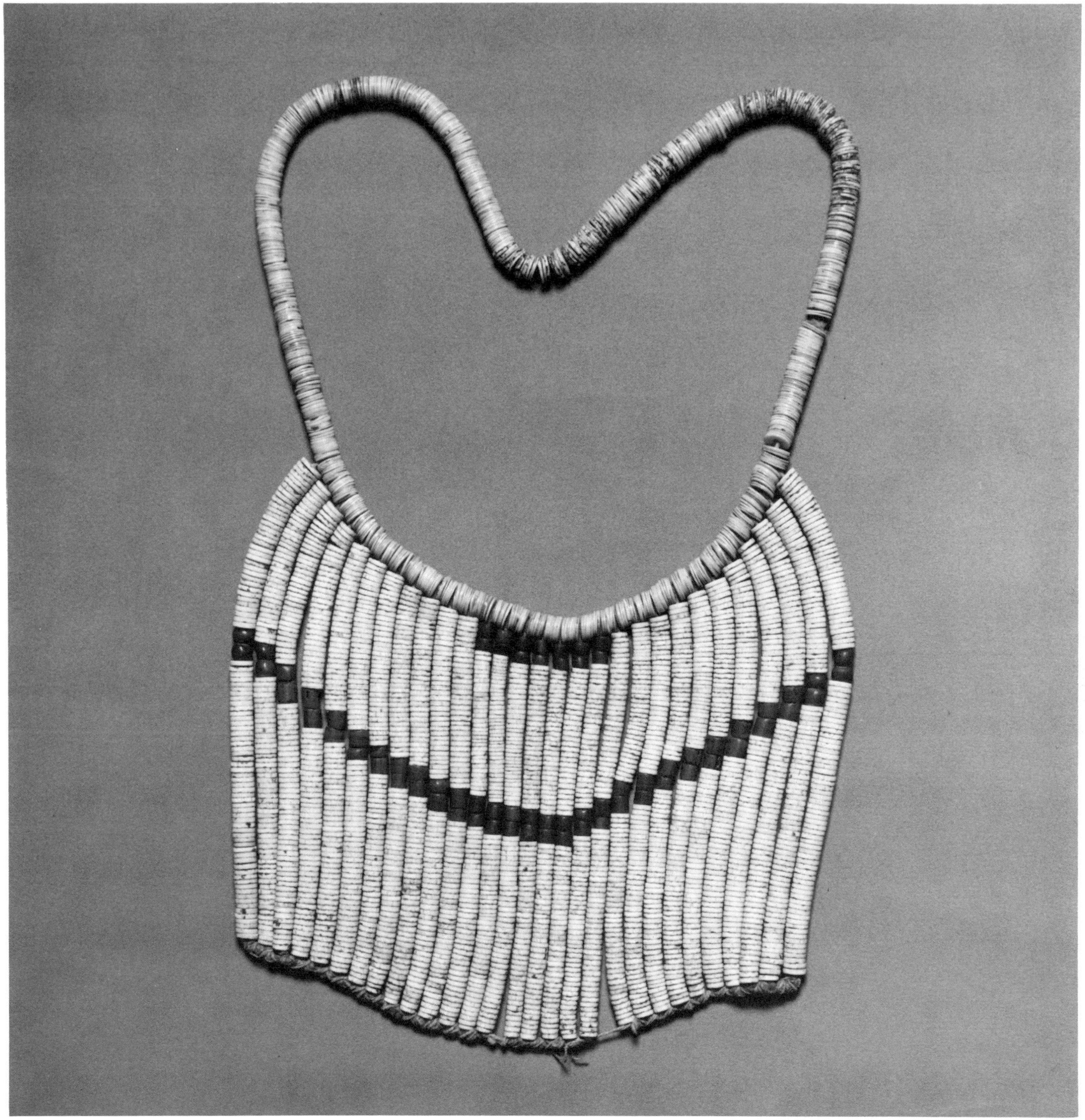

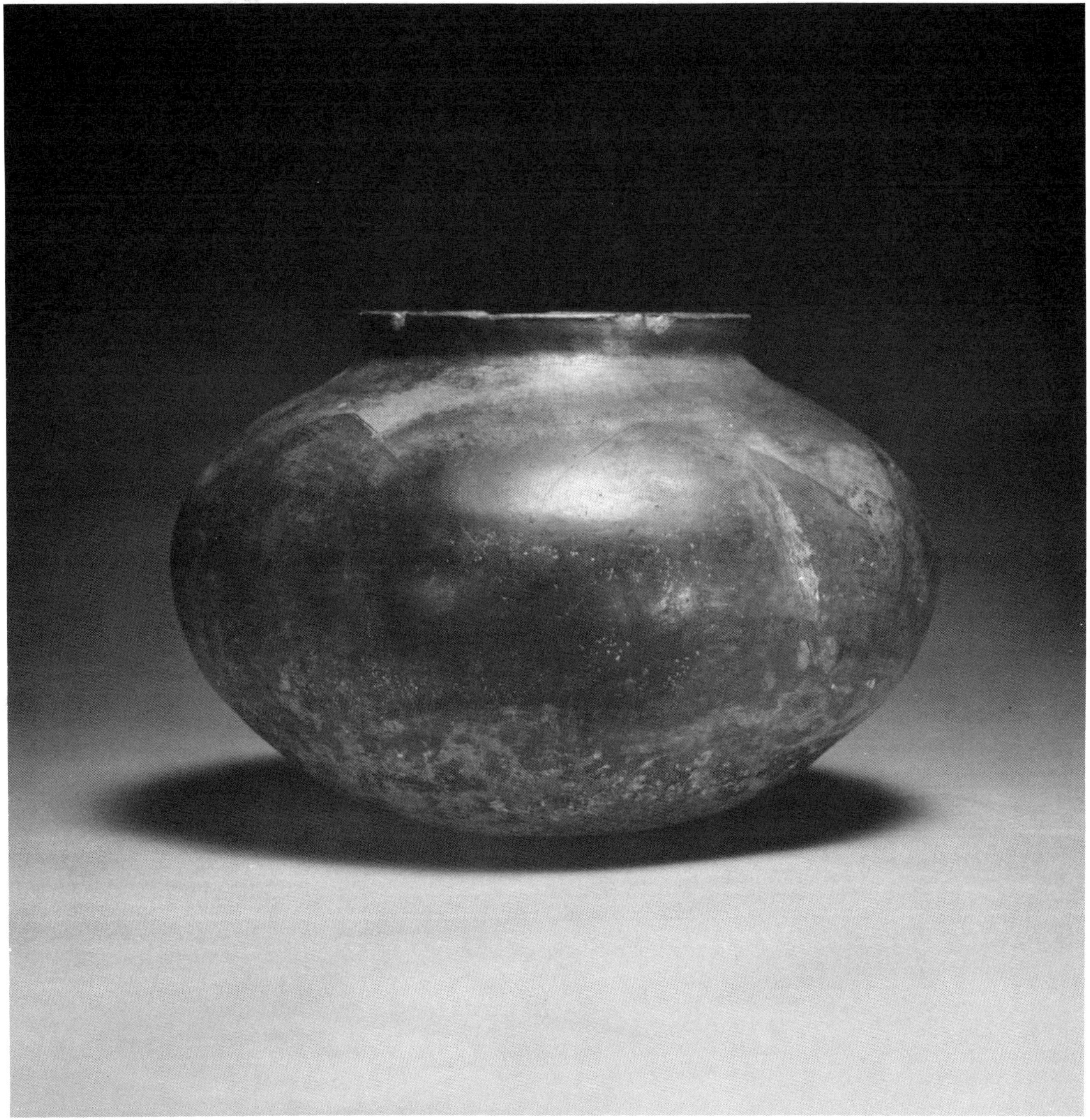

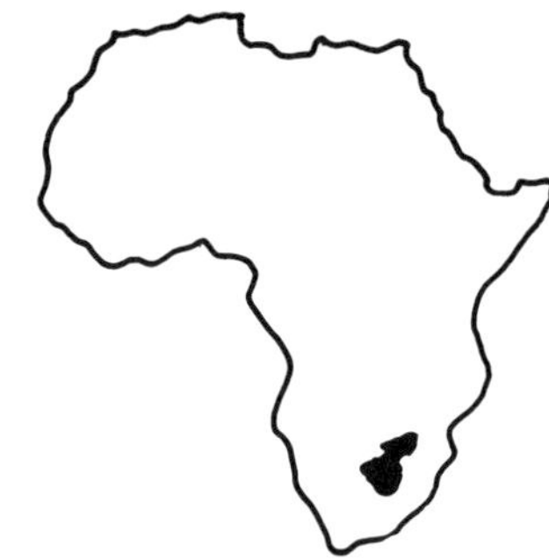

Pot (E62,934)

Sotho-Tswana,
South Africa

Earthenware

H. 25 cm.

The western Sotho, or Tswana, is comprised of several groups whose territory extends into the Bushmen country of South Africa. Unlike the Bushmen, the Sotho make pottery including large containers such as this, used for native beer or for water. The exterior is decorated with an ochre slip and incised lines to produce a chevron pattern. *Museum purchase, 1979. Collected by Alfred Hawes, 1874-1893.*

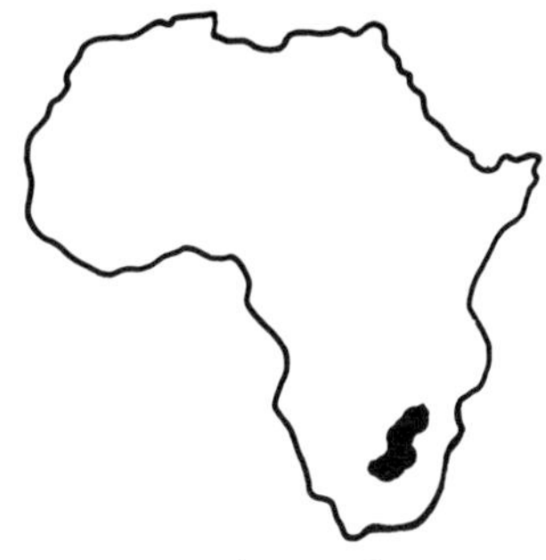

Knife and Sheath (E9,987)

Sotho-Tswana,
South Africa

Ivory, iron, vegetable fiber,
pigment

L. 36 cm.

Tswana knife handles and
sheaths are usually carved from
wood; examples in ivory, such as
this, are uncommon and must
have been an item of prestige.
Donor unknown, prior to 1908.

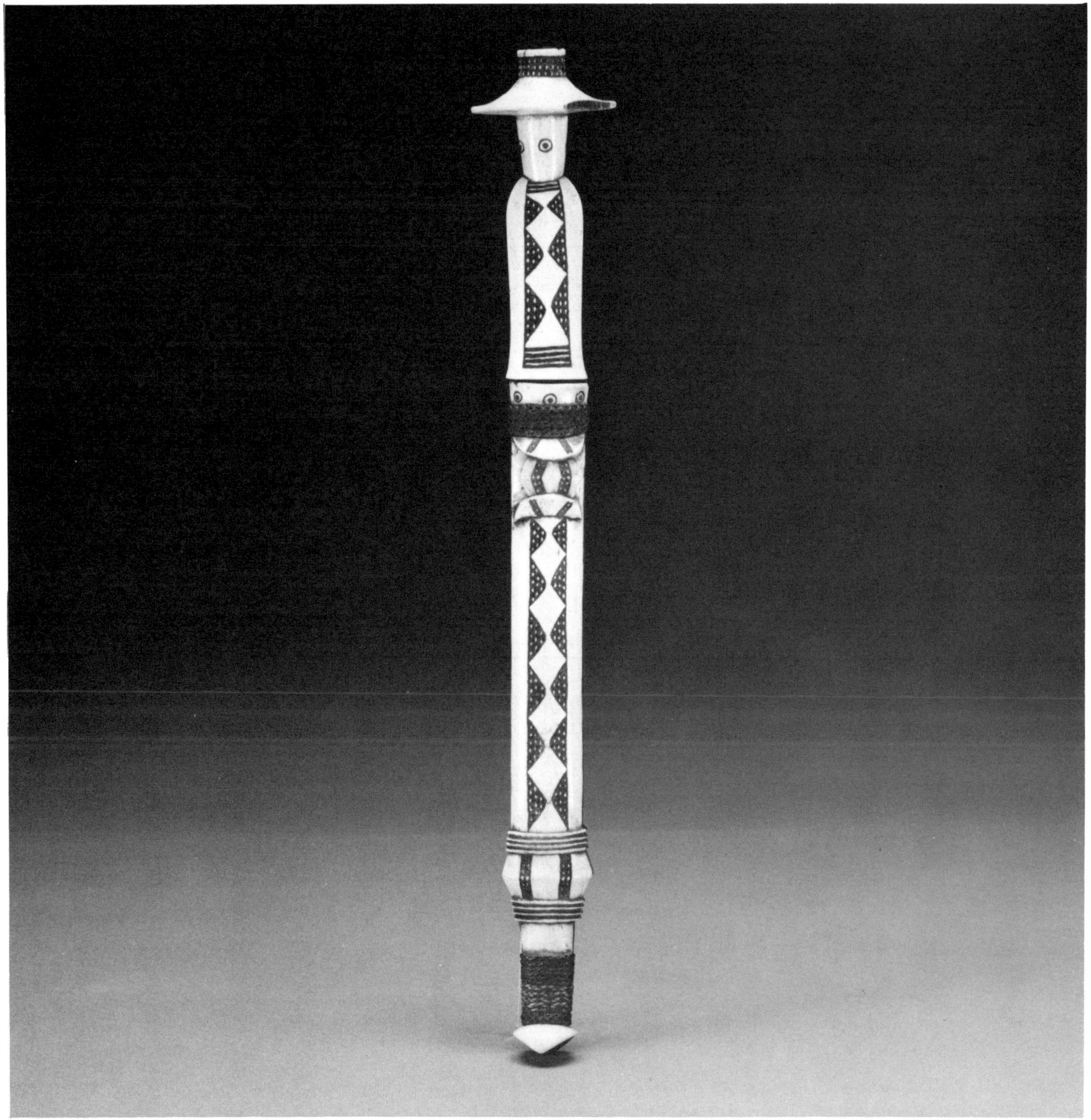

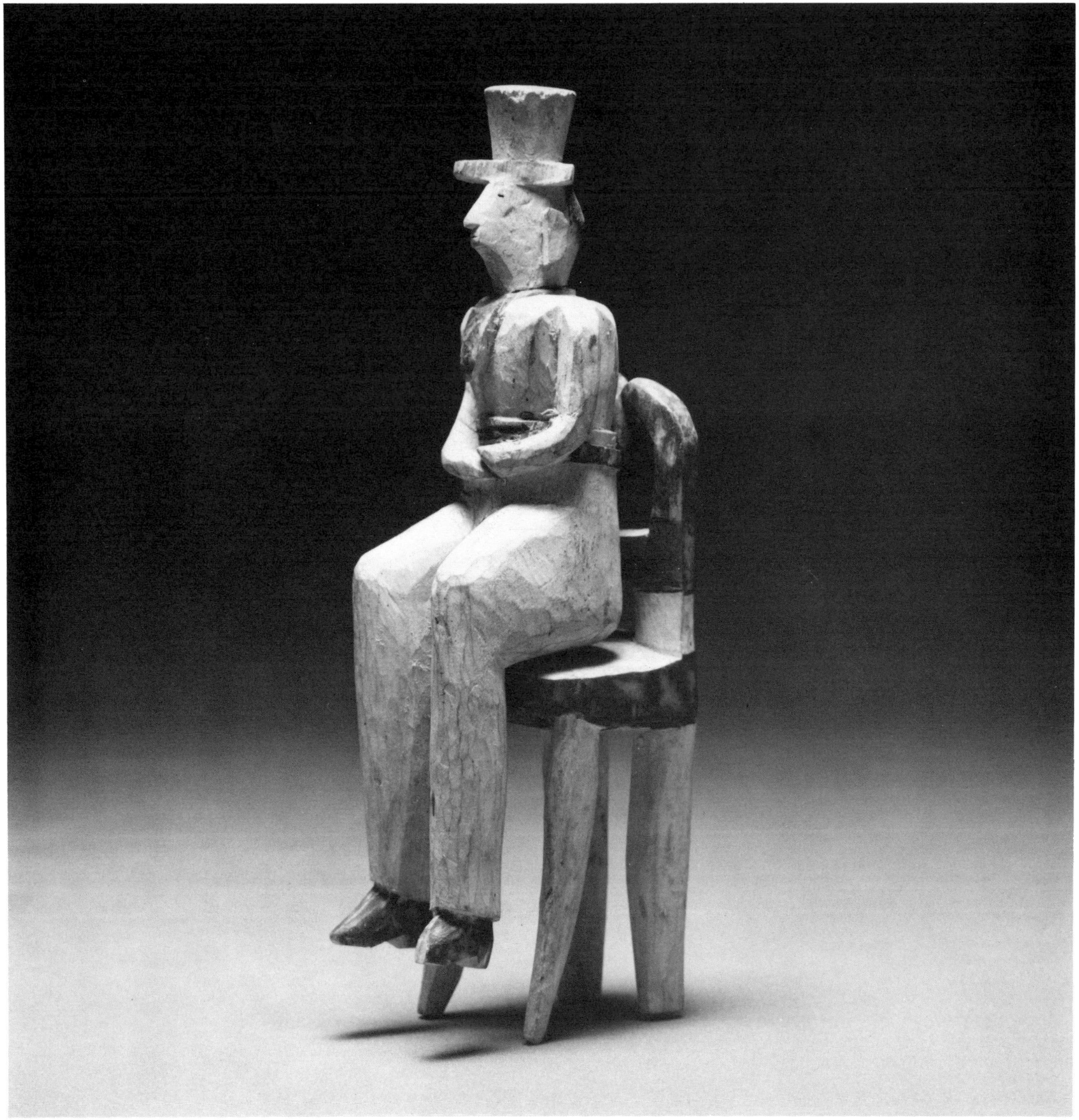

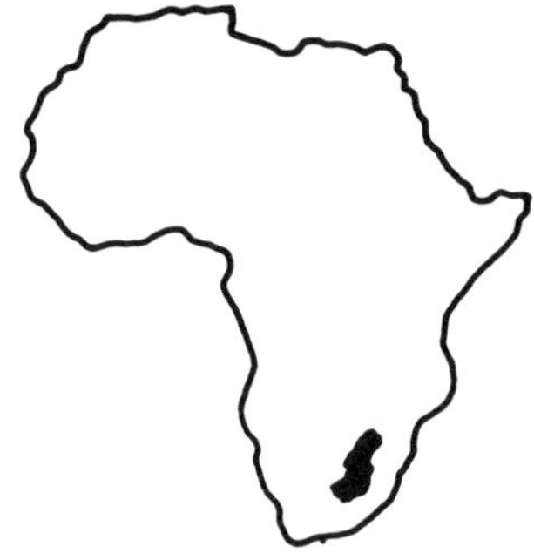

Figure (E8,575 & E8,576)

Sotho-Tswana,
South Africa

Wood

H. (composite) 32 cm.

A rare example of South African sculpture, this figure is of a seated European, possibly a Boer. *Gift of Dr. Charles G. Weld, 1906.*

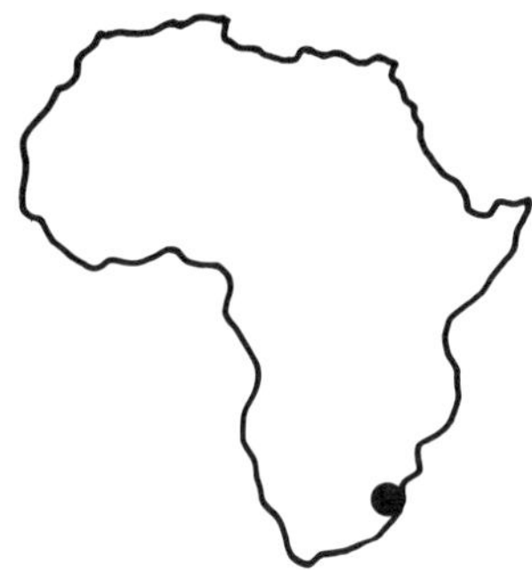

Container (E53,420)

Nguni (Zulu),
South Africa-Lesotho

Wood

H. 23 cm.

The Zulu have occupied portions of what is now eastern South Africa and Lesotho for several centuries coexisting with other Nguni groups. In the early 19th century, however, the Zulu began a period of militarism, greatly expanding their territory and subordinating neighboring groups. Zulu economy is based on both agriculture and animal husbandry, while family life is centered around the *kraal*, consisting of a group of huts surrounding a corral. Zulu art is almost exclusively confined to the decoration of functional objects and dress. Geometric motifs, constructed of bands of parallel lines, are common on wood objects, such as this container for milk or beer. *Ex American Board of Commissioners for Foreign Missions collection, 1976. Collected ca. 1860?*

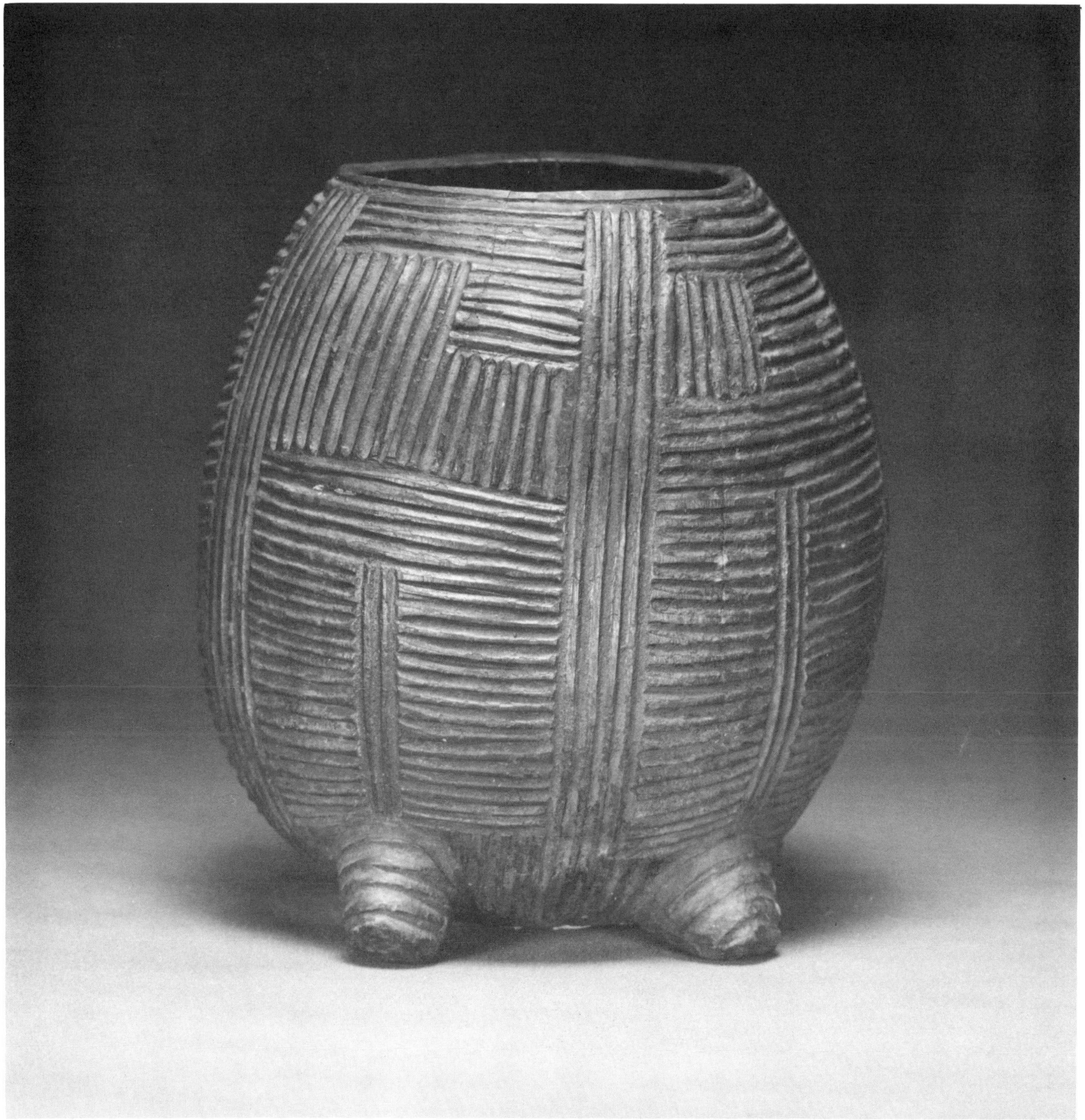

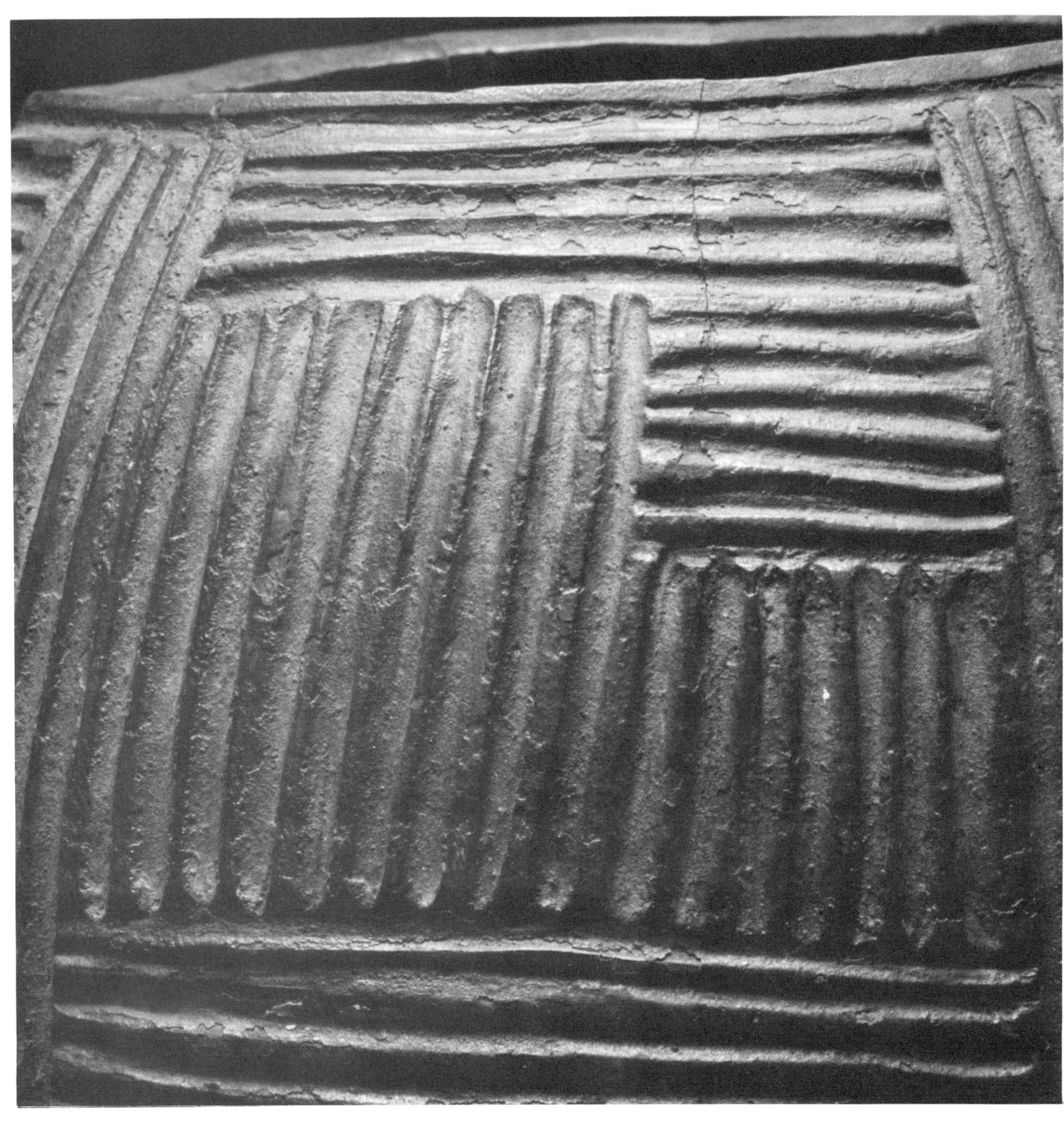

Detail of Zulu container (preceding page).

96

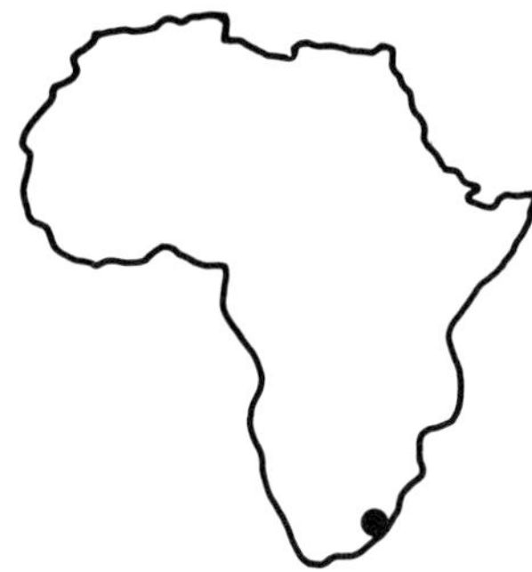

Headrest (E53,566)

Nguni (Zulu),
South Africa-Lesotho

Wood

H. 17 cm.

Headrests, or *izigqiki*, are con-
sidered private property and are
often buried with their owners
upon their death. *Ex American
Board of Commissioners for
Foreign Missions collection, 1976.
Collected ca. 1836-1850.*

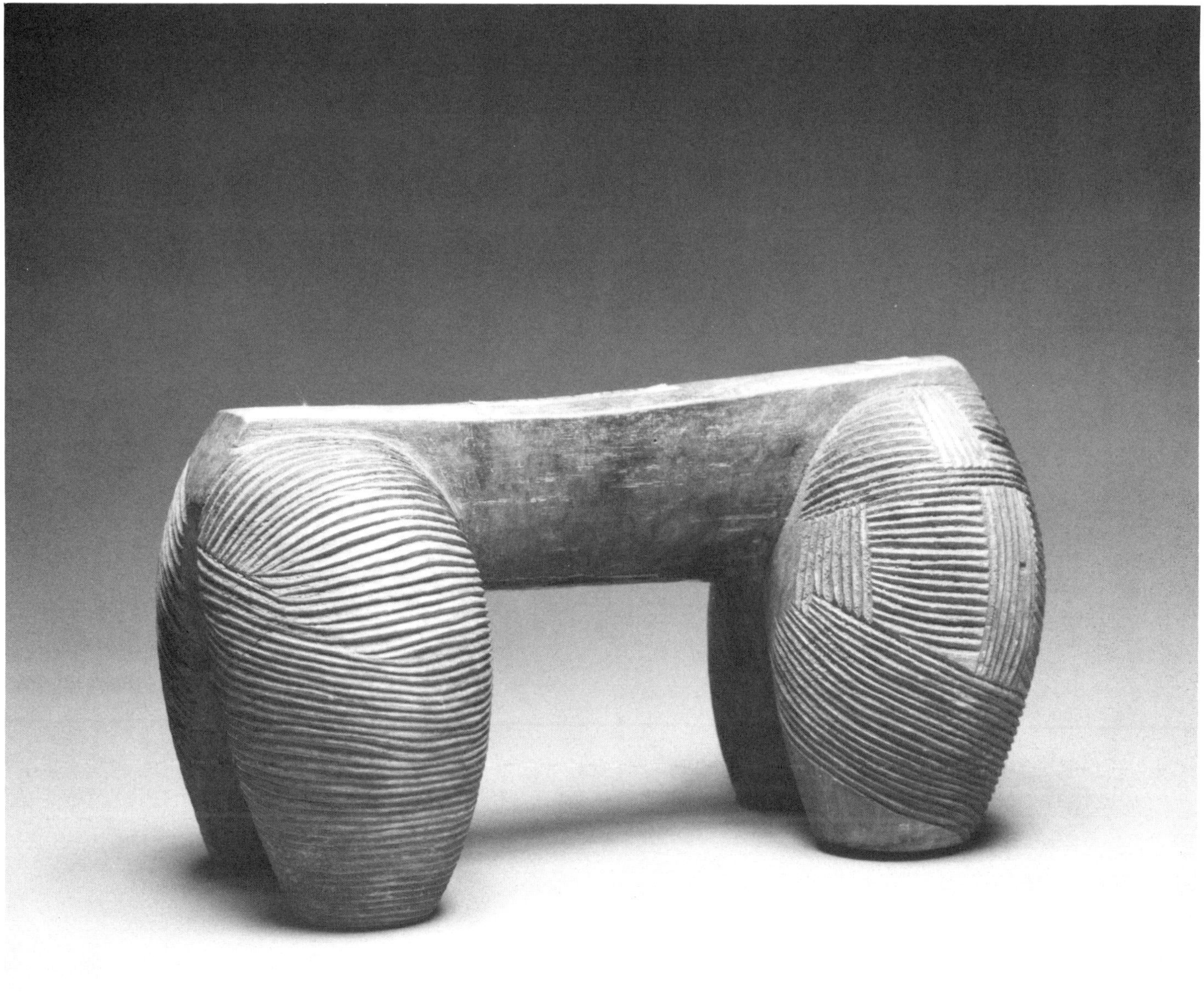

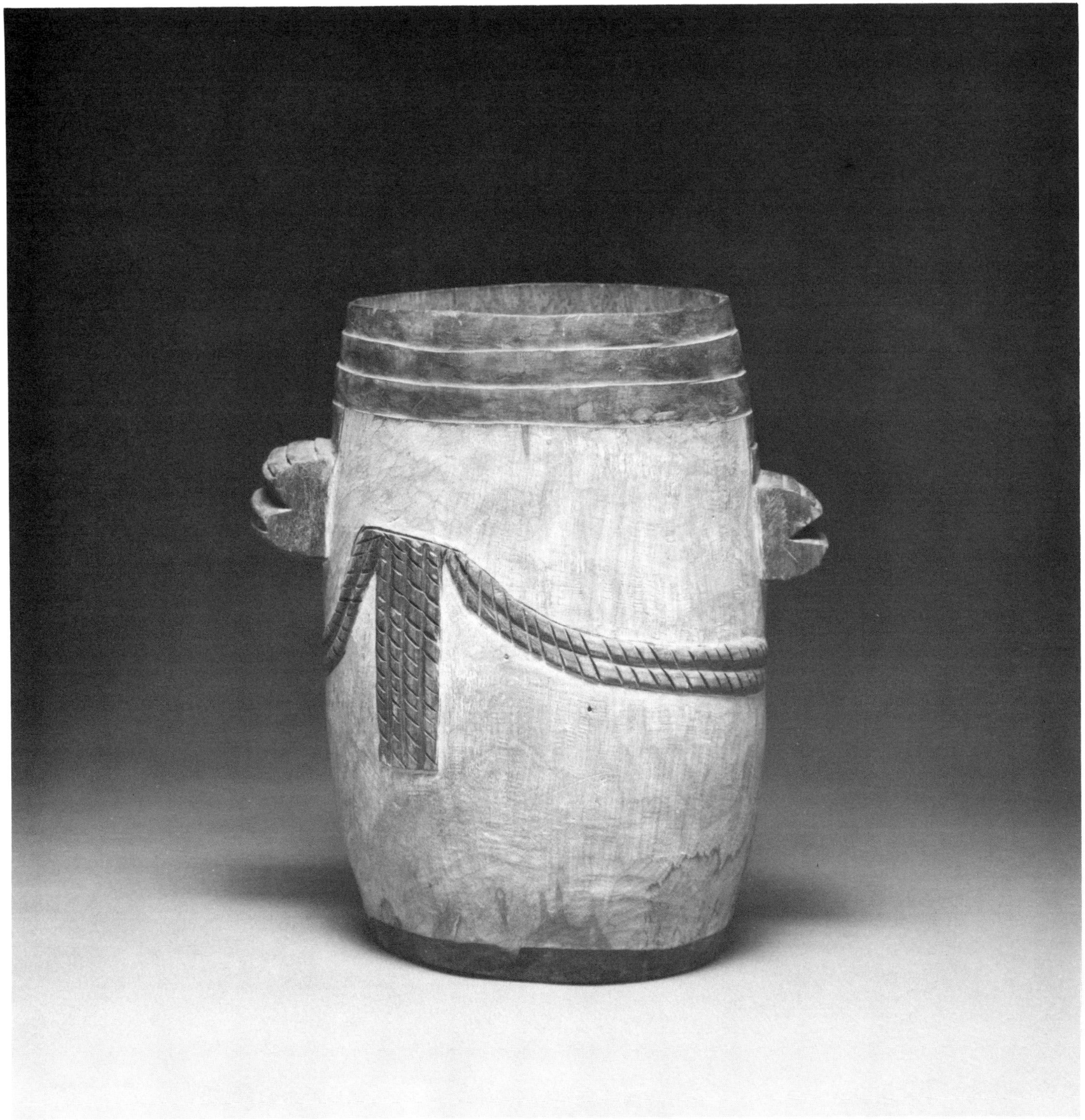

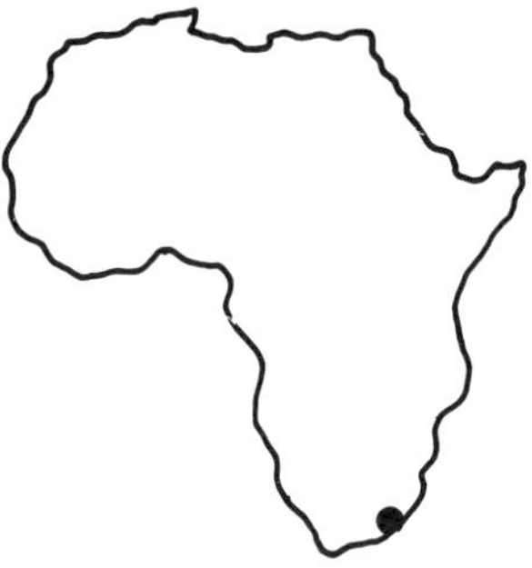

Milk Bucket (E53,421)

Nguni (Zulu), South Africa-Lesotho

Wood

H. 31 cm.

Cow's milk is an important staple among the Zulu, who eat it curdled and mixed with corn mash. Zulu men use buckets called *ithunga* to collect the milk; the lugs on the side of the bucket are used to hold it securely between the knees while milking. *Ex American Board of Commissioners for Foreign Missions collection, 1976. Collected ca. 1860?*

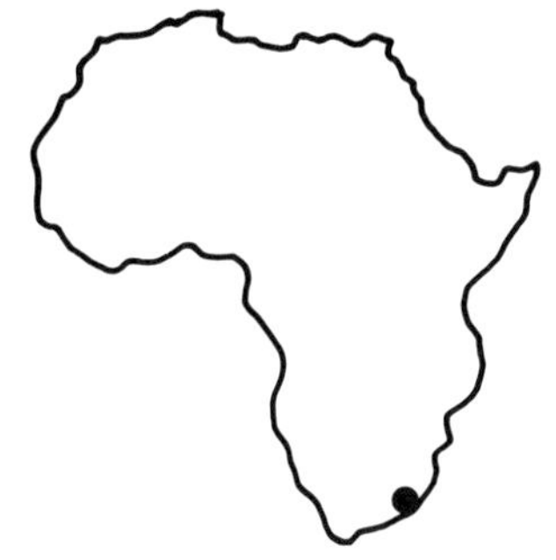

Left

Spoon (E53,547)

Nguni (Zulu), South Africa-Lesotho

Wood

L. 39 cm.

Right

Spoon (E53,532)

Nguni (Zulu), South Africa-Lesotho

Wood

L. 41 cm.

Each Zulu family member owned a spoon with which to eat the yogurt-corn porridge. That of the family head, together with a spoon for mixing the porridge, were stored in a basketry case when not in use. *E53,547 & E53,532, Ex American Board of Commissioners for Foreign Missions Collection, 1976. Collected ca. 1836-1850.*

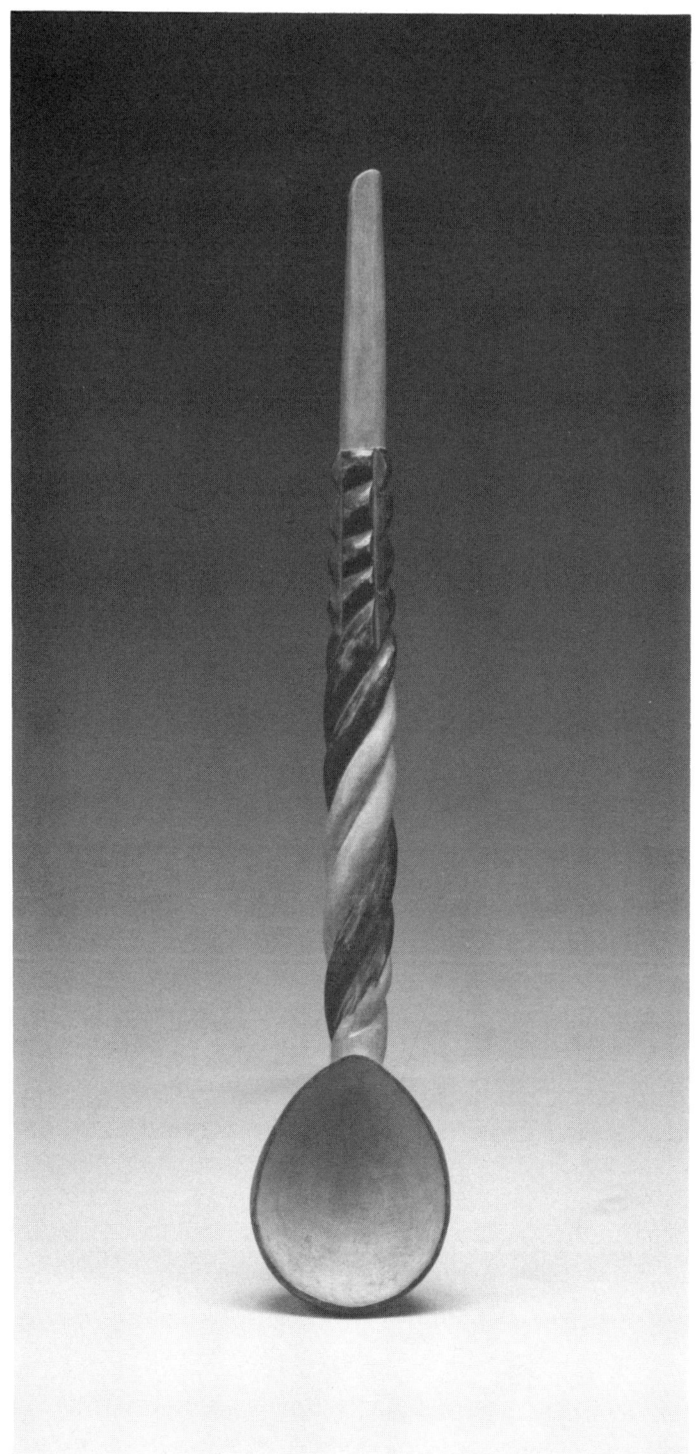

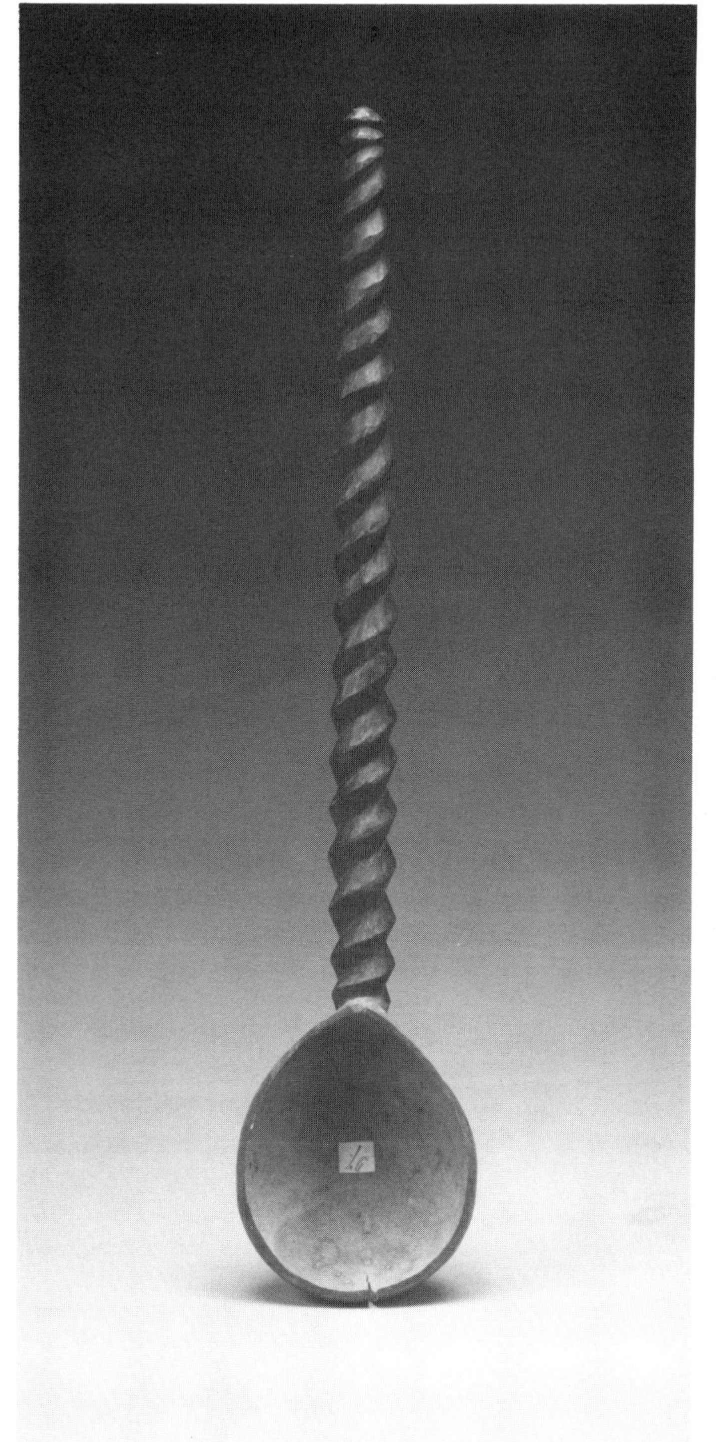

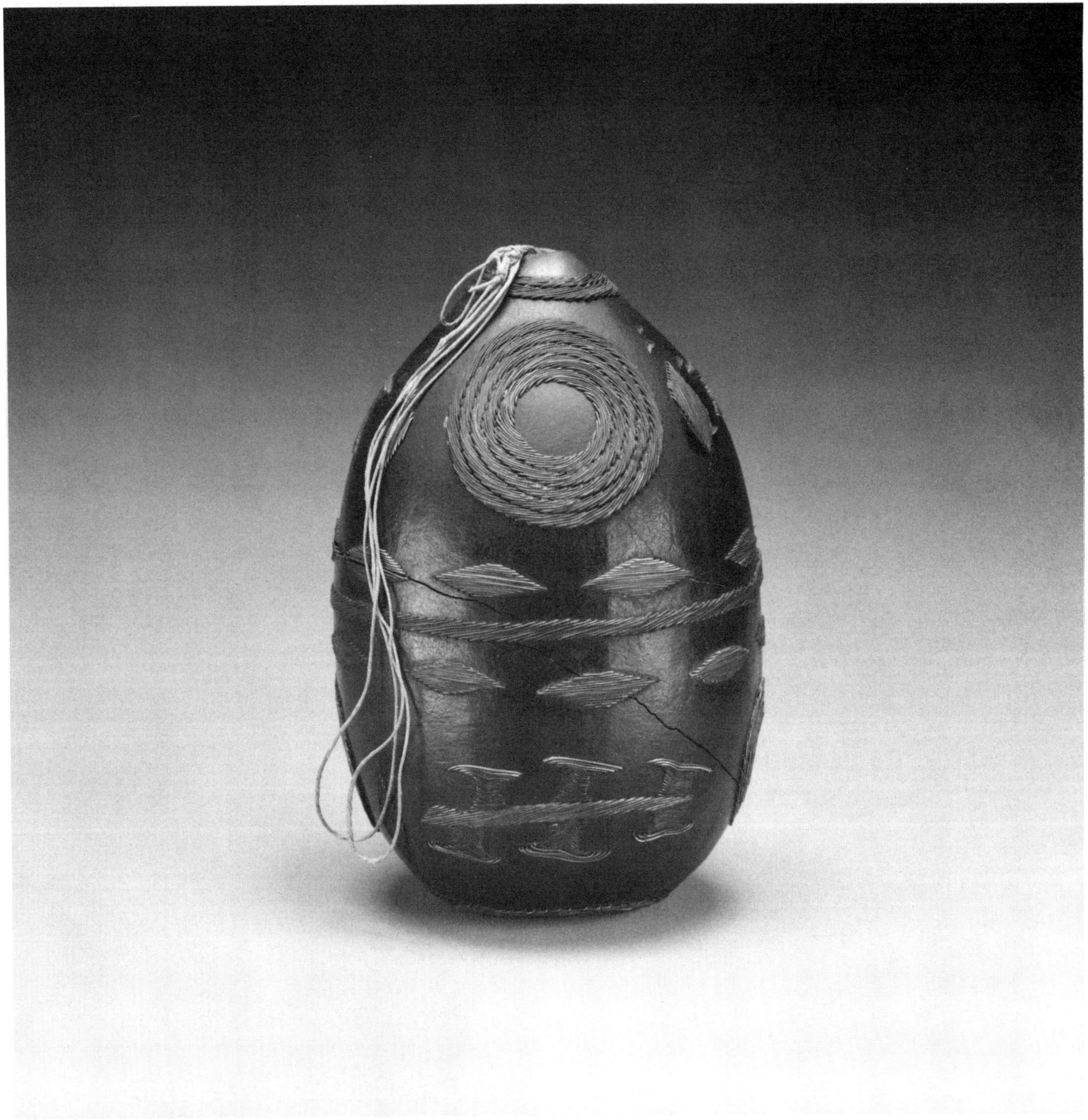

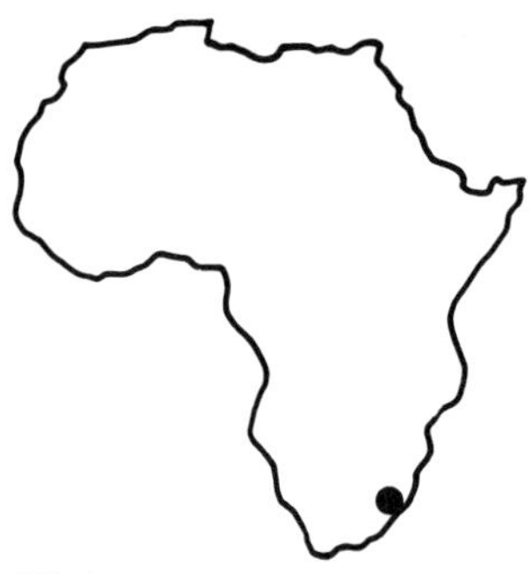

Snuff Container (E14,392)

Nguni (Zulu), South Africa-Lesotho

Gourd, brass wire

H. 19 cm.

Many Zulu men and women carry small containers for snuff, worn either around the neck or on a waistband. An important individual might keep a large container, such as this, in the home. Brass wire was an expensive commodity, and its use in the decoration of this container is a further indication of the owner's high status. *Gift of Dr. Charles G. Weld, 1910.*

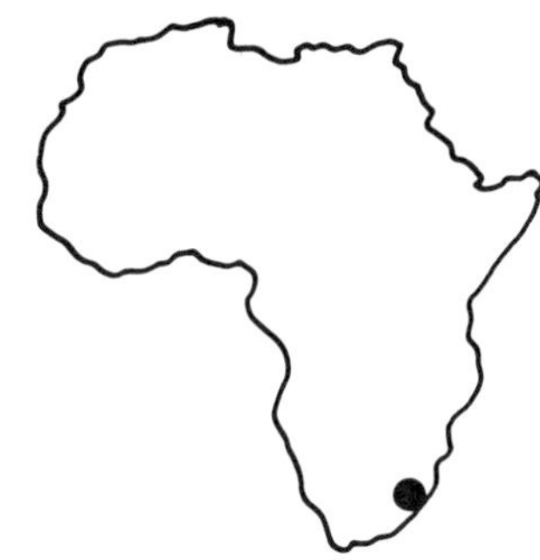

Snuff Spoon (E67,107)

Nguni (Zulu), South
Africa-Lesotho

Bone or ivory, pigment

L. 18 cm.

Small bone or ivory spoons, ornamented with intricate engraved
designs, were used for taking
snuff. When not in use, they served as a hair ornament and
perspiration swipe. *Museum purchase, 1980.*

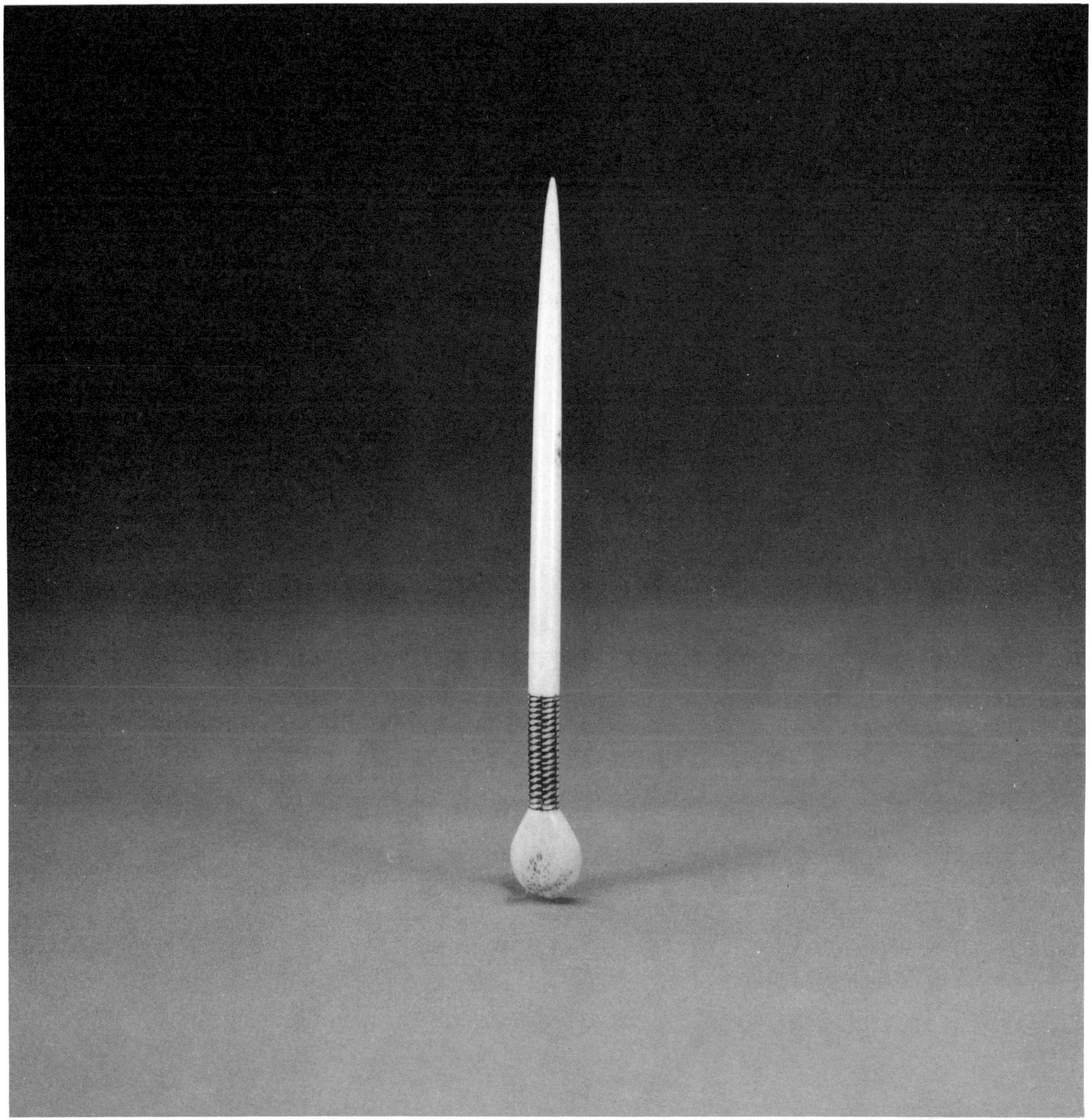

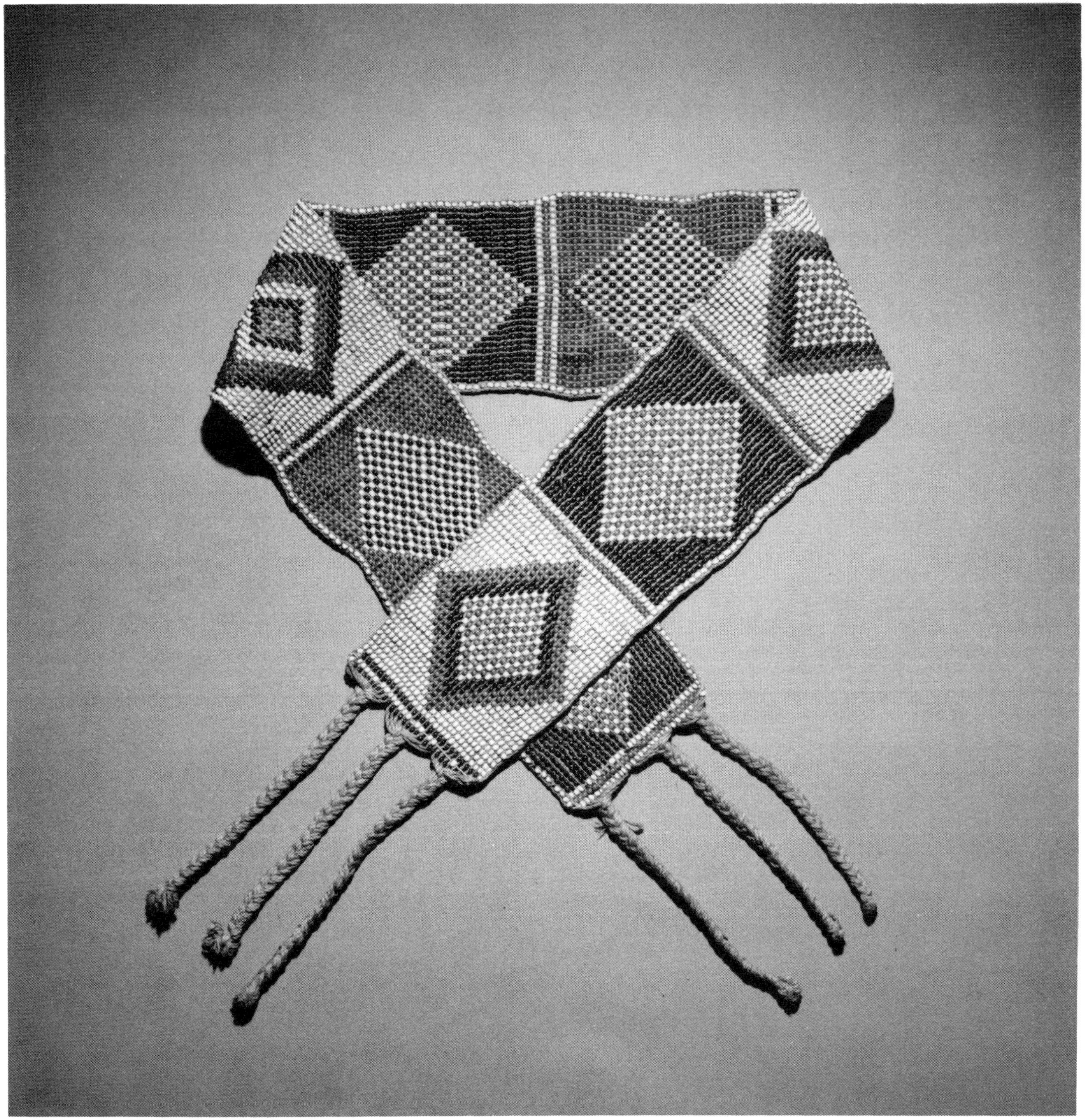

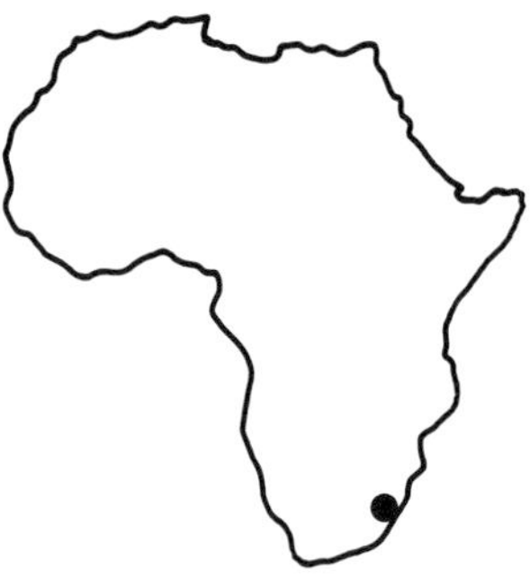

Waistband (E21,933)

Nguni (Zulu), South Africa-Lesotho

Glass beads, cordage

L. 101 cm.

By the mid 19th century, quantities of glass trade beads in various colors became available to the Zulu, who readily incorporated them into articles of dress. *Gift of the heirs of George C. Stone, 1936.*

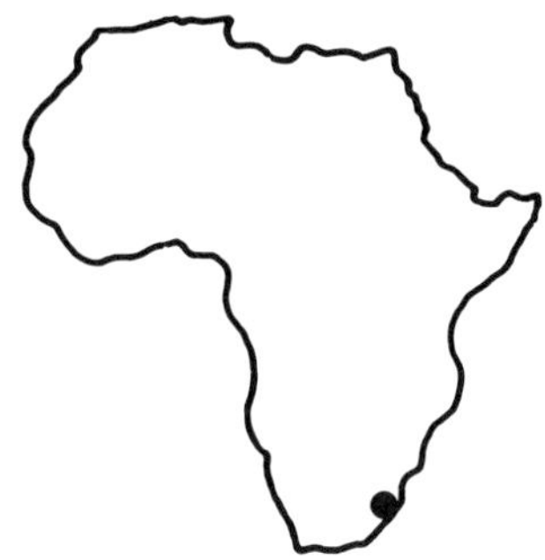

Skirt (E8,609)

Nguni (Zulu), South Africa-Lesotho

Glass beads, cordage

L. (fringed portion) 79 cm.

Pre-pubescent Zulu girls customarily wore a small skirt, either fringed or with a small beaded panel in the front. This skirt is particularly elaborate. *Gift of Dr. Charles G. Weld, 1906.*

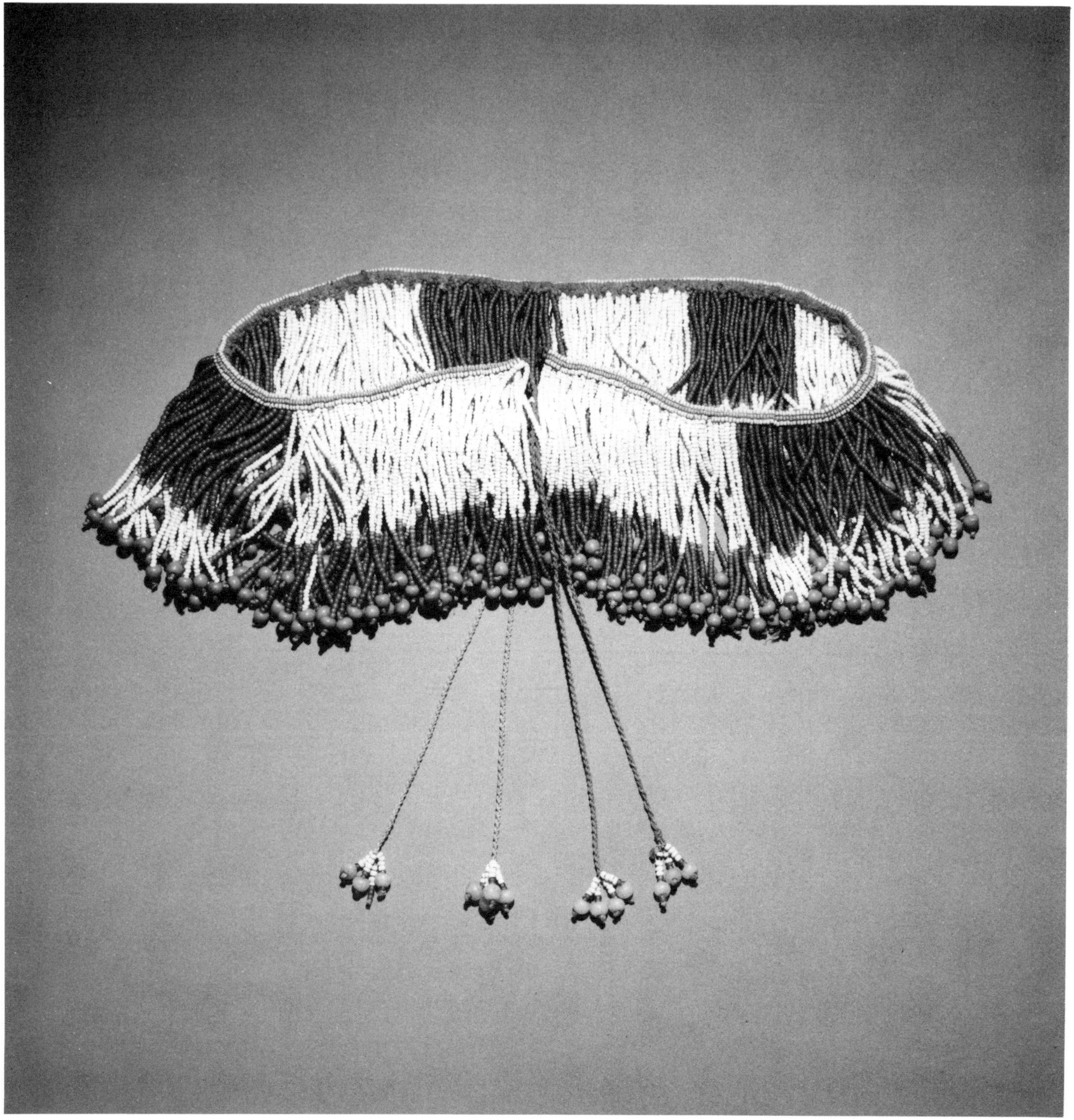

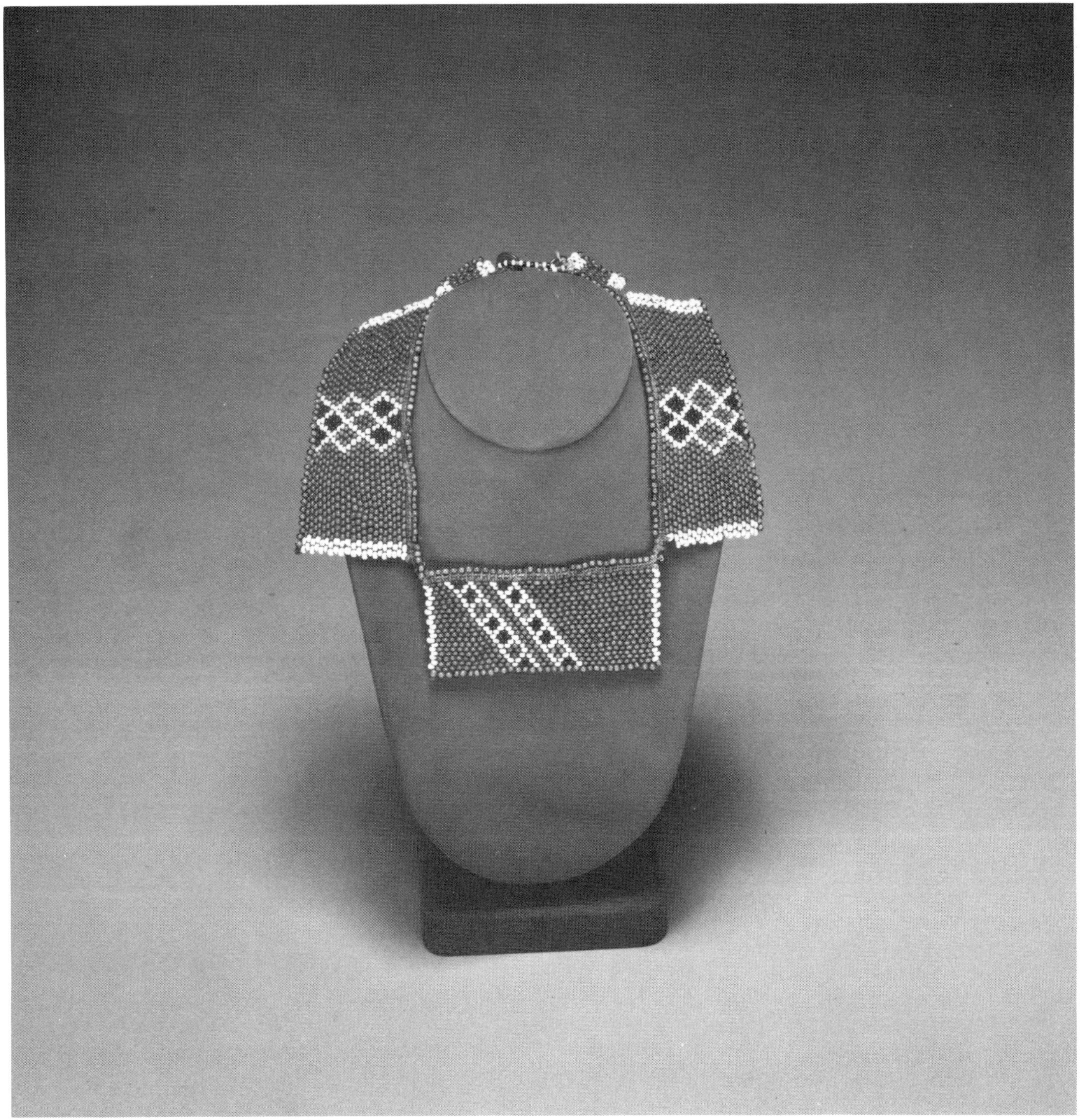

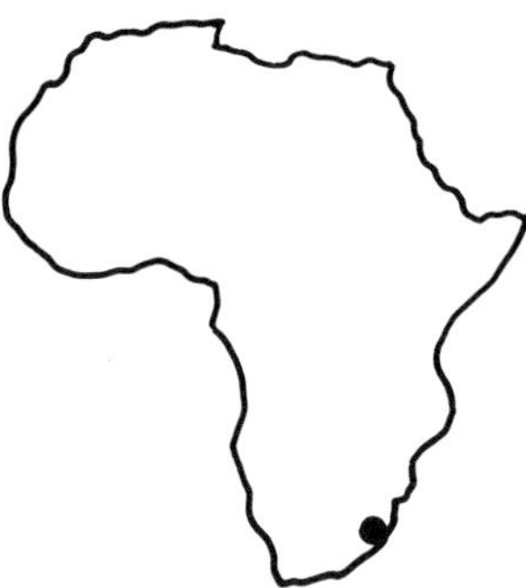

Necklace (E18,240)

Nguni (Zulu), South
Africa-Lesotho

Glass beads, vegetable
fiber, brass buttons

L. 42 cm.

Both sexes wore beaded articles of
dress, particularly in adolescence
when they attracted the attention
of potential mates. During court-
ship, girls would often make beaded necklaces, called *amabheque*,
for their boyfriends. The colors
and designs of the beaded panels
were understood as a sort of non-
verbal language, different com-
binations conveying messages of
affection, fidelity, etc. *Gift of Amy
and Clara Curtis, 1921.*

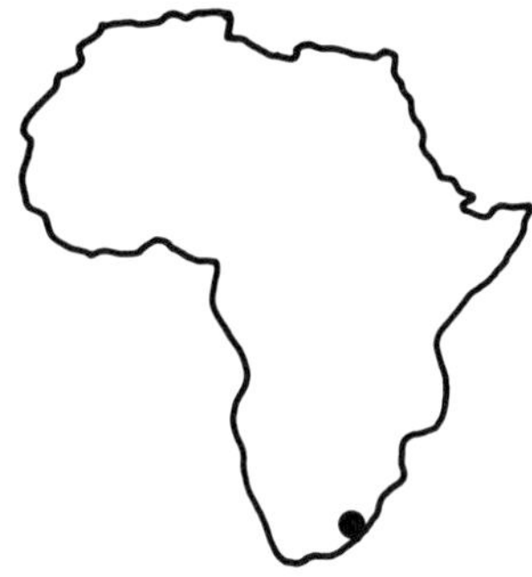

Collar (E18,250)

Nguni (Zulu), South
Africa-Lesotho

Vegetable fiber

D. 21 cm.

The Zulu were skilled basket-
workers, as exemplified by this
beautifully woven fiber collar. *Gift
of Amy and Clara Curtis, 1921.*

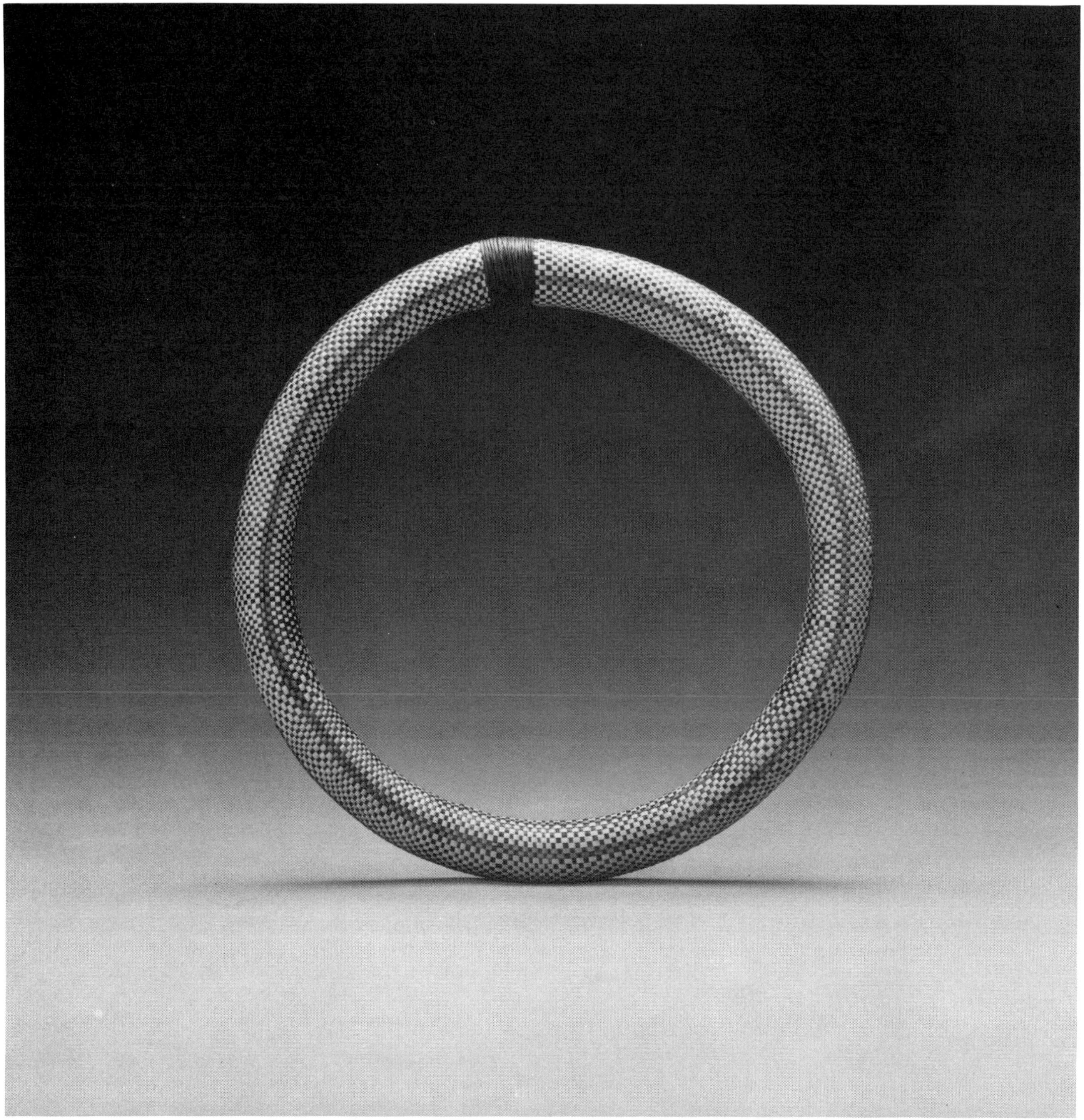

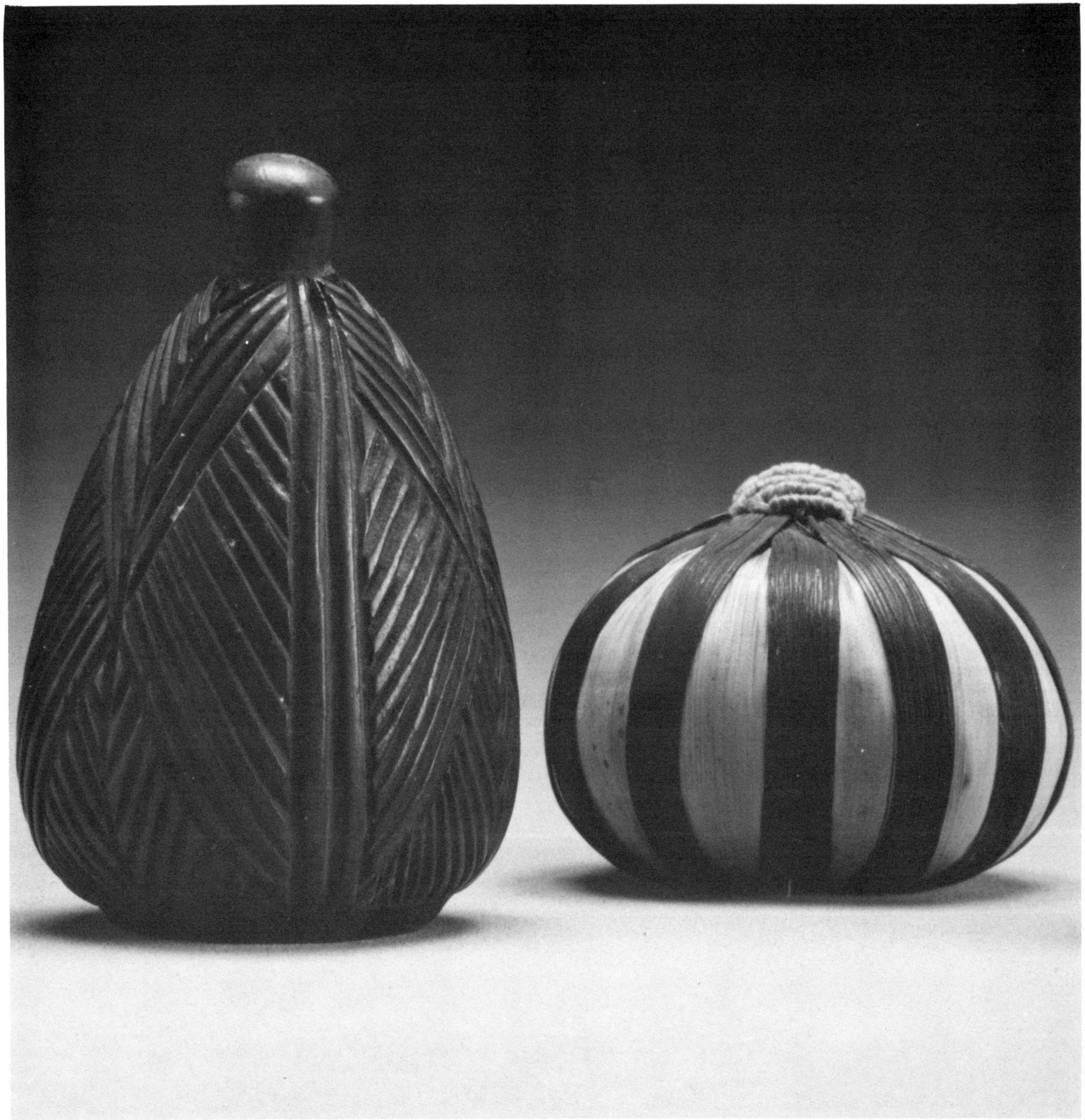

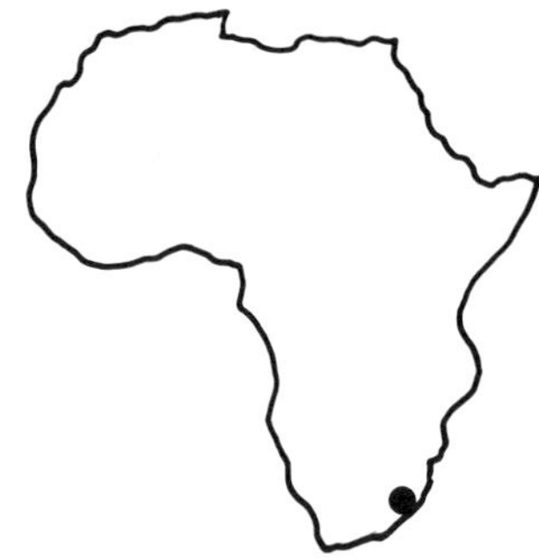

Penis Cap (E62,938)

Nguni (Zulu), South
Africa-Lesotho

Wood

H. 8 cm.

Penis Cap (E7,932)

Nguni (Zulu), South
Africa-Lesotho

Banana leaves, cordage

H. 4 cm.

For the adult Zulu male, the minimum modest attire consisted of a penis cap, called *umncwado*, made of banana leaves, wood or a small gourd. *E62,938, gift of Mr. John Swain Carter, 1979. Collected by Alfred Hawes, ca. 1874-1893. E7,932, museum purchase, 1905.*

106

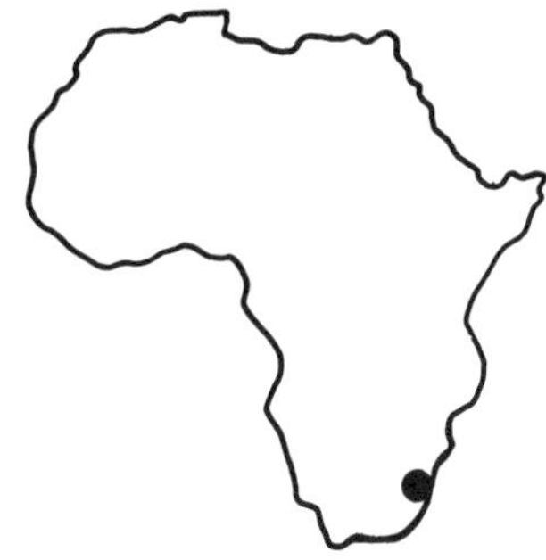

Staff (E7,035)

Nguni (Zulu), South
Africa-Lesotho

Wood

H. 97 cm. *Detail*

Staffs were carried by Zulu elders
as a sign of prestige. *Gift of Mrs.
Annie M. Lyman, 1891.*

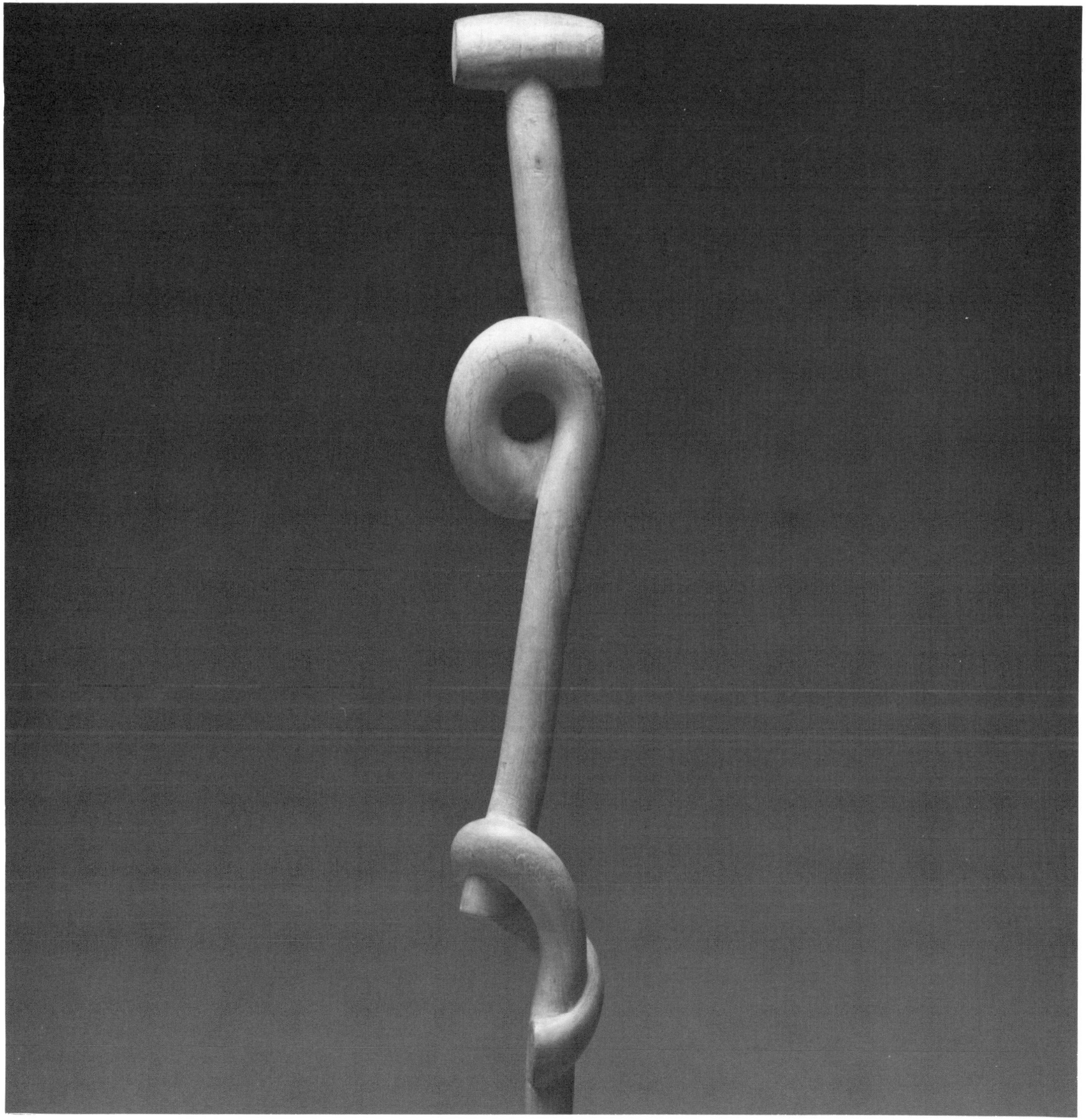

Index of Tribal Designations

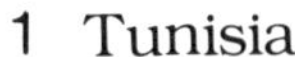

1 Tunisia
2 Western Sahara
3 Senegal
4 Gambia
5 Guinea-Bissau
6 Guinea
7 Sierra Leone
8 Liberia
9 Ivory Coast
10 Upper Volta
11 Ghana
12 Togo
13 Benin
14 Cameroon
15 Rio Muni
16 Gabon
17 Central African Republic
18 Congo
19 Somalia
20 Uganda
21 Rwanda
22 Burundi

23 Malawi
24 Mozambique
25 Zimbabwe
26 Botswana
27 Swaziland
28 Lesotho

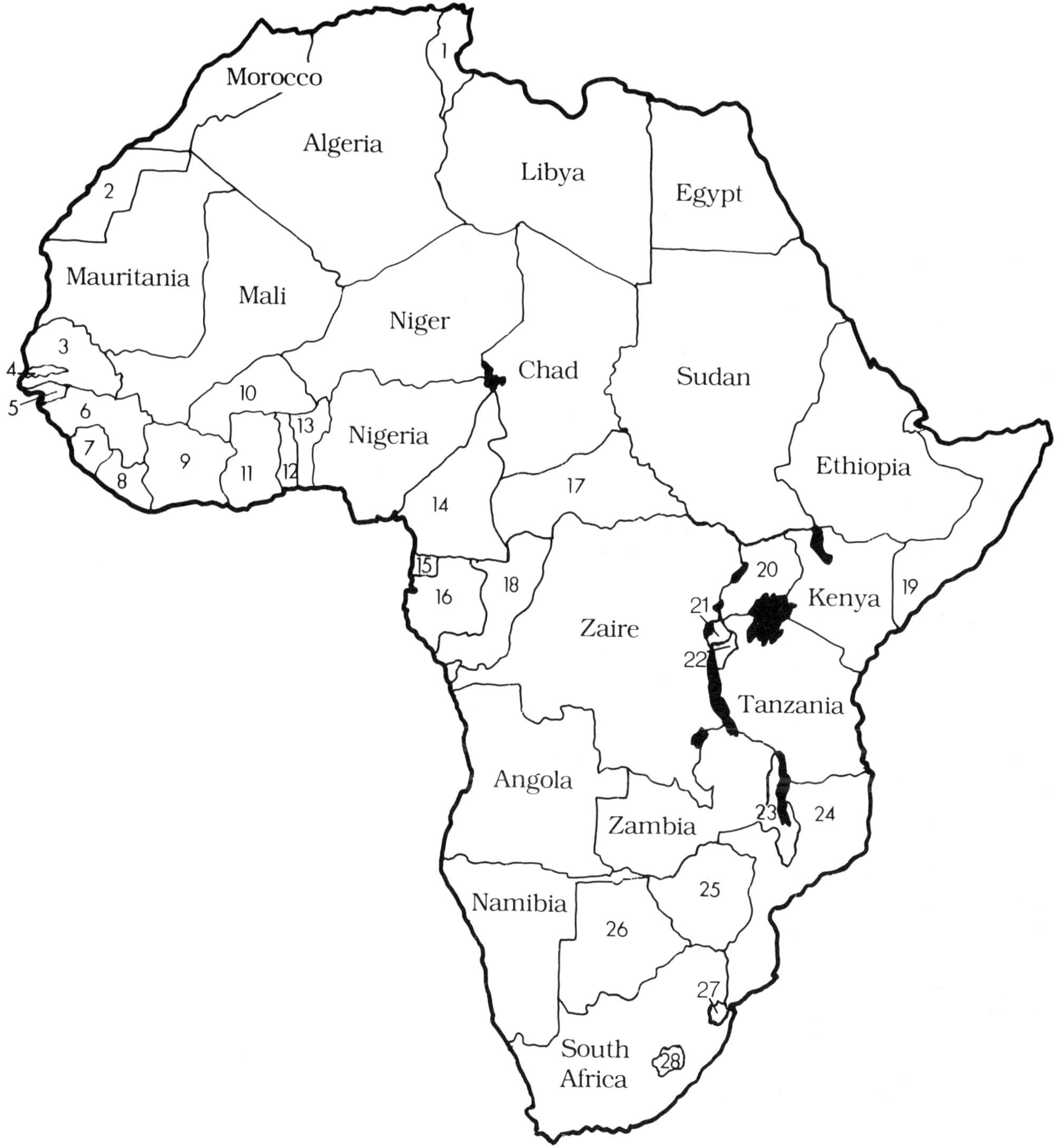

Bibliography

Adams, Monni. "African Treasures of the Peabody Museum, Harvard." *African Arts*, Vol. XV, No. 4 (1982), pp. 28-40.

__________. "An Evening with William Fagg." *African Arts*, Vol. X, No. 4 (1977), pp. 38-43.

__________. *Designs for Living: Symbolic Communication in African Art.* Cambridge: Harvard University, 1982.

__________. "Kuba Embroidered Cloth." *African Arts*, Vol. XII, No. 1 (1978), pp. 24-39.

Bascom, William. *African Art in Cultural Perspective.* New York: W.W. Norton & Co., 1973.

Bennett, Norman R. *The Zanzibar Letters of Edward D. Ropes, Jr.* Boston: Boston University Press, 1973.

Bennett, Norman R. and George E. Brooks, Jr., eds. *New England Merchants in Africa.* Boston: Boston University Press, 1965.

Bravmann, Rene A. *West African Sculpture.* Seattle: University of Washington Press, 1970.

Brooks, George E., Jr. *Yankee Traders, Old Coasters and African Middlemen.* Boston: Boston University Press, 1970.

Conner, Michael W. and Diane Pelrine. *The Geometric Vision: Arts of the Zulu.* Lafayette: Perdue Research Foundation, 1983.

Cornet, Joseph. *Art of Africa: Treasures from the Congo.* London: Phaidon Press Ltd., 1971.

Delange, Jacqueline. *The Art and Peoples of Black Africa.* New York: E.P. Dutton, 1974.

Dietz, Betty Warner and Babatunde Olatunji. *Musical Instruments of Africa.* New York: John Day Company, 1965.

Dodge, Ernest S. and Charles P. Copeland. *Handbook to the Collections of the Peabody Museum of Salem.* Salem: Peabody Museum, 1949.

Donnan, Elizabeth. *Documents Illustrative of the History of the Slave Trade to America.* Vol. III, *New England and the Middle Colonies.* Washington: Carnegie Institution, 1932.

Drewal, Henry John. *African Artistry: Technique and Aesthetics in Yoruba Sculpture.* Atlanta: High Museum of Art, 1980.

East India Marine Society, The. *Catalog of the Articles in the Museum.* Salem: Palfray, Ives, Foote and Brown, 1831 (with manuscript additions).

Fagg, William. *African Sculpture.* Washington: International Exhibitions Foundation, 1969.

__________. *Divine Kingship in Africa.* London: Shenval Press, 1970.

Fagg, William and John Picton. *The Potter's Art in Africa.* London: Shenval Press, 1970.

Feest, Christian. *The Art of War.* London: Thames and Hudson, 1980.

Fischer, Werner and Manfred A. Zirngibl. *African Weapons.* Passau: Prinz-Verlog, 1978.

Glave, E.J. *In Savage Africa.* New York: R.H. Russell & Son., 1892.

Goldwater, Robert. *Bambara Sculpture from the Western Sudan.* New York: The Museum of Primitive Art, 1960.

Guggenheim, Hans. *Dogon Art.* Cambridge: Massachusetts Institute of Technology, 1974.

Gunn, Harold D. *A Handbook of the African Collections of the Commercial Museum, Philadelphia.* Philadelphia: The Commercial Museum, n.d.

Hall, H. *The Sherbro of Sierra Leone.* Philadelphia: The University Press, 1938.

Hibbert, Christopher. *Africa Explored: Europeans in the Dark Continent, 1769-1889.* New York: W.W. Norton & Co., 1982.

History of American Missions. Worcester: Spooner & Howland, 1840.

Imperato, Pascal James. "Dogan Door Locks." *African Arts*, Vol. XI, No. 4 (1978), pp. 54-57.

Johnston, Sir Harry. *The Uganda Protectorate.* London: Hutchinson and Co., 1902.

Kresby, John D. *The Cultural Regions of East Africa.* New York: Academic Press, 1977.

Kollman, Paul. *The Victoria Nyanza.* London: Swan Sonneschein and Co., Ltd., 1899.

Laude, Jean. *African Art of the Dogon.* New York: The Viking Press, 1973.

McLeod, M.D. *The Asante.* London: British Museum Publications, Ltd., 1981.

Mount, Sigrid Docken. "African Art at the Cincinnati Art Museum." *African Arts,* Vol. XIII, No. 4 (1980), pp. 40-46.

Muller, Hendrik P.N. and J.F. Snelleman. *Industrie des Cafres du Sud-est de l'Afrique.* Leyde: E.J. Brill, n.d.

Mordock, George Peter. *Africa: Its Peoples and Their Culture History.* New York: McGraw-Hill Book Company, 1959.

Nketia, J.H. Kwabena. *The Music of Africa.* New York: W.W. Norton and Co., 1974.

Osae, T.A., S.N. Nwabara and A.T.O. Odunsi. *A Short History of West Africa: A.D. 1000 to the Present.* New York: Hill and Wang, 1973.

Picton, John and John Mack. *African Textiles.* London: British Museum Publications, Ltd., 1979.

Roy, Christopher D. *The Dogon of Mali and Upper Volta.* Munich: Galerie fur afrikanische Kunst, 1983.

Sadler, Michael E., ed. *Arts of West Africa.* London: Oxford University Press, 1935.

Schmeltz, J.D.E. *Ethnographisch Album Van Het Stroomgebied Van Den Congo.* Gravenhage: Martinus Nijhoff, 1916.

Segy, Ladislas. *African Sculpture Speaks.* New York: Lawrence Hill and Company, 1955.

_________________. *Masks of Black Africa.* New York: Dover Publications, Inc., 1976.

Sieber, Roy. *African Furniture and Household Objects.* Bloomington: Indiana University Press, 1980.

Societe des Amis du Musee de l'Homme. *Arts Connus et Arts Meconnus de L'Afrique Noire.* Paris: Musee de l'Homme, 1966.

Stedman, Susan. "The Peabody Museum of Salem." *African Arts,* Vol. X, No. 1 (1977), pp. 42-47.

Stow, George W. *The Native Races of South Africa.* New York: The Mac-Millan Co., 1905.

Teel, William. *An Outline of African Art.* Cambridge: The University Prints, 1970.

Thompson, Robert Farris. *African Art in Motion.* Los Angeles: University of California Press, 1974.

_________________. *Black Gods and Kings.* Bloomington: Indiana University Press, 1976.

Weule, Karl. *Native Life in East Africa.* New York: D. Appleton and Company, 1909.

Wingert, Paul S. *African Negro Sculpture.* New York: Columbia University Press, 1948.

Wittmer, Marcilene K. and William Arnett. *Three Rivers of Nigeria.* Atlanta: High Museum of Art, 1978.

Zaslavsky, Claudia. *Africa Counts: Number and Pattern in African Culture.* Boston: Prindle, Wever and Schmidt, Inc., 1973.

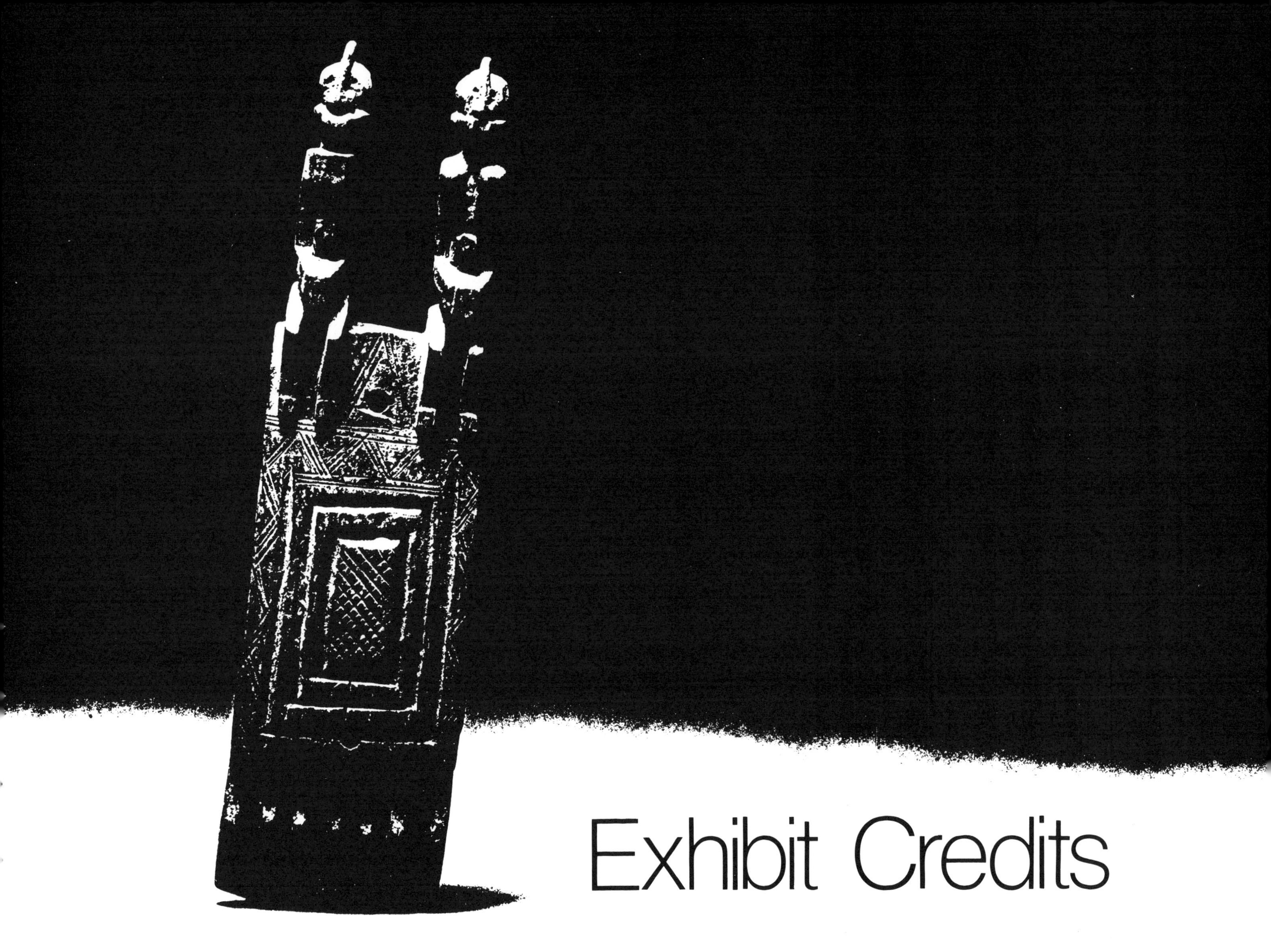
Exhibit Credits

CURATOR   John R. Grimes

DESIGNER   Frederick MacDougall Johnson

ADVISOR ON AFRICAN ART   William Teel

PROJECT MANAGER   Gregor Trinkaus-Randall

STRUCTURAL ENGINEER   Frank Duley

EXHIBITS TECHNICIAN AND LIGHTING ENGINEER   Campbell Seamans

OBJECTS CONSERVATOR AND INSTALLER   William L. Phippen

PHOTOGRAPHER   Markham Sexton

CURATORIAL ASSISTANT   Margaret D. Warner

GRAPHICS ASSISTANTS   Kathleen Smith, Marjorie Detkin

EXHIBIT ASSISTANTS   Brian Thomas, Jeffrey Demirs, Beth Grimes and William Eldridge